DANTDM (REAL NAME DAN MIDDLETON) IS ONE OF THE WORLD'S TOP YOUTUBERS. DAN STARTED MAKING VIDEOS WHILE HE WAS A STUDENT AT THE UNIVERSITY OF NORTHAMPTON. SOON AFTER, IN 2012, HIS CURRENT MINECRAFT-FOCUSED CHANNEL WAS BORN—*THE DIAMOND MINECART //
DANTDM*. HE NOW HAS FANS ALL AROUND THE GLOBE AND MAKES VIDEOS THAT ARE WATCHED BY MILLIONS OF PEOPLE EVERY DAY.

DAN LIVES IN THE UK WITH HIS WIFE, JEMMA, (ALSO KNOWN AS *XXJEMMAXX*) AND THEIR TWO PUGS, ELLIE AND DARCIE. THIS IS HIS FIRST BOOK.

D0473327

THIS BOOK IS FOR MY WIFE, JEMMA.

MY PUGS. EVERY SINGLE MEMBER OF TEAMTDM.

AND EVERY MEMBER OF MY FAMILY THAT

SUPPORTS ME; YOU KNOW WHO YOU ARE.

TRAYAURUS AND THE ENCHANTED CRYSTAL

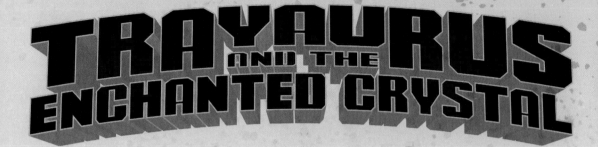

DANTDM

ILLUSTRATED BY
DOREEN MULRYAN AND MIKE LOVE

HARPER
An Imprint of HarperCollins*Publishers*

DANTDM: TRAYAURUS AND THE ENCHANTED CRYSTAL
COPYRIGHT © 2016 BY DANIEL MIDDLETON
ALL RIGHTS RESERVED. MANUFACTURED IN U.S.A.
NO PART OF THIS BOOK MAY BE USED OR REPRODUCED IN ANY MANNER WHATSOEVER WITHOUT
WRITTEN PERMISSION EXCEPT IN THE CASE OF BRIEF QUOTATIONS EMBODIED IN CRITICAL
ARTICLES AND REVIEWS. FOR INFORMATION ADDRESS HARPERCOLLINS CHILDREN'S BOOKS,
A DIVISION OF HARPERCOLLINS PUBLISHERS, 195 BROADWAY, NEW YORK, NY 10007.
WWW.HARPERCOLLINSCHILDRENS.COM

ISBN 978-0-06-257432-9 (TRADE BDG.)—ISBN 978-0-06-267653-5 (SPECIAL EDITION)

17 18 19 20   LSCC   10 9 8 7 6
❖
FIRST AMERICAN EDITION
ORIGINALLY PUBLISHED IN GREAT BRITAIN IN 2016 BY TRAPEZE,
AN IMPRINT OF THE ORION PUBLISHING GROUP LTD.
THIS EDITION INTENDED FOR THE SCHOOL MARKET ONLY.

TRAYAURUS AND THE ENCHANTED CRYSTAL

DanTDM

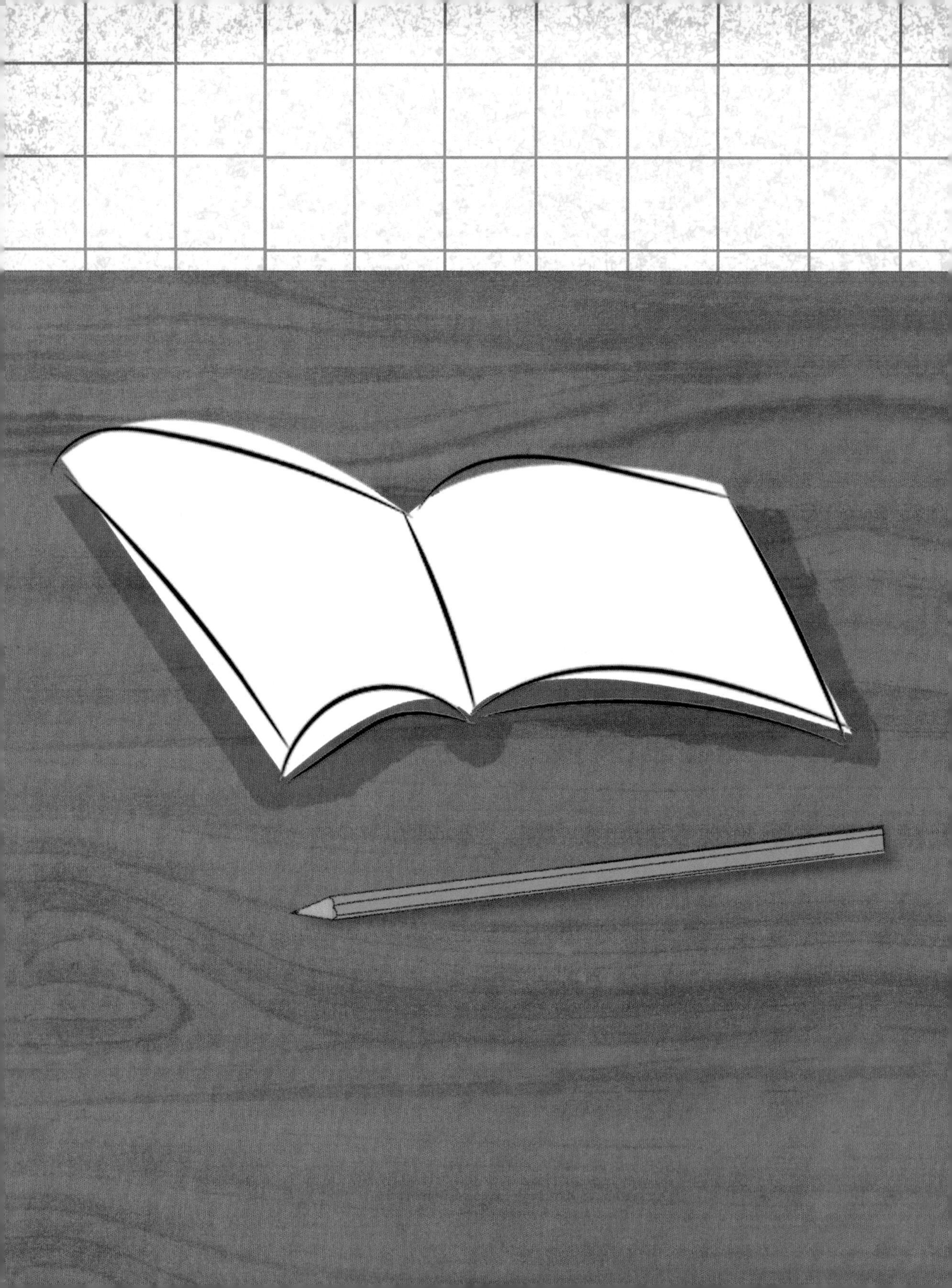

HEY THERE, EVERYONE—DAN HERE AND WELCOME TO MY BOOK! THANK YOU SO MUCH FOR CHOOSING TO BUY MY FIRST EVER GRAPHIC NOVEL. IT'S BEEN A VERY SPECIAL PROJECT, AND I'M SO GLAD YOU'VE DECIDED TO TAKE THIS JOURNEY WITH ME.

YOU MIGHT KNOW ME FROM MY VIDEOS, ESPECIALLY MESSING AROUND WITH MY FAVORITE MINECRAFT CHARACTERS LIKE TRAYAURUS, GRIM, CRAIG, AND MANY OTHERS. I LOVE CREATING STORIES AND ADVENTURES FOR THEM ONLINE SO MUCH THAT I WANTED TO TAKE THEIR STORY FURTHER IN A MEGA-QUEST—AND THAT'S RIGHT HERE IN THE FOLLOWING PAGES. WITH NO LIMITS TO THE KIND OF ESCAPADES WE COULD GET UP TO IN THIS BOOK, WE DELVE HEADFIRST INTO AN EPIC ADVENTURE, A STRUGGLE FOR POWER, AND WE MAKE BOTH FRIENDS AND ENEMIES ALONG THE WAY.

I DECIDED TO WRITE THIS BOOK FOR THE SAME REASONS I STARTED DOING YOUTUBE VIDEOS—BECAUSE I LOVE BEING CREATIVE, PLAYING GAMES, INVENTING STORIES AND HAVING FUN IN THE PROCESS. WHEN I FIRST BEGAN MAKING VIDEOS, HARDLY ANYONE VIEWED THEM, BUT NOW I HAVE ONE OF THE MOST-WATCHED CHANNELS IN THE WORLD—AND IT'S ALL DOWN TO YOU GUYS! YOU HAVE ALL BEEN A HUGE SUPPORT; WATCHING, LIKING, AND INTERACTING WITH MY VIDEOS EVERY SINGLE DAY, MAKING ALL OF THE HARD WORK WORTHWHILE. I HOPE THIS PROVES THAT IF YOU KEEP DOING SOMETHING WITH PASSION, WORK HARD, AND NEVER GIVE UP, YOU'LL EVENTUALLY HAVE OPPORTUNITIES TO DO BRILLIANT THINGS.

THIS GRAPHIC NOVEL IS ONE OF THOSE THINGS. THE IDEA CAME ABOUT BECAUSE I WANTED TO CREATE SOMETHING NEW FOR ALL OF US TO ENJOY, AND THIS HAS DEFINITELY BEEN ONE OF THE MOST EXCITING THINGS I'VE WORKED ON. FROM PLOTTING THE STORY, EVOLVING MY CHARACTERS, ADJUSTING THE COLORS, PLANNING THE BACKGROUNDS, AND LAYING IT ALL OUT, THIS BOOK HAS SURE BEEN A WHIRLWIND COMPARED TO MAKING VIDEOS! I HAVE LOVED BEING ABLE TO TELL A STORY VISUALLY, AND HAVING THE CHANCE TO WORK WITH AMAZING ARTISTS HAS BEEN A BLAST. I AM A HUGE GRAPHIC NOVEL FAN, AND I HOPE THAT BY READING THIS, YOU WILL BE TOO (IF YOU'RE NOT ALREADY).

SO HERE GOES. THIS IS MY WORLD OF IMAGINATION ON A PAGE—YOU CAN NOW SIT DOWN WITH A STORY STRAIGHT OUTTA MY BRAINBOX! HOPEFULLY YOU WILL ENJOY IT AND IT WILL INSPIRE YOU TO KEEP BEING CREATIVE, FOLLOWING YOUR DREAMS, AND MAKING STUFF—JUST LIKE DAN AND TRAYAURUS IN THEIR LAB.

OK, INTRODUCTION OVER. LET'S DO THIS!

Dan◆TDM

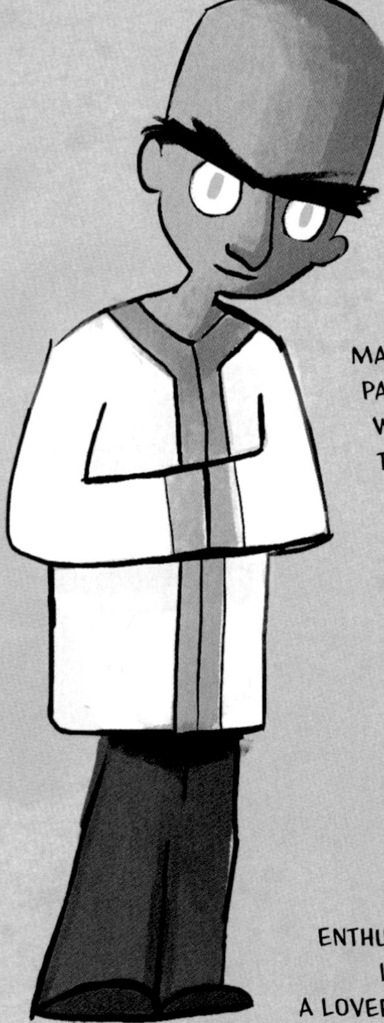

TRAYAURUS

DR. TRAYAURUS (OR JUST TRAYAURUS FOR SHORT) IS A BUDDING SCIENTIST WITH HIS VERY OWN LAB. FROM A YOUNG AGE, TRAYAURUS STARTED MIXING LIQUIDS, COMBINING MATERIALS, AND STUDYING ANYTHING HE COULD TO FULFILL HIS PASSION FOR SCIENCE. UNFORTUNATELY FOR HIM, HE WAS BORN WITH EXTREME CLUMSINESS, A CONDITION THAT CAUSES HIM TO MAKE LITTLE MISTAKES IN HIS AMBITIOUS EXPERIMENTS WITH DISASTROUS RESULTS. HOWEVER, WITH HELP FROM HIS BEST FRIEND, DAN, THINGS ALWAYS WORK OUT IN THE END, NO MATTER HOW BIG THE MESS.

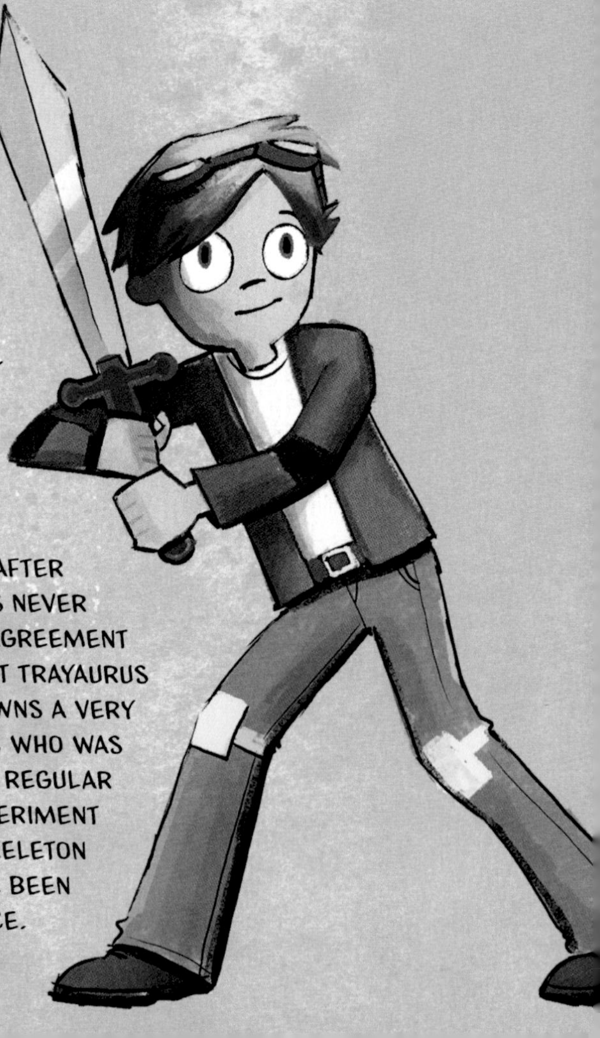

DAN

DAN IS A HAPPY, ENTHUSIASTIC, AND FUN-LOVING INDIVIDUAL. A LOVER OF ADVENTURE AND PURSUER OF ALL THINGS EXTRAORDINARY. DAN AIDS TRAYAURUS WITH HIS EXPERIMENTS DAY IN, DAY OUT, INTENT ON EXPLORING ALL THINGS WEIRD. DAN MET TRAYAURUS AFTER MOVING NEXT DOOR TO HIS LAB AND HAS NEVER LOOKED BACK, DESPITE A SLIGHT DISAGREEMENT ABOUT A GIANT PET DRAGON THAT TRAYAURUS ONCE OWNED. DAN ALSO OWNS A VERY SPECIAL DOG CALLED GRIM, WHO WAS ONCE A PERFECTLY HEALTHY, REGULAR DOG, BUT ONE UNFORTUNATE EXPERIMENT LATER, GRIM IS NOW A LIVING SKELETON VERSION OF HIMSELF. THEY HAVE BEEN INSEPARABLE EVER SINCE.

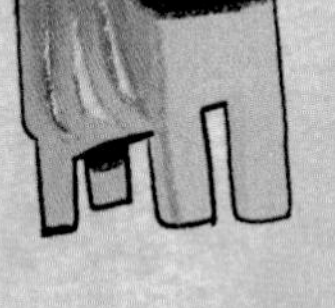

DENTON

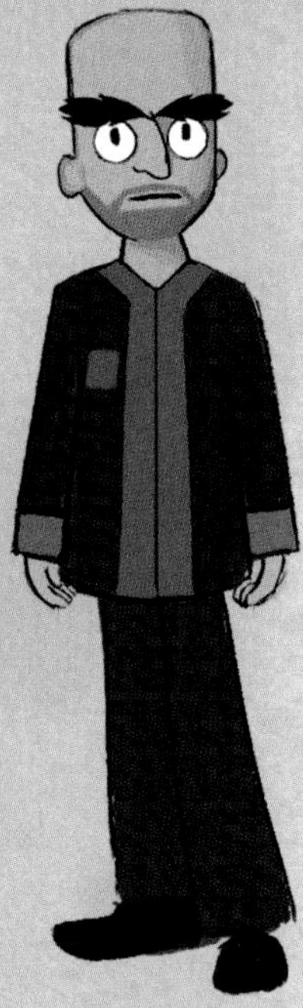

NO ONE IS SURE WHERE DENTON CAME FROM OR WHY HE IS SO UPSET WITH EVERYONE HE MEETS. HE RUNS HIS OWN LAB, WHERE HE CONDUCTS EVIL EXPERIMENTS TO AID HIS ULTIMATE PLAN OF WORLD DOMINATION. AT HIS COMMAND IS A GROUP OF ELVES, ALL OF WHOM WERE EMPLOYED BY HIM AFTER HE BUILT OVER THEIR SETTLEMENT WITH HIS GIANT LABORATORY. WITH THEIR LEADER, FIN, AS DENTON'S RIGHT-HAND MAN, THE ELVES NOW AID DENTON IN HIS EVIL PLANS. DAN, TRAYAURUS, AND DENTON HAVE CROSSED PATHS IN THE PAST, WITH DENTON BEING BEATEN EACH TIME, LEAVING HIM WITH A STRONG DISLIKE TOWARD DAN AND TRAYAURUS AND SEEKING REVENGE!

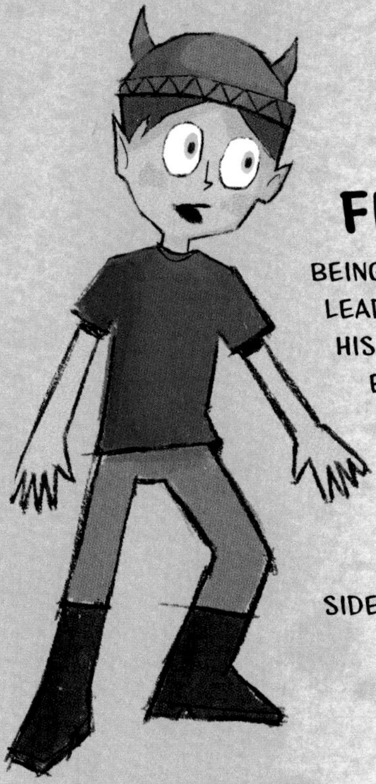

FIN

BEING THE LARGEST IN SIZE, FIN WAS THE NATURAL LEADER OF THE ELF COMMUNITY. BUT WHEN DENTON BUILT HIS LAB OVER THEIR SETTLEMENT, IT THREATENED THEIR VERY EXISTENCE. NATURALLY PERSUASIVE, FIN USED HIS CHARMS TO ENCOURAGE DENTON TO TAKE HIM AND THE ELVES ON AS LAB ASSISTANTS SO THEY WOULDN'T BE LEFT HOMELESS. DENTON RECOGNIZED FIN'S QUICK THINKING AND EFFICIENCY AND EMPLOYED HIM AS HIS SECOND-IN-COMMAND. EVER SINCE, FIN HAS STOOD LOYALLY BY DENTON'S SIDE, LEADING MANY OF HIS EXPERIMENTS.

PIGS

THE PIGS WERE YOUR NORMAL, EVERYDAY PIGS UNTIL ONE OF THE YOUNGER FEMALES WAS BESTOWED WITH THE POWER OF SPEECH. IT TURNS OUT THAT SHE IS VERY GRUMPY MOST OF THE TIME, THOUGH SHE HARBORS A SECRET SOFT SPOT FOR DAN AND TRAYAURUS. BUT DON'T YOU GO TELLING THEM THAT!

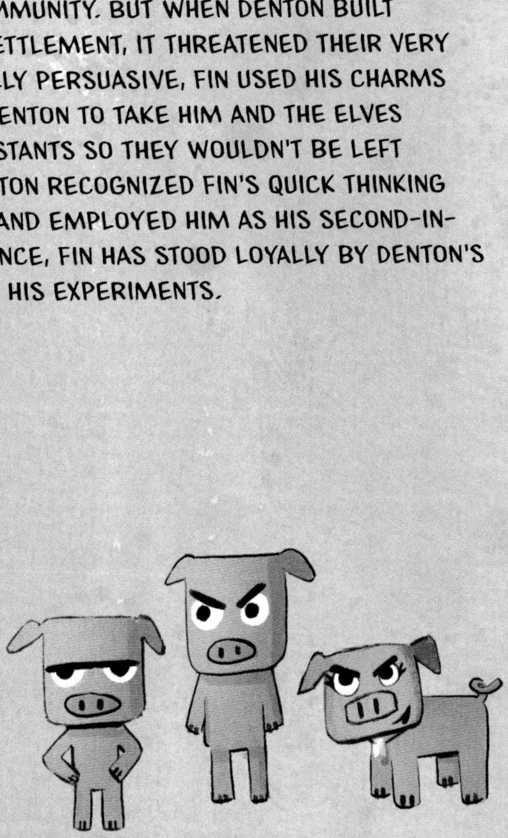

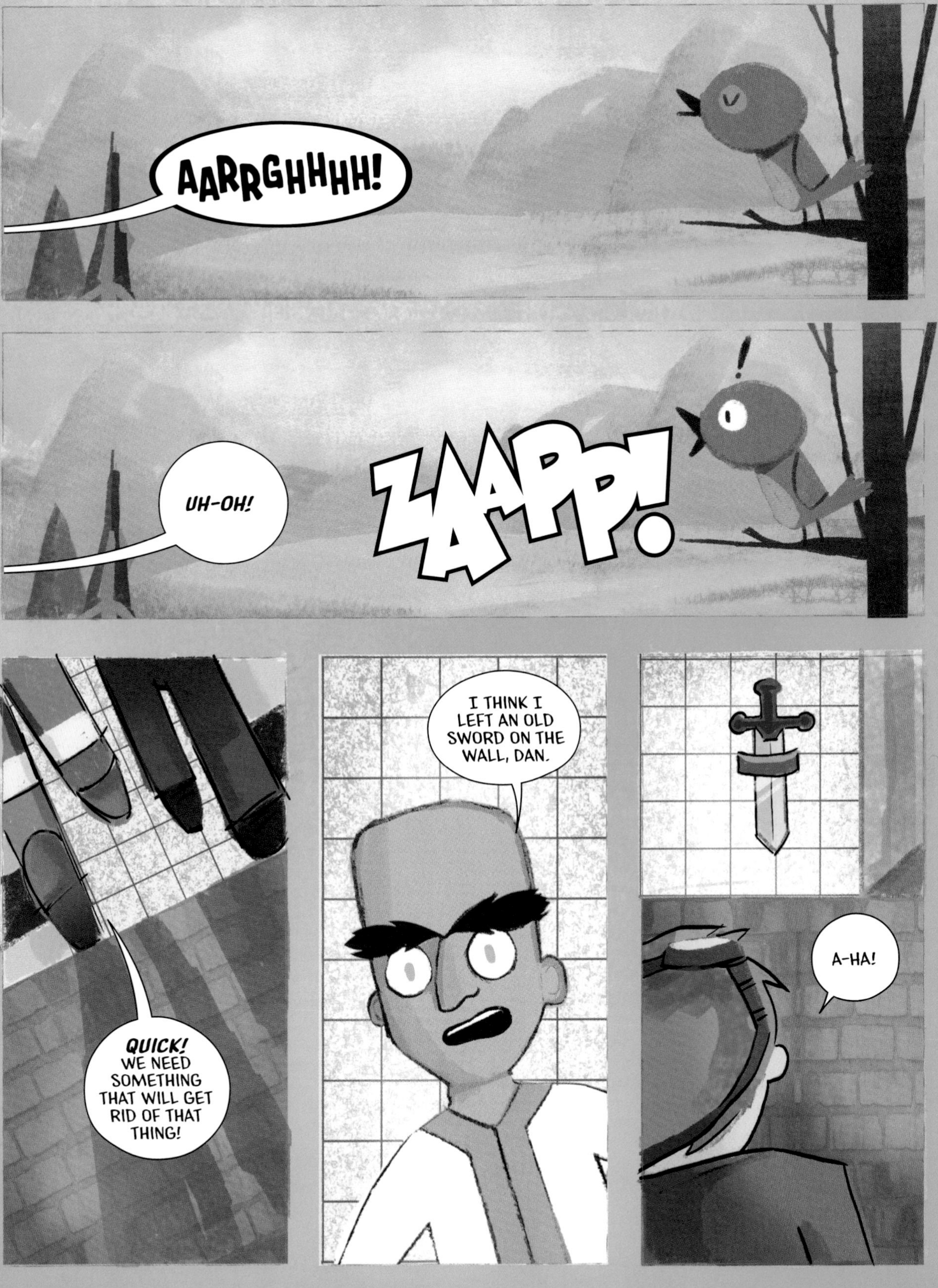
AARRGHHHH!
UH-OH!
ZAAPP!
QUICK! WE NEED SOMETHING THAT WILL GET RID OF THAT THING!
I THINK I LEFT AN OLD SWORD ON THE WALL, DAN.
A-HA!

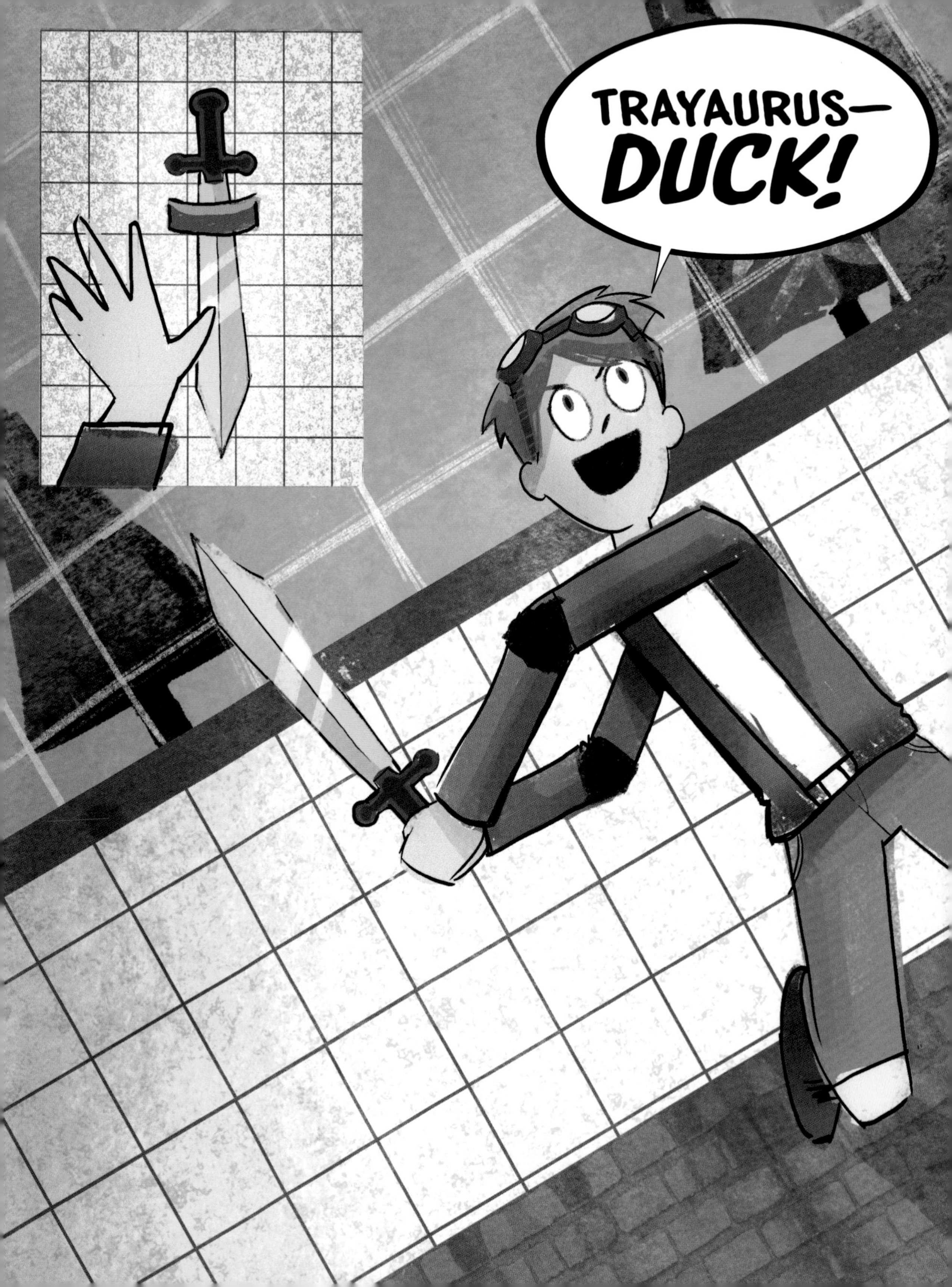
TRAYAURUS—
DUCK!

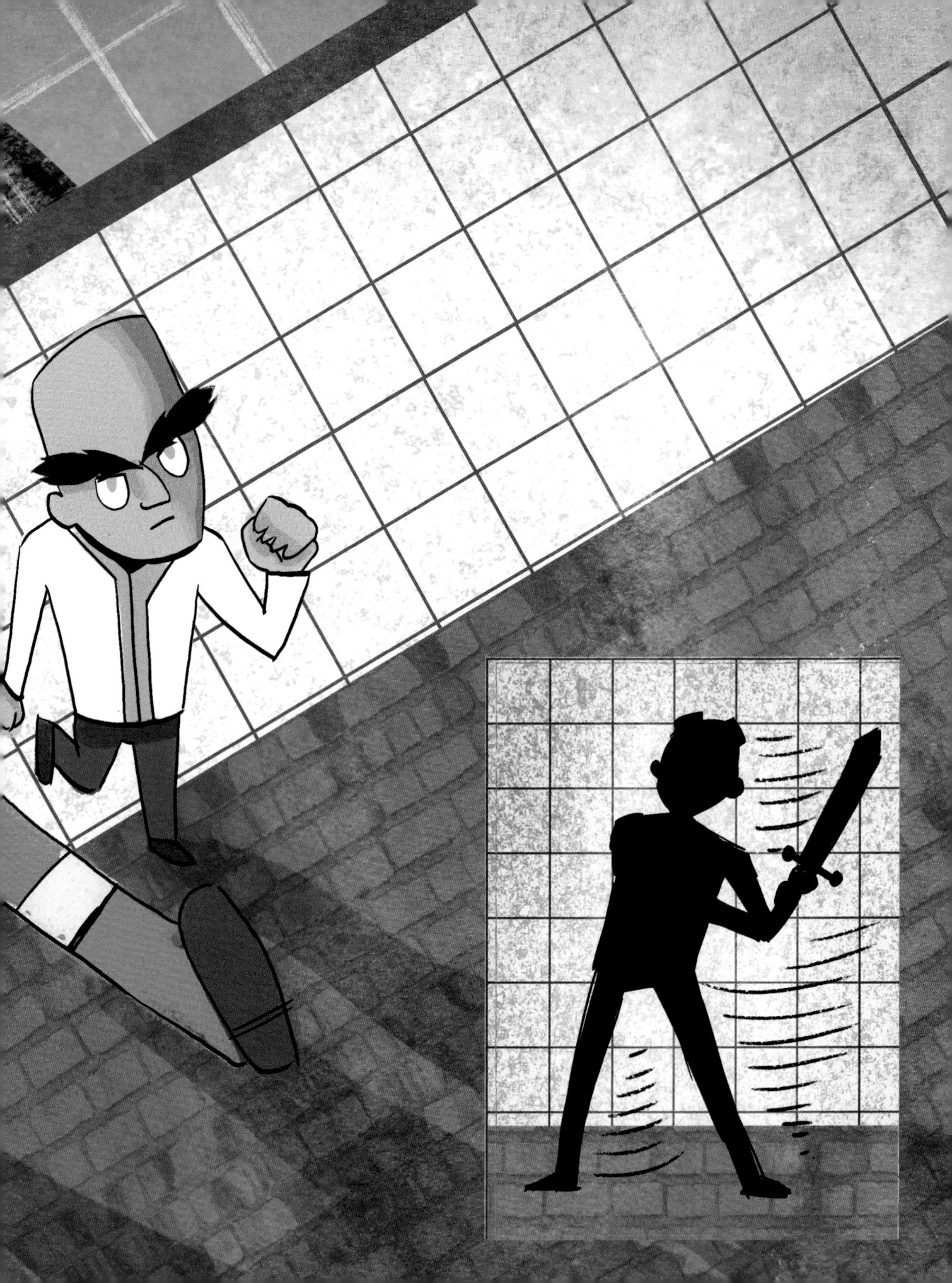

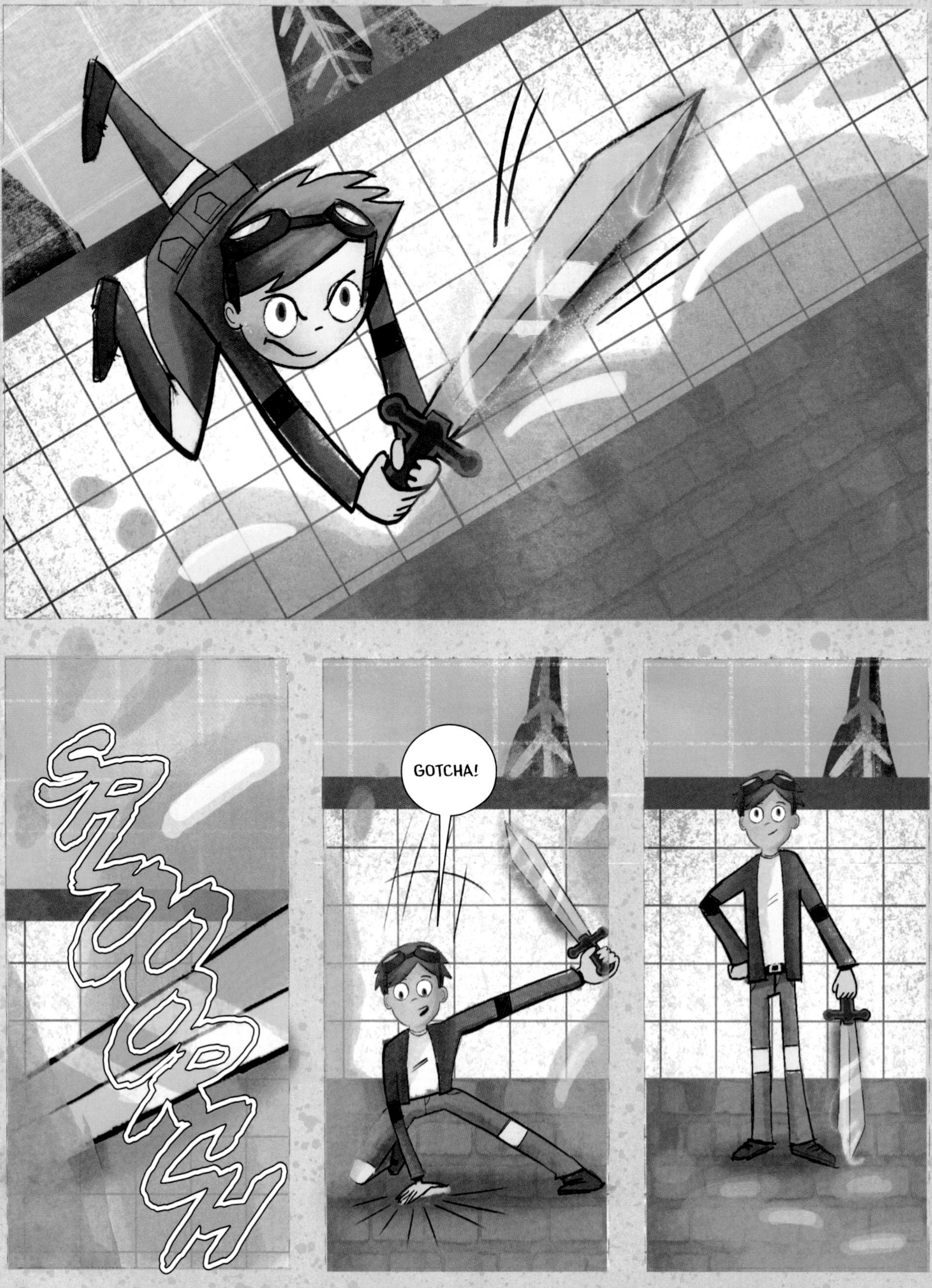
GOTCHA!

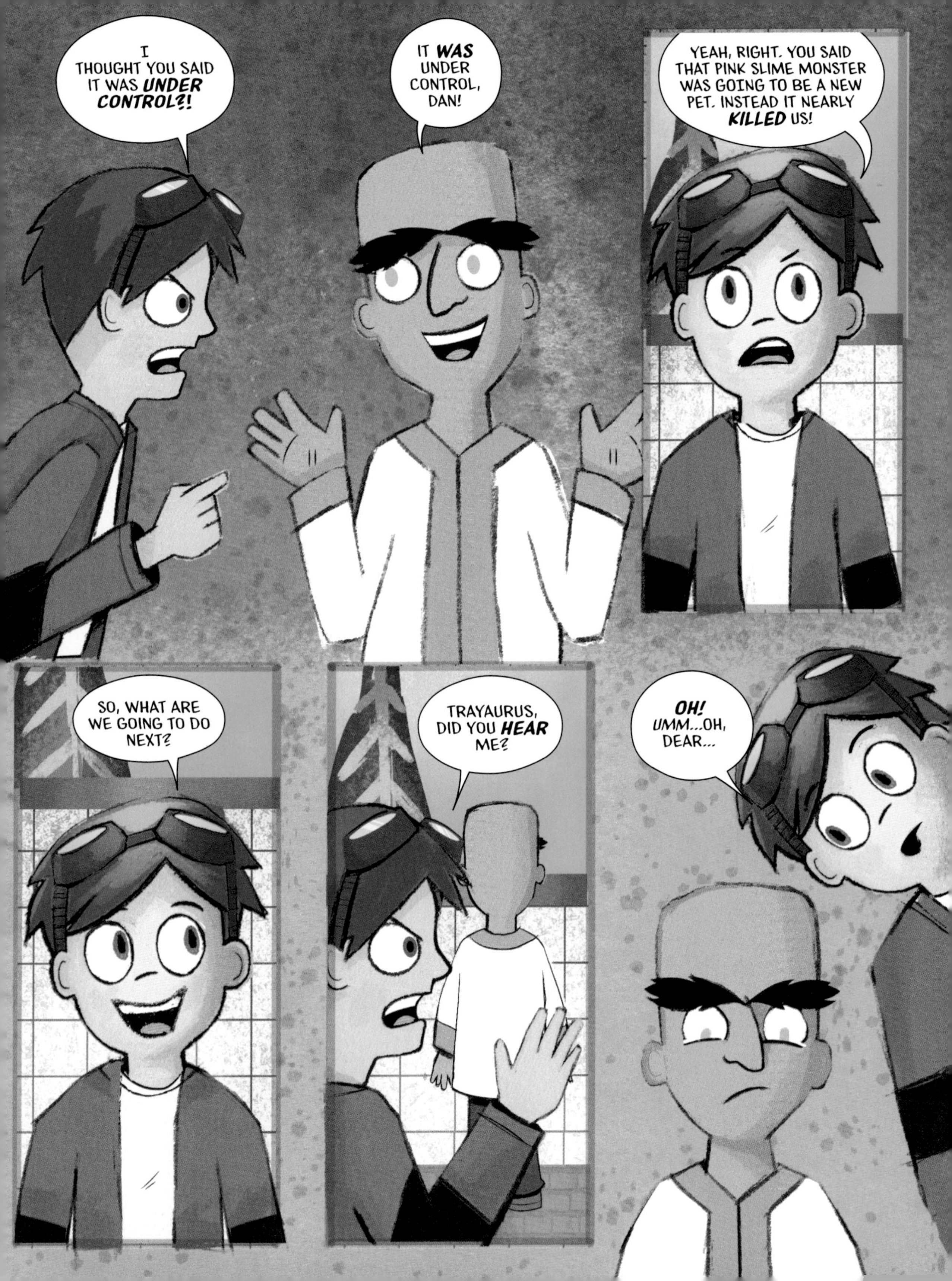
I THOUGHT YOU SAID IT WAS UNDER CONTROL?!
IT WAS UNDER CONTROL, DAN!
YEAH, RIGHT. YOU SAID THAT PINK SLIME MONSTER WAS GOING TO BE A NEW PET. INSTEAD IT NEARLY KILLED US!
SO, WHAT ARE WE GOING TO DO NEXT?
TRAYAURUS, DID YOU HEAR ME?
OH! UMM...OH, DEAR...

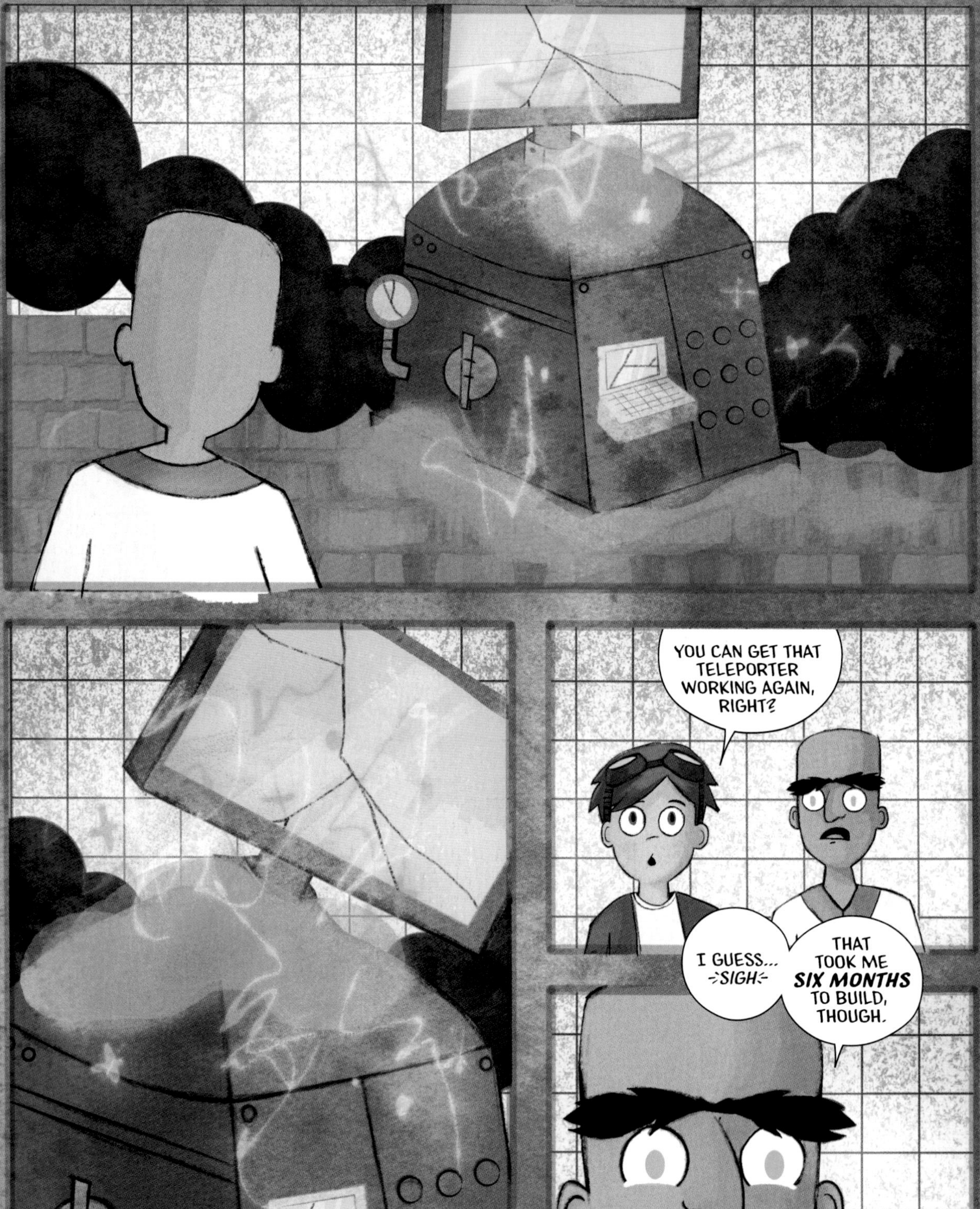
YOU CAN GET THAT TELEPORTER WORKING AGAIN, RIGHT?
I GUESS... ~SIGH~
THAT TOOK ME **SIX MONTHS** TO BUILD, THOUGH.

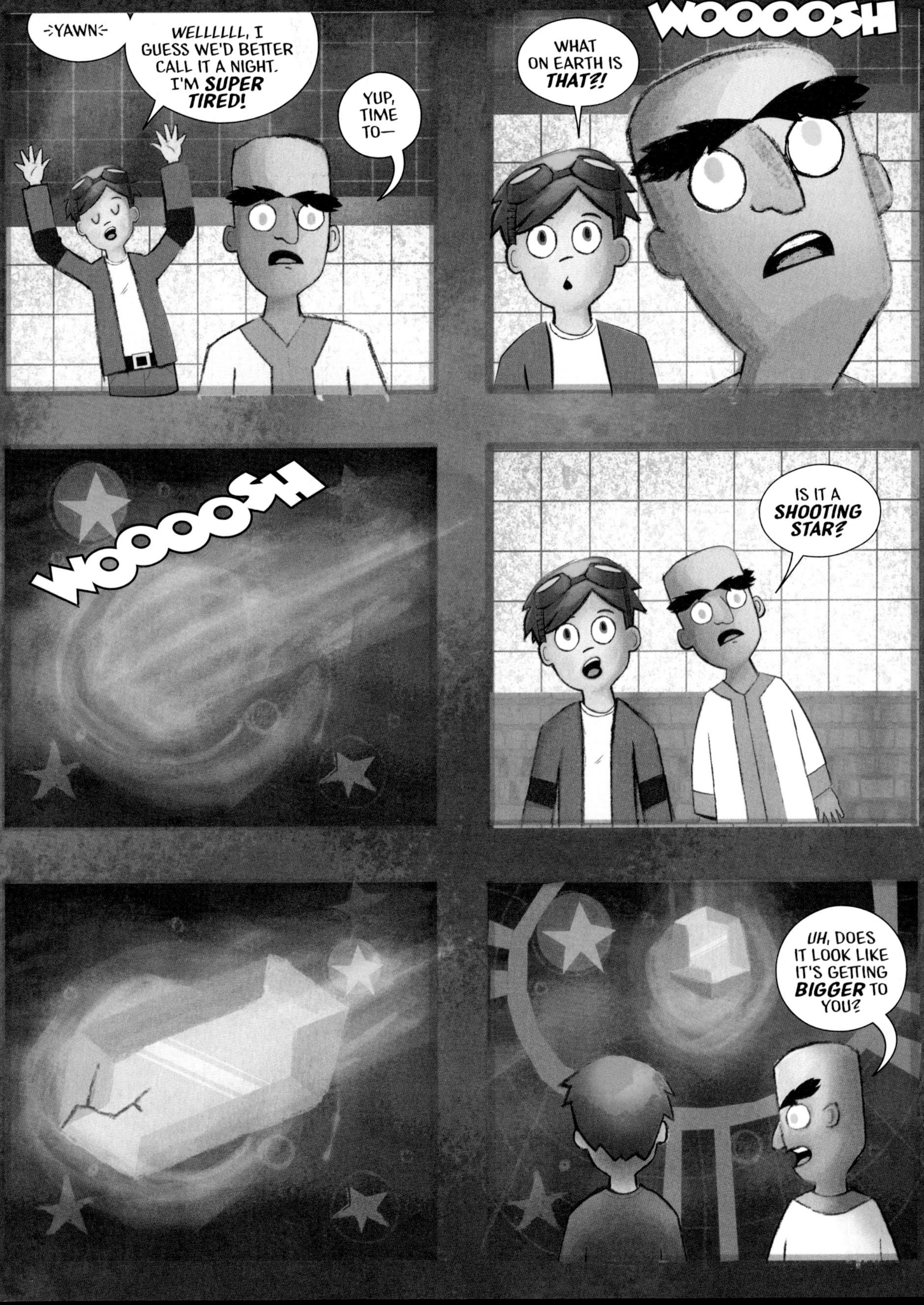
-YAWN-
WELLLLLLL, I GUESS WE'D BETTER CALL IT A NIGHT. I'M SUPER TIRED!
YUP, TIME TO—
WOOOOSH
WHAT ON EARTH IS THAT?!
WOOOOSH
IS IT A SHOOTING STAR?
UH, DOES IT LOOK LIKE IT'S GETTING BIGGER TO YOU?

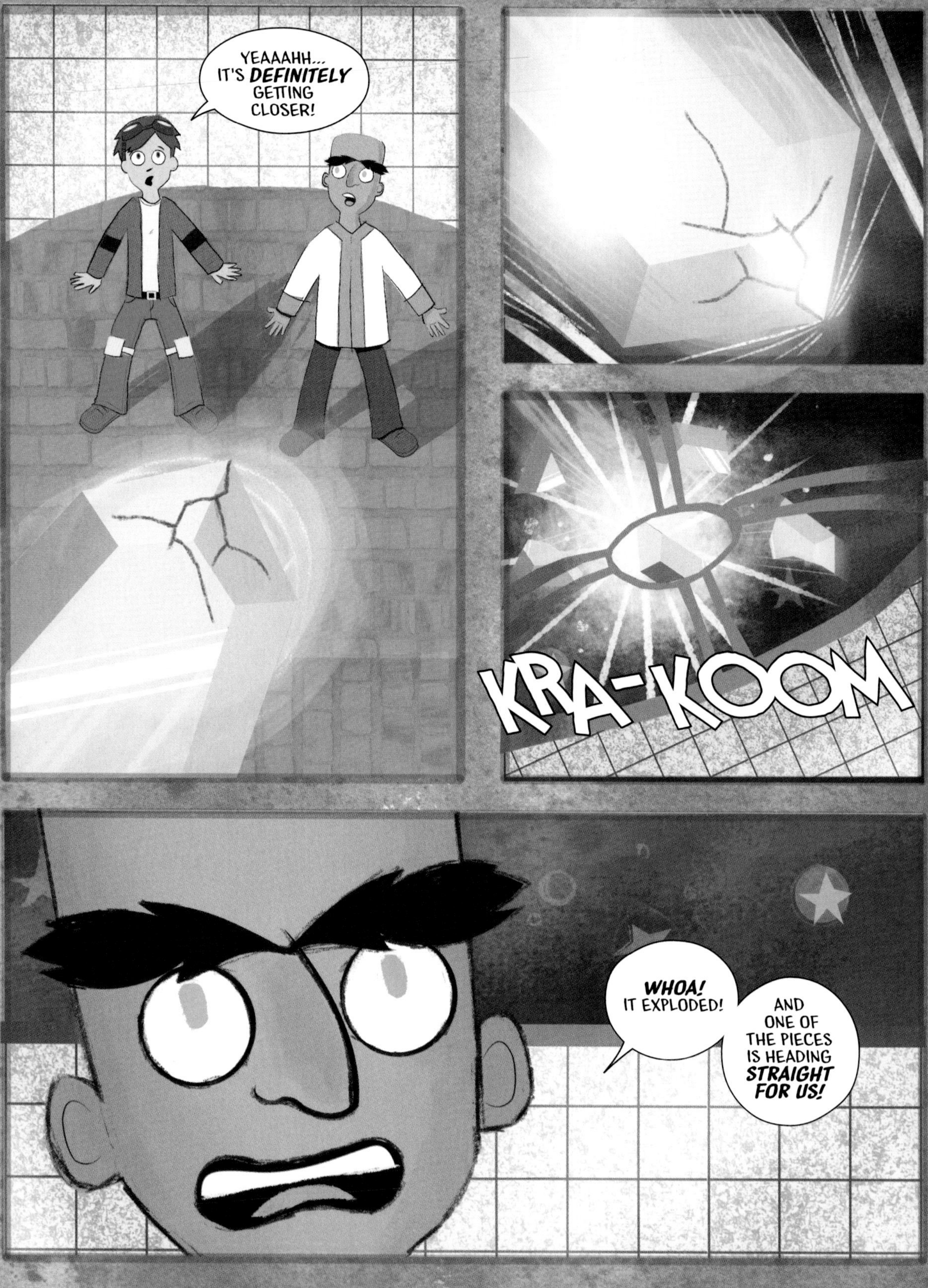

YEAAAHH... IT'S DEFINITELY GETTING CLOSER!
KRA-KOOM
WHOA! IT EXPLODED!
AND ONE OF THE PIECES IS HEADING STRAIGHT FOR US!

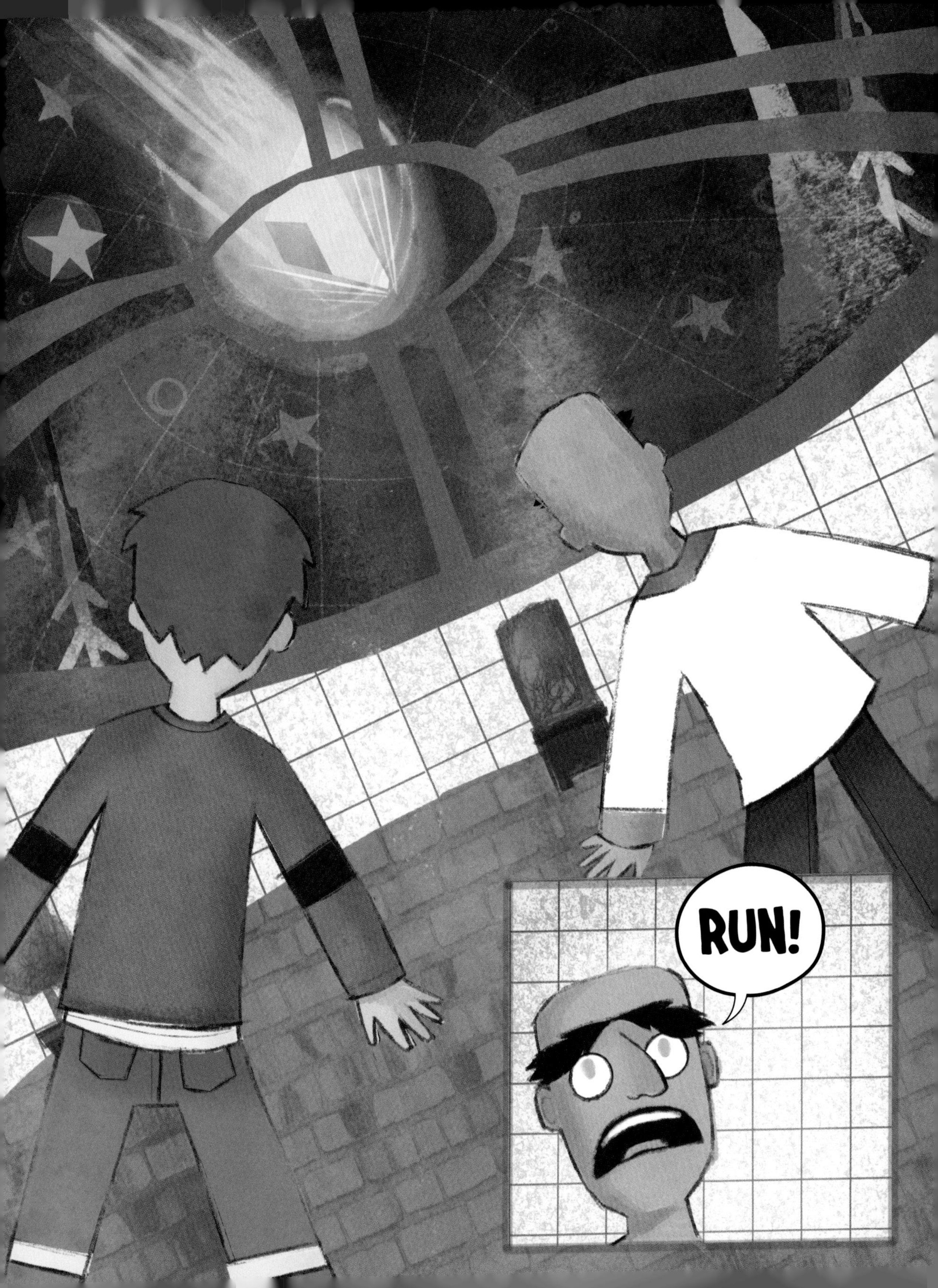
RUN!

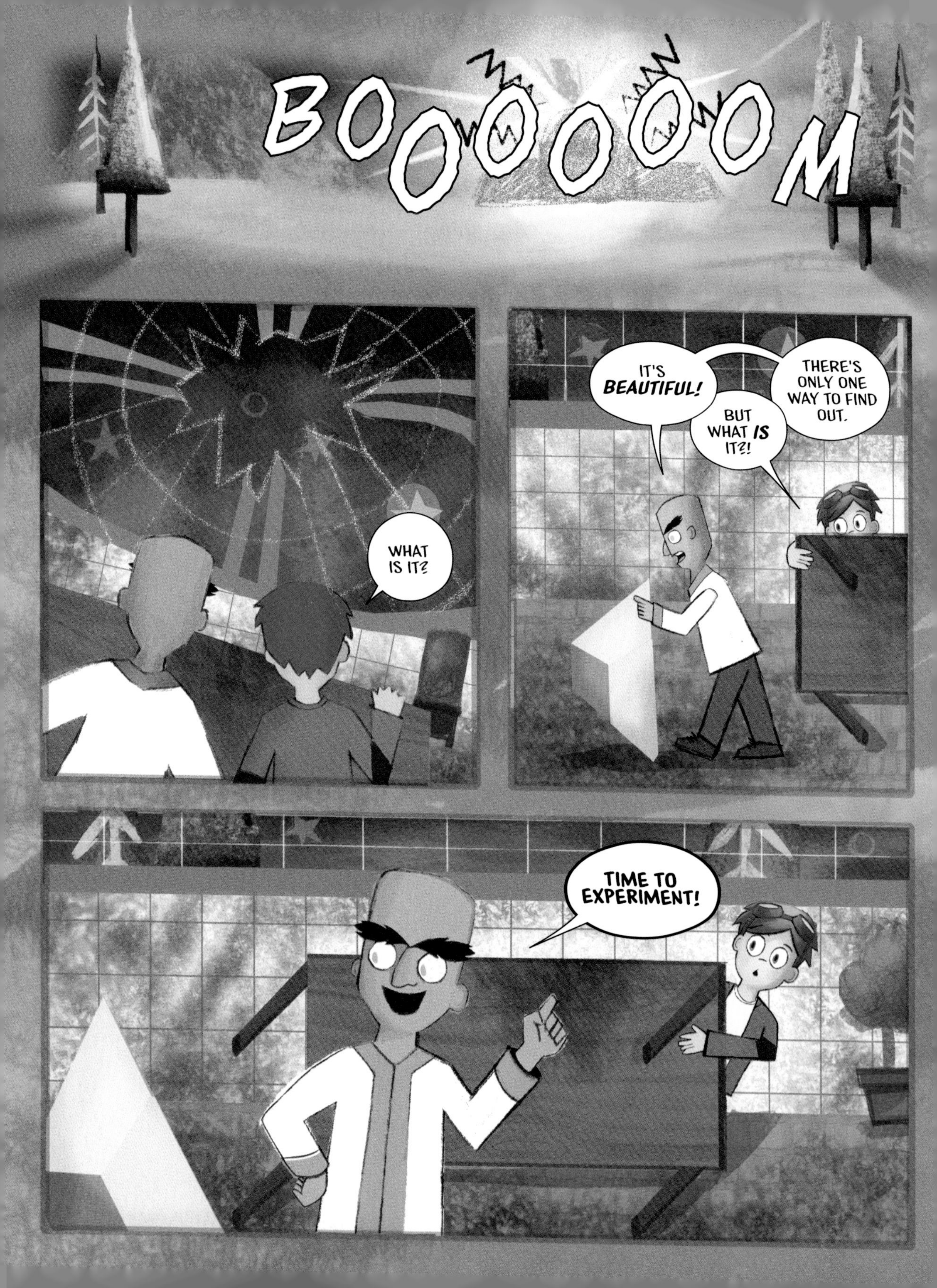
BOOOOOOM
WHAT IS IT?
IT'S BEAUTIFUL!
BUT WHAT IS IT?!
THERE'S ONLY ONE WAY TO FIND OUT.
TIME TO EXPERIMENT!

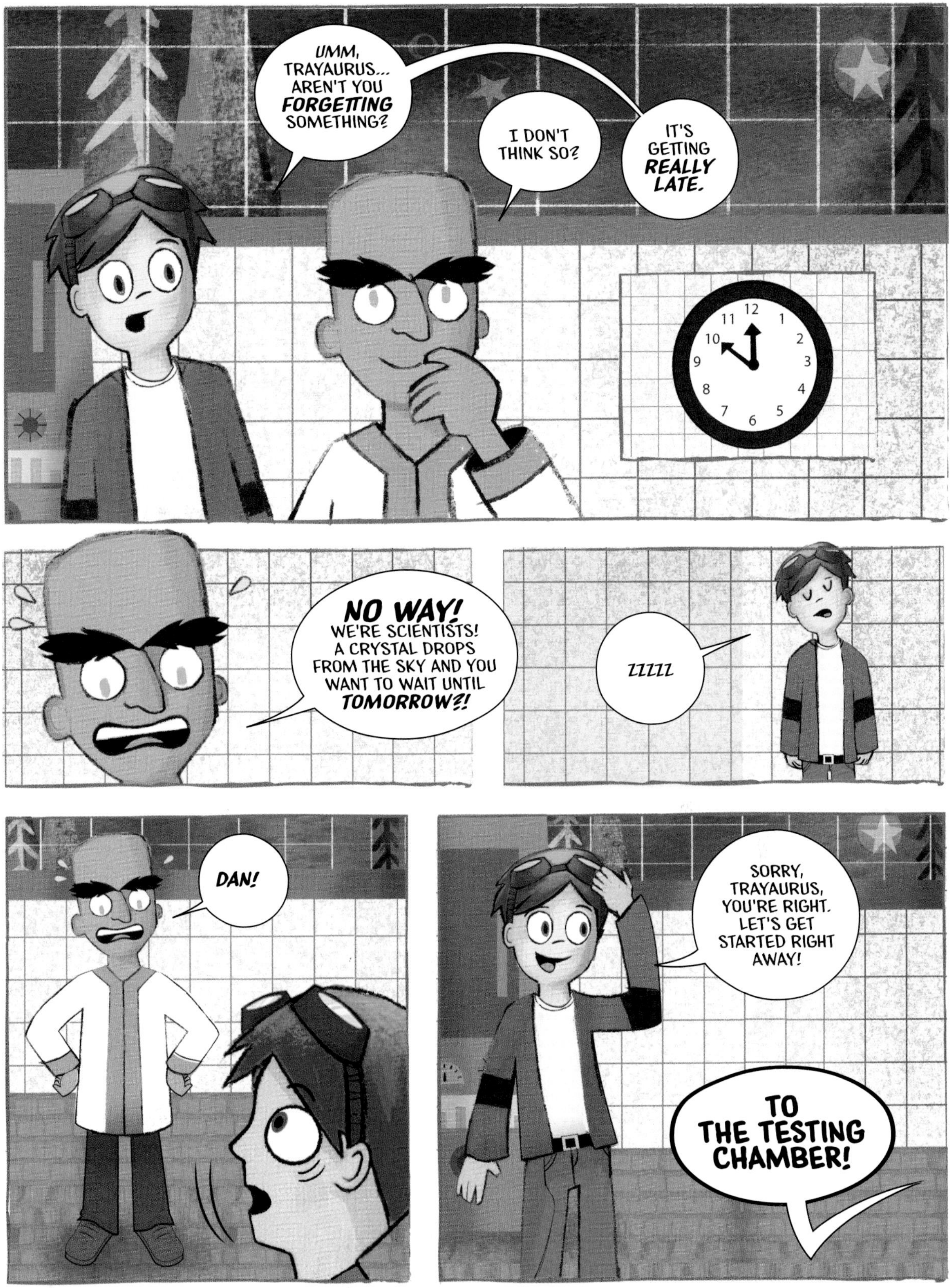
UMM, TRAYAURUS... AREN'T YOU FORGETTING SOMETHING?
I DON'T THINK SO?
IT'S GETTING REALLY LATE.
NO WAY! WE'RE SCIENTISTS! A CRYSTAL DROPS FROM THE SKY AND YOU WANT TO WAIT UNTIL TOMORROW?!
ZZZZZ
DAN!
SORRY, TRAYAURUS, YOU'RE RIGHT. LET'S GET STARTED RIGHT AWAY!
TO THE TESTING CHAMBER!

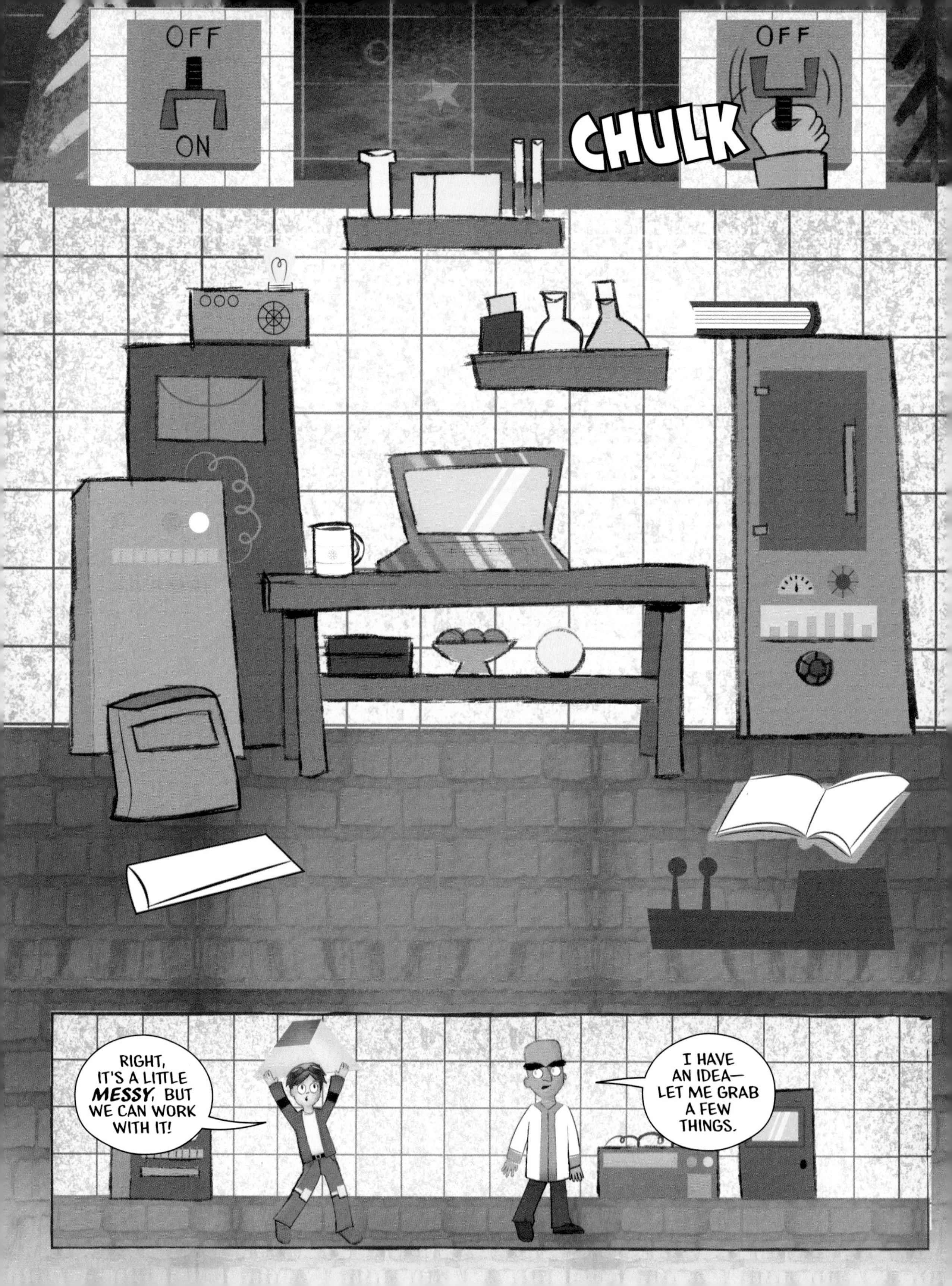
OFF
ON
OFF
CHULK
RIGHT, IT'S A LITTLE *MESSY,* BUT WE CAN WORK WITH IT!
I HAVE AN IDEA— LET ME GRAB A FEW THINGS.

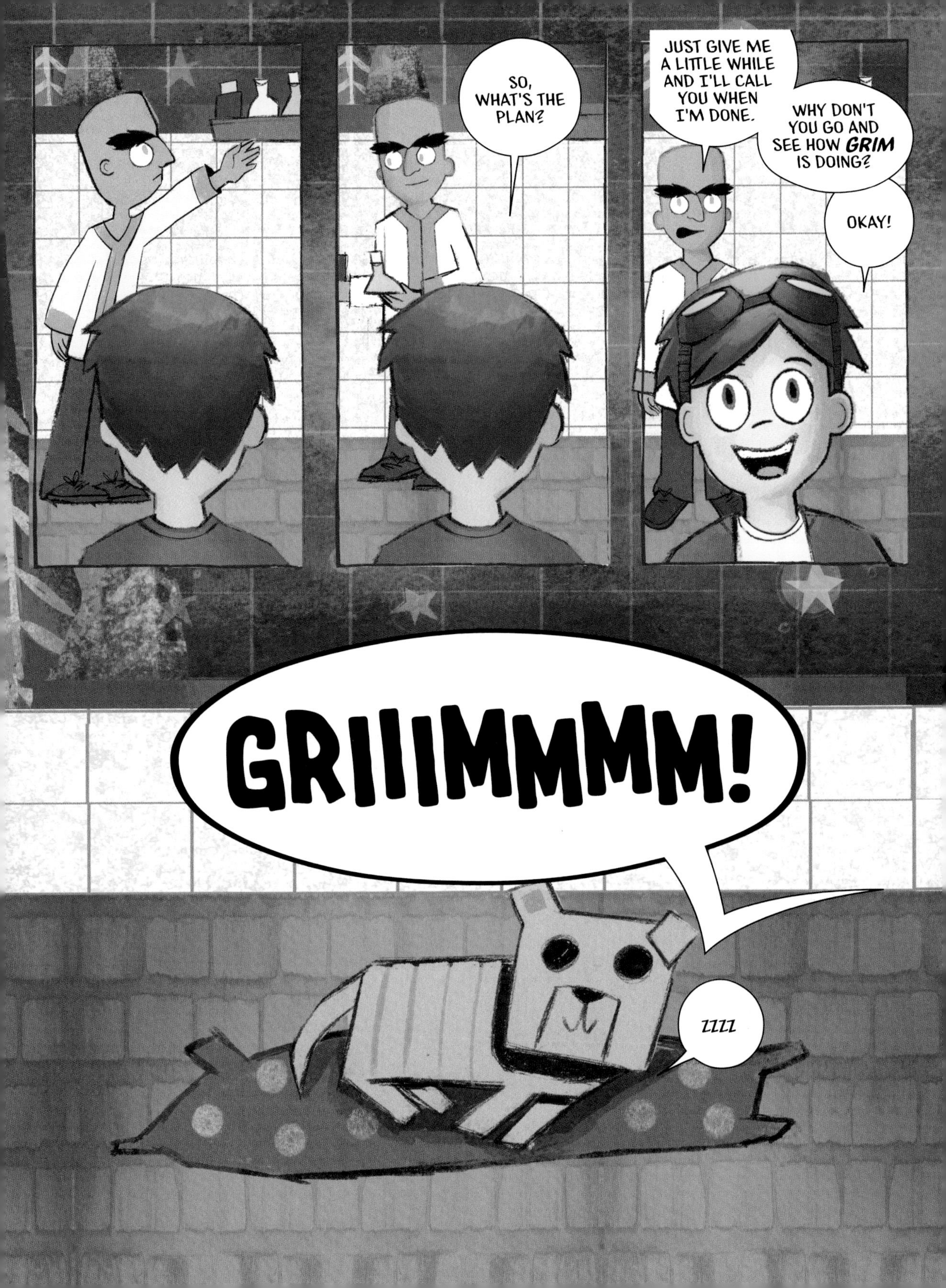
SO, WHAT'S THE PLAN?
JUST GIVE ME A LITTLE WHILE AND I'LL CALL YOU WHEN I'M DONE.
WHY DON'T YOU GO AND SEE HOW GRIM IS DOING?
OKAY!
GRIIIMMMMM!
ZZZZ

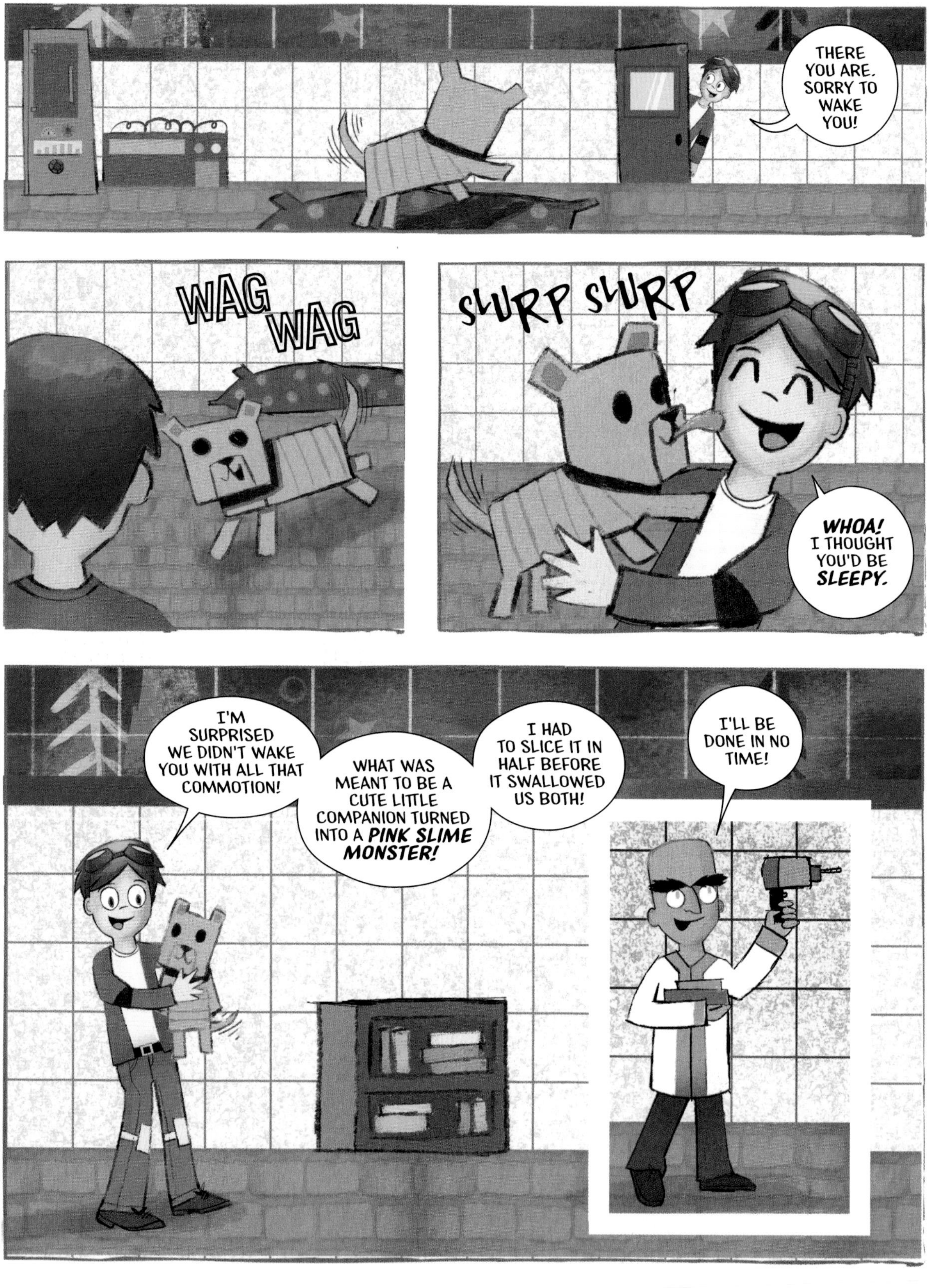
THERE YOU ARE. SORRY TO WAKE YOU!
WAG WAG
SLURP SLURP
WHOA! I THOUGHT YOU'D BE SLEEPY.
I'M SURPRISED WE DIDN'T WAKE YOU WITH ALL THAT COMMOTION!
WHAT WAS MEANT TO BE A CUTE LITTLE COMPANION TURNED INTO A PINK SLIME MONSTER!
I HAD TO SLICE IT IN HALF BEFORE IT SWALLOWED US BOTH!
I'LL BE DONE IN NO TIME!

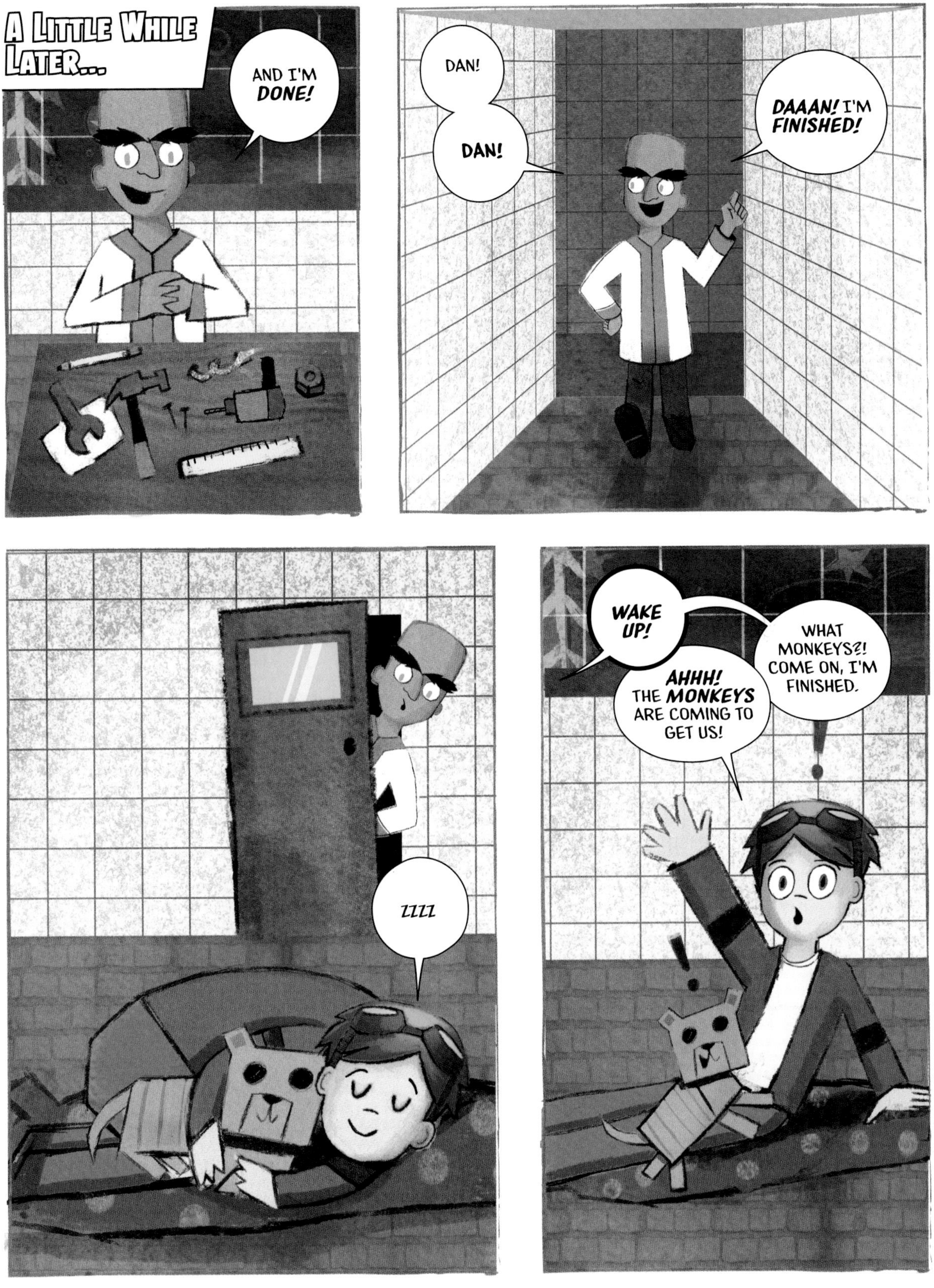
A LITTLE WHILE LATER...
AND I'M DONE!
DAN!
DAN!
DAAAN! I'M FINISHED!
ZZZZ
WAKE UP!
AHHH! THE MONKEYS ARE COMING TO GET US!
WHAT MONKEYS?! COME ON, I'M FINISHED.

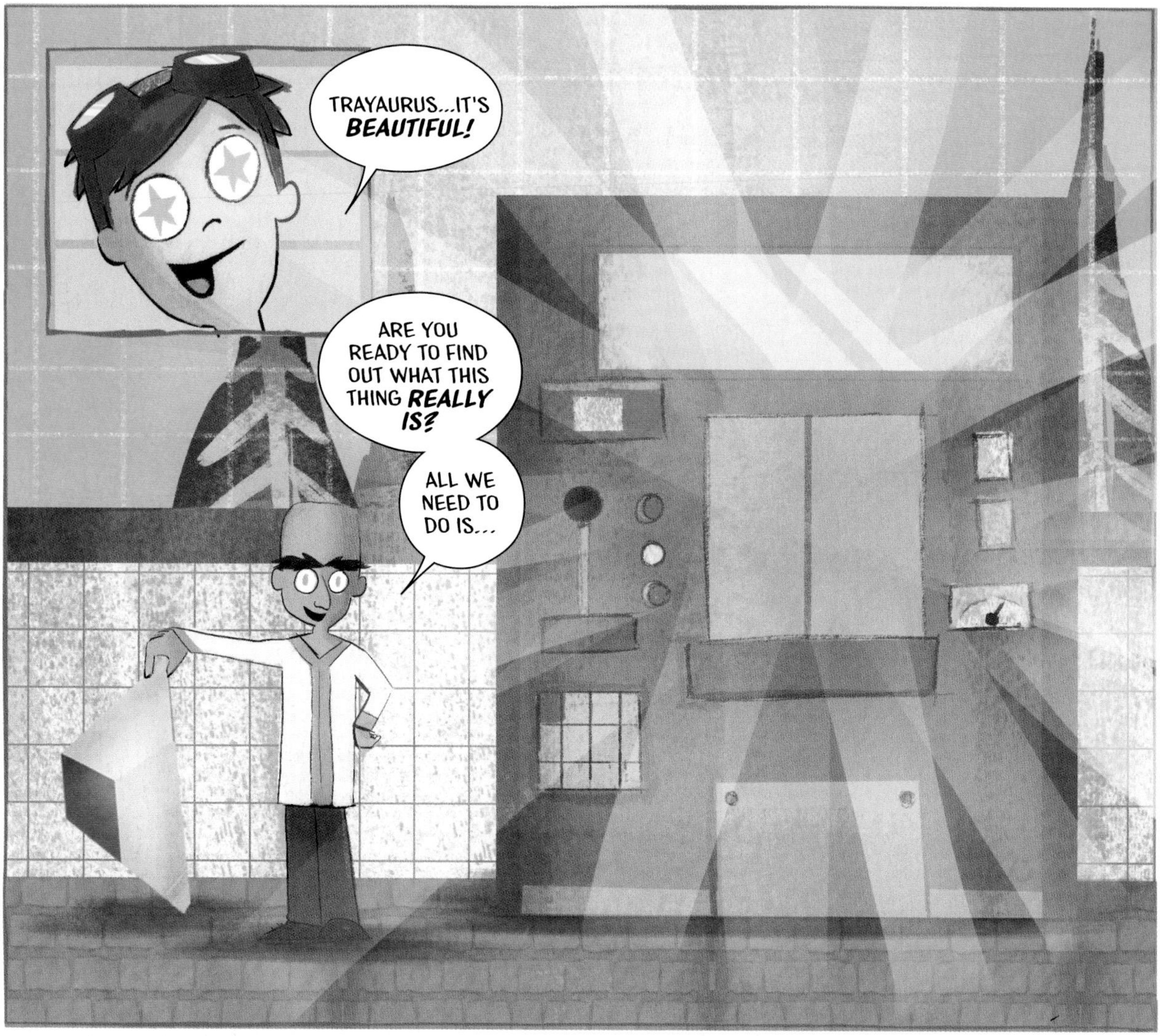
TRAYAURUS...IT'S *BEAUTIFUL!*
ARE YOU READY TO FIND OUT WHAT THIS THING *REALLY IS?*
ALL WE NEED TO DO IS...

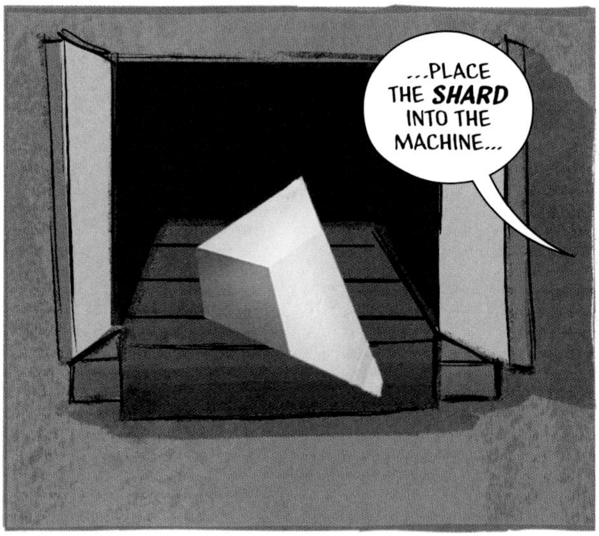
...PLACE THE *SHARD* INTO THE MACHINE...

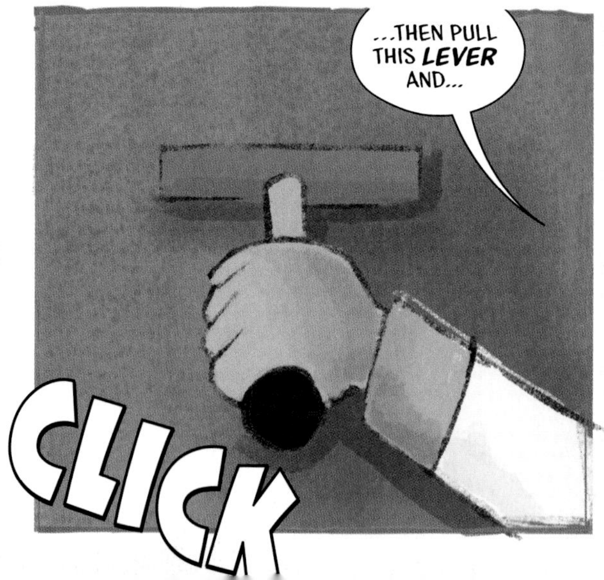
...THEN PULL THIS *LEVER* AND...
CLICK

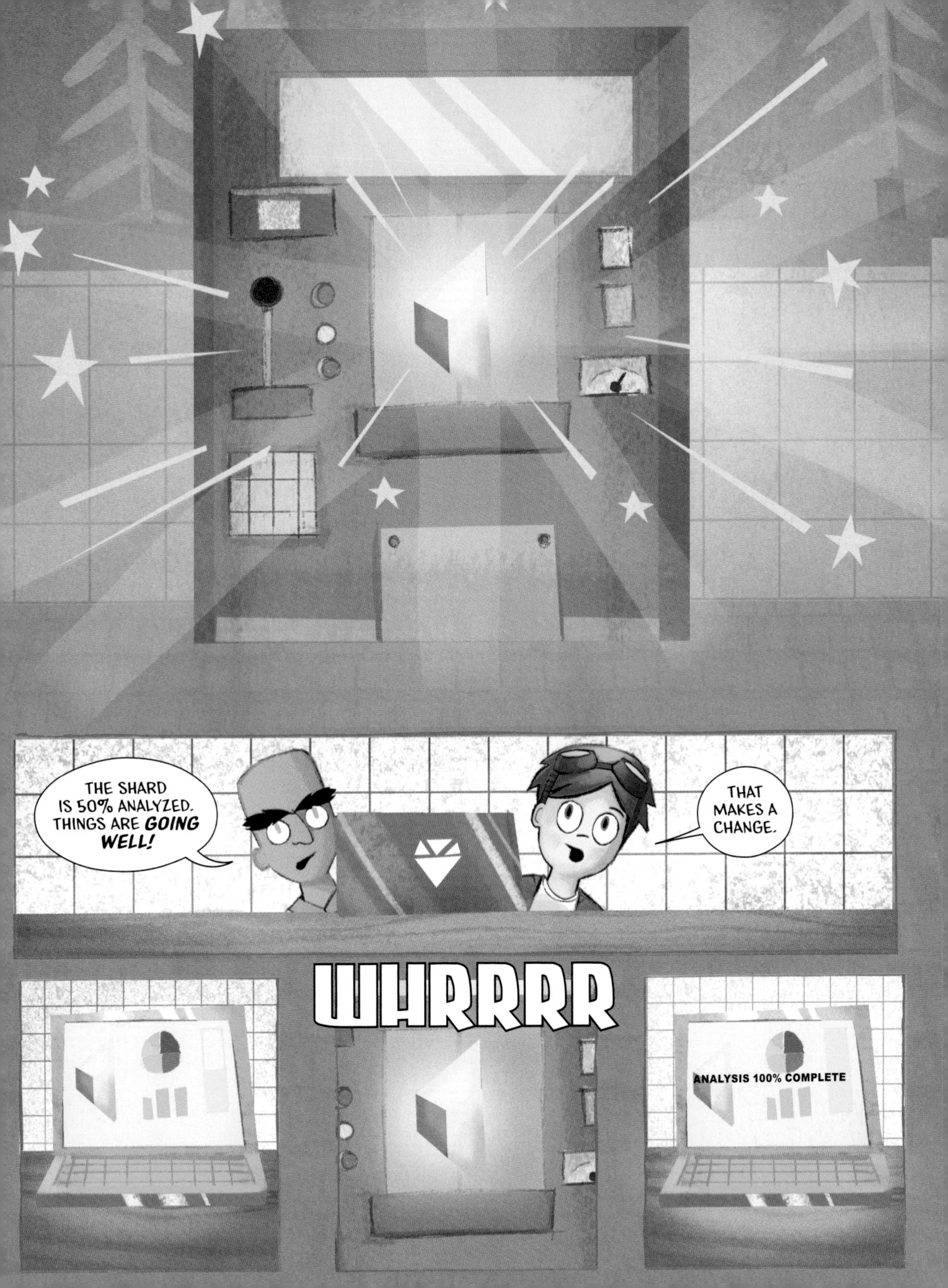
THE SHARD IS 50% ANALYZED. THINGS ARE GOING WELL!
THAT MAKES A CHANGE.
WHRRRR
ANALYSIS 100% COMPLETE

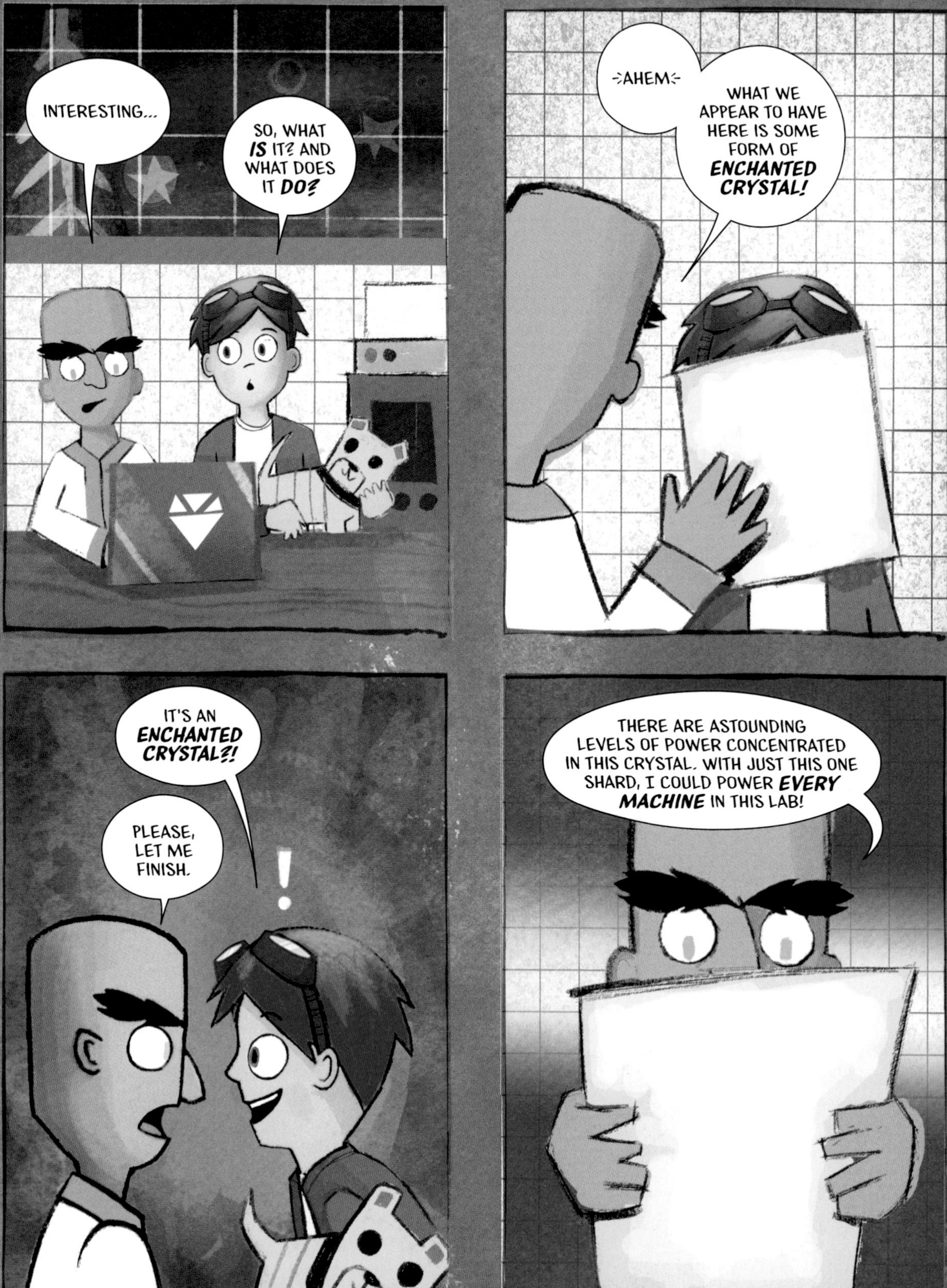
INTERESTING...
SO, WHAT **IS** IT? AND WHAT DOES IT **DO?**
-AHEM-
WHAT WE APPEAR TO HAVE HERE IS SOME FORM OF **ENCHANTED CRYSTAL!**
IT'S AN **ENCHANTED CRYSTAL?!**
PLEASE, LET ME FINISH.
!
THERE ARE ASTOUNDING LEVELS OF POWER CONCENTRATED IN THIS CRYSTAL. WITH JUST THIS ONE SHARD, I COULD POWER **EVERY MACHINE** IN THIS LAB!

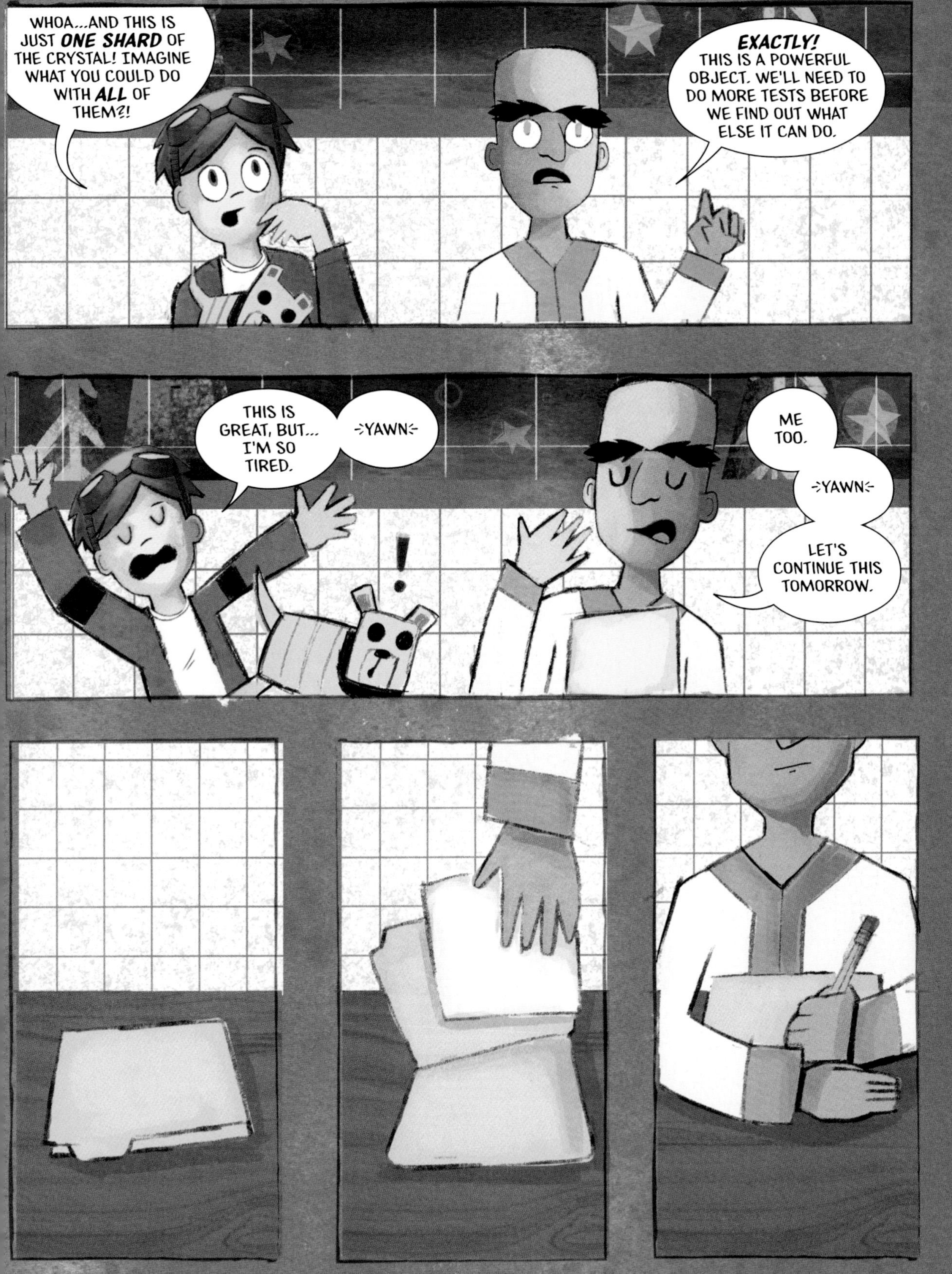
WHOA...AND THIS IS JUST ONE SHARD OF THE CRYSTAL! IMAGINE WHAT YOU COULD DO WITH ALL OF THEM?!
EXACTLY! THIS IS A POWERFUL OBJECT. WE'LL NEED TO DO MORE TESTS BEFORE WE FIND OUT WHAT ELSE IT CAN DO.
THIS IS GREAT, BUT... I'M SO TIRED.
YAWN
ME TOO.
YAWN
LET'S CONTINUE THIS TOMORROW.
!

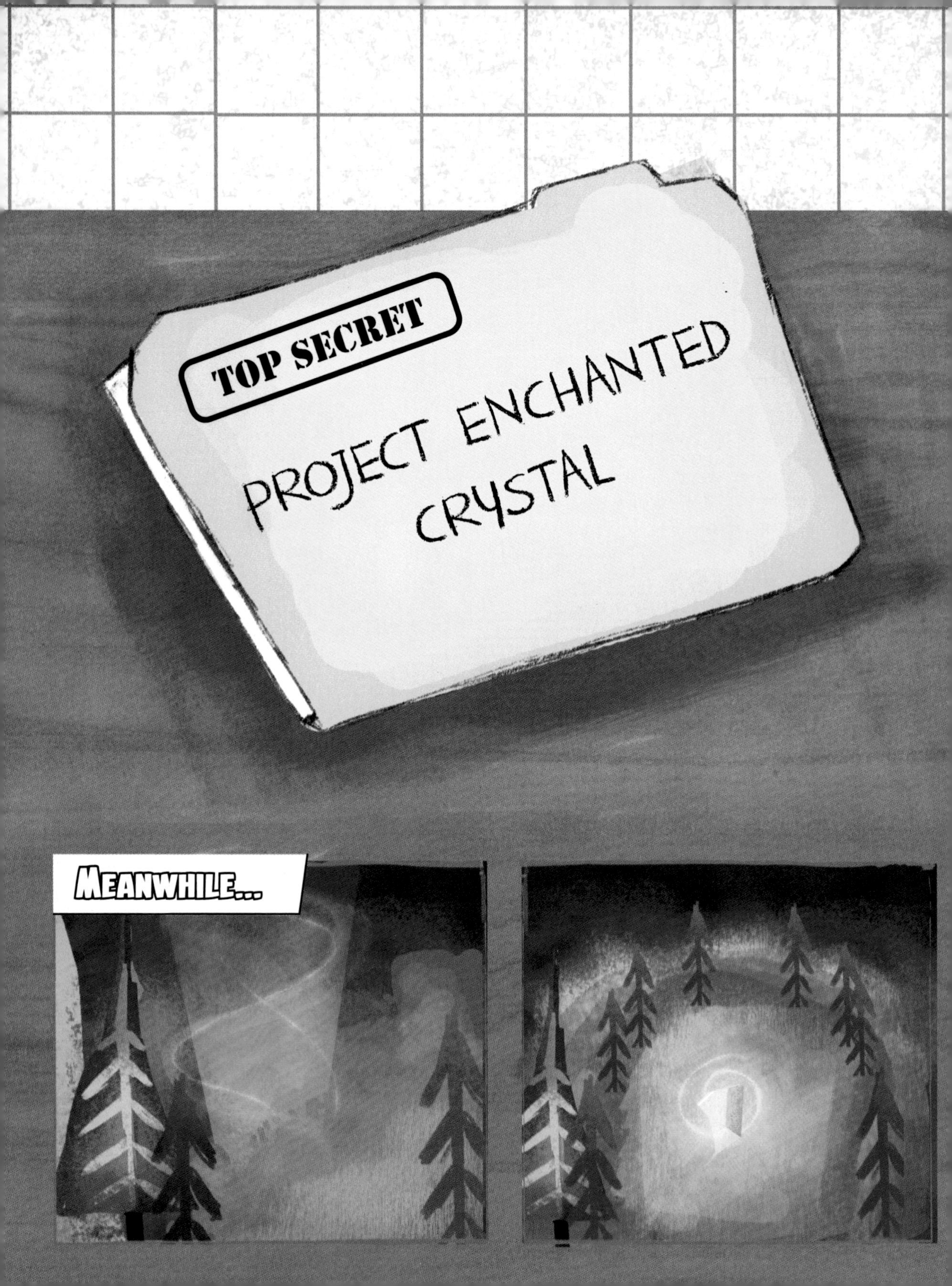
TOP SECRET
PROJECT ENCHANTED CRYSTAL
MEANWHILE...

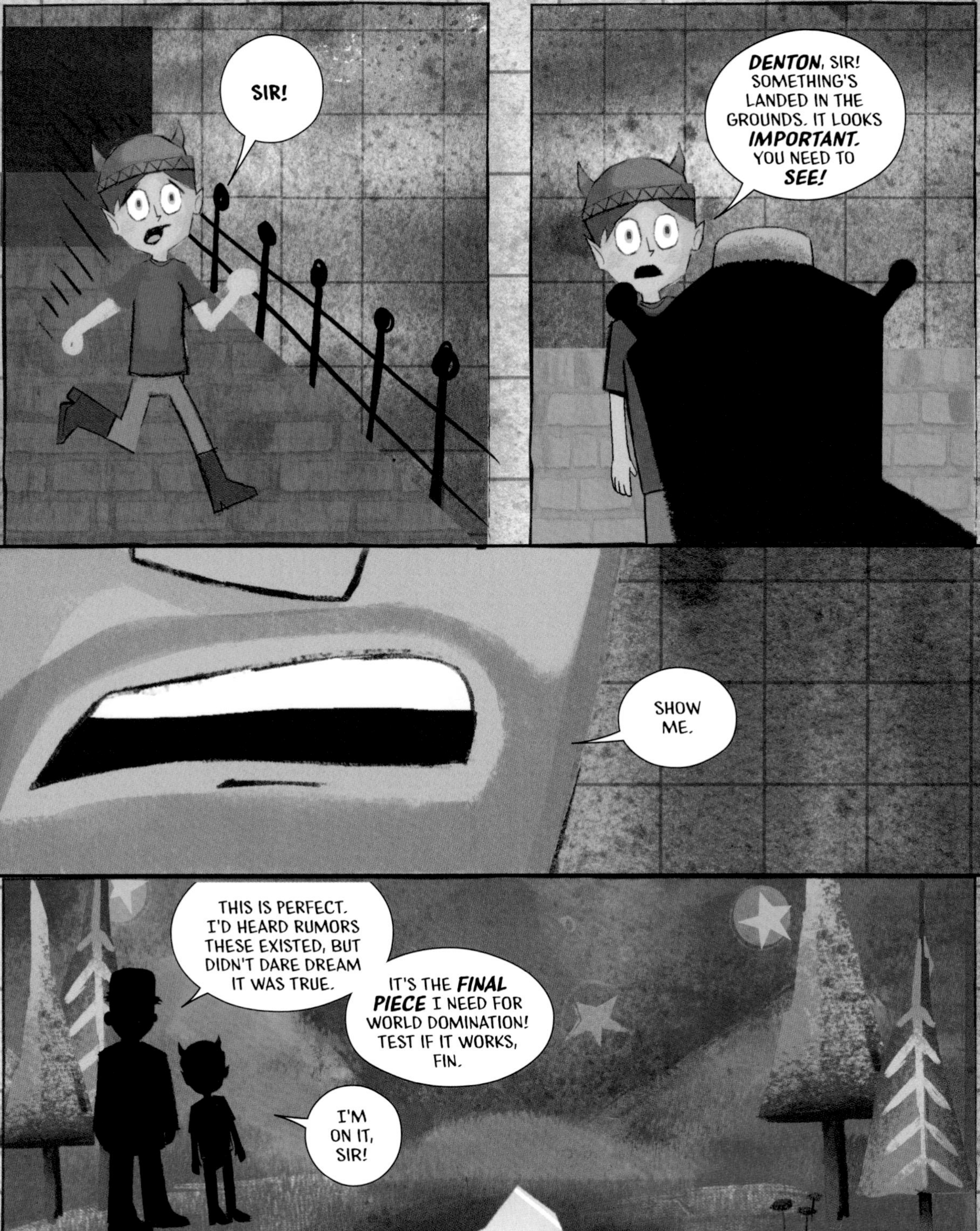
SIR!
DENTON, SIR! SOMETHING'S LANDED IN THE GROUNDS. IT LOOKS IMPORTANT. YOU NEED TO SEE!
SHOW ME.
THIS IS PERFECT. I'D HEARD RUMORS THESE EXISTED, BUT DIDN'T DARE DREAM IT WAS TRUE.
IT'S THE FINAL PIECE I NEED FOR WORLD DOMINATION! TEST IF IT WORKS, FIN.
I'M ON IT, SIR!

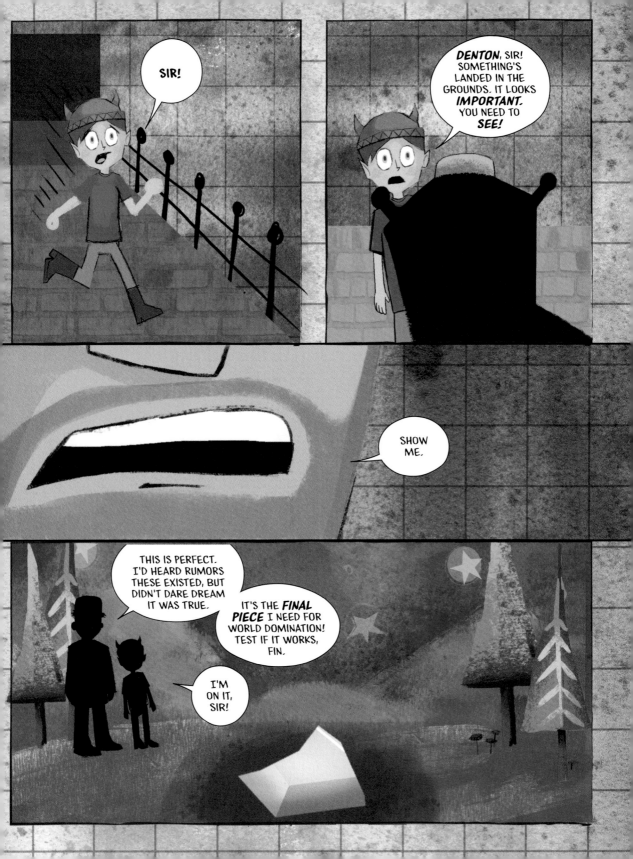

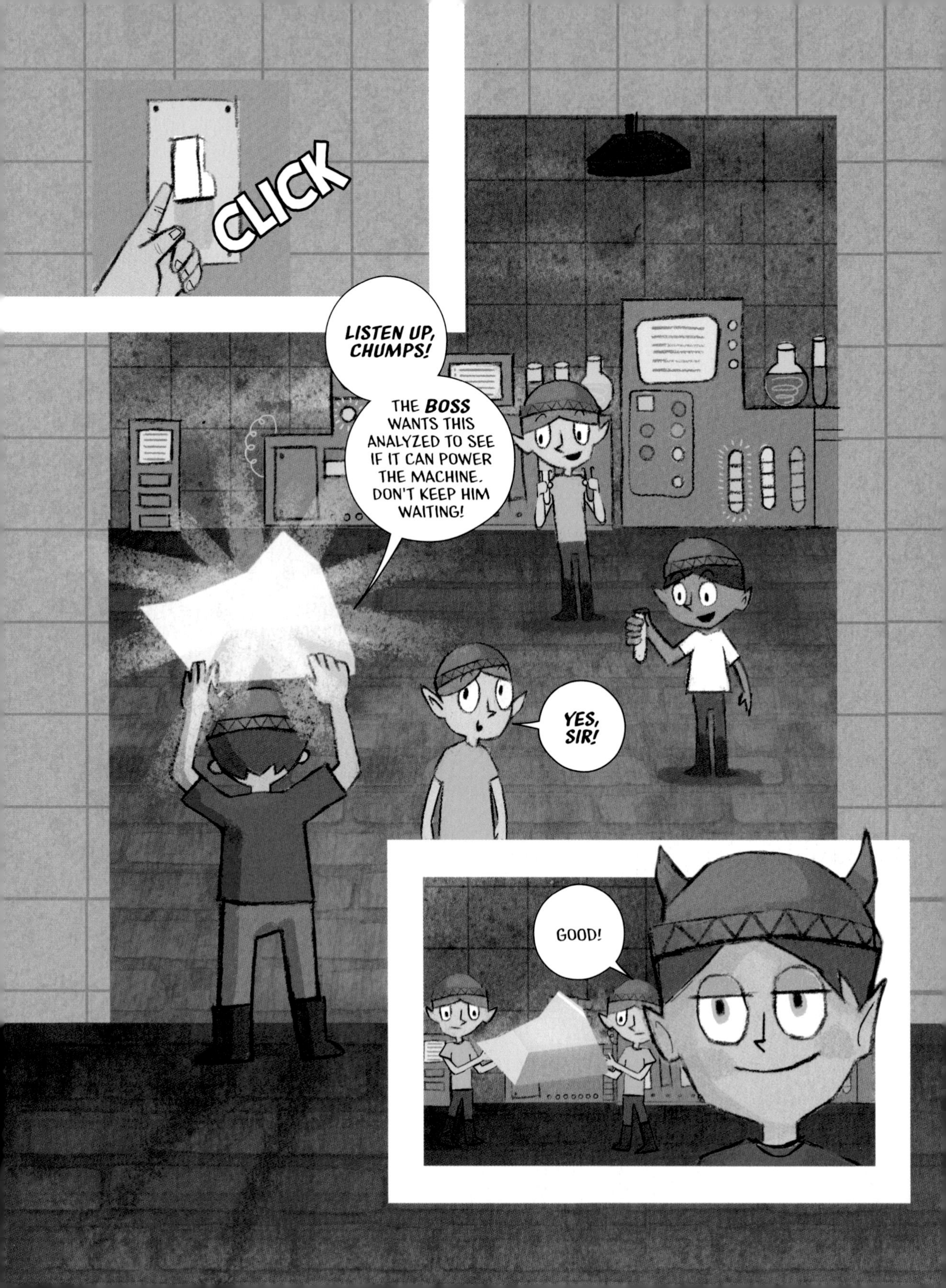
CLICK
LISTEN UP, CHUMPS!
THE BOSS WANTS THIS ANALYZED TO SEE IF IT CAN POWER THE MACHINE. DON'T KEEP HIM WAITING!
YES, SIR!
GOOD!

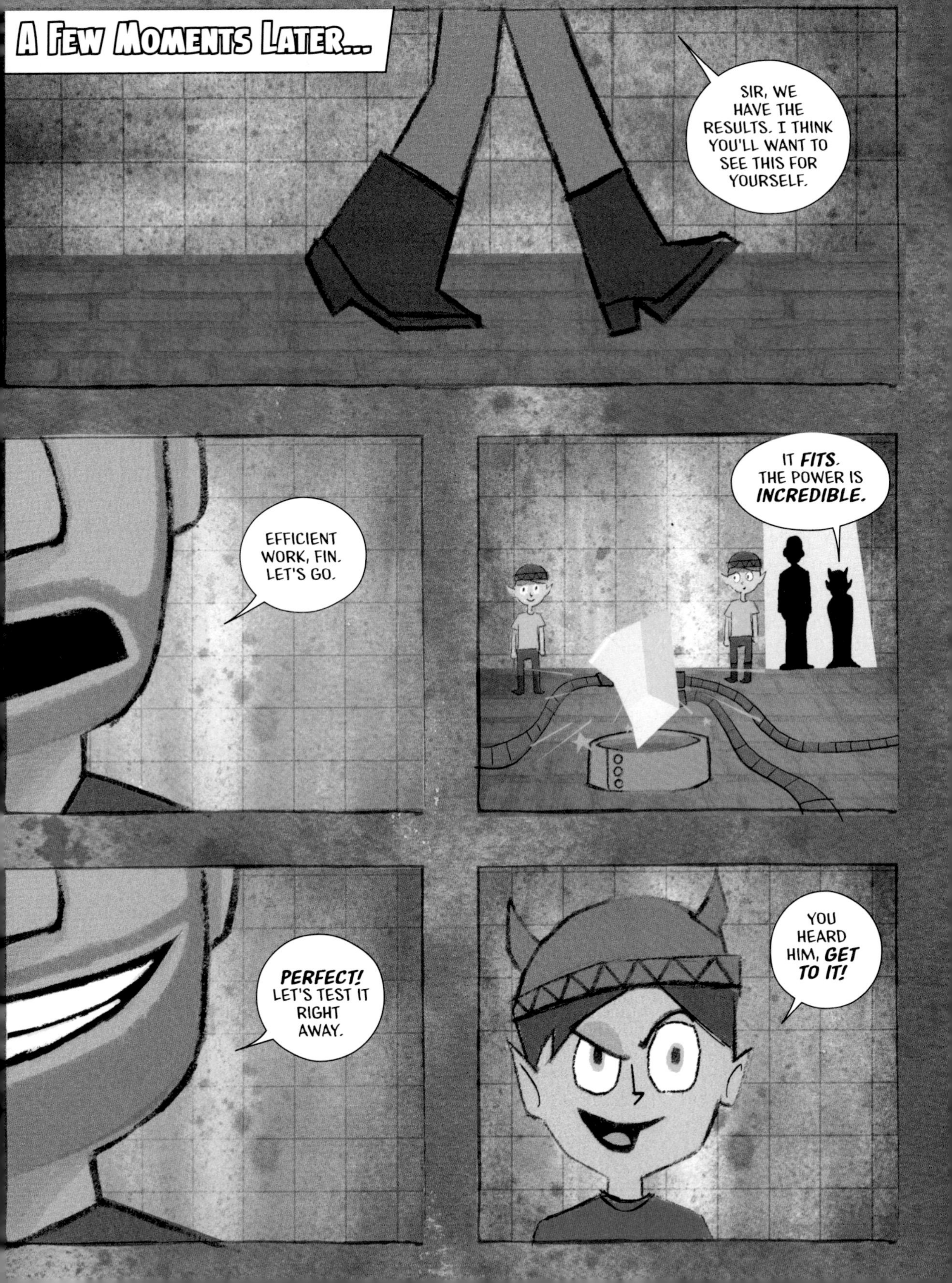
A FEW MOMENTS LATER...
SIR, WE HAVE THE RESULTS. I THINK YOU'LL WANT TO SEE THIS FOR YOURSELF.
EFFICIENT WORK, FIN. LET'S GO.
IT FITS. THE POWER IS INCREDIBLE.
PERFECT! LET'S TEST IT RIGHT AWAY.
YOU HEARD HIM, GET TO IT!

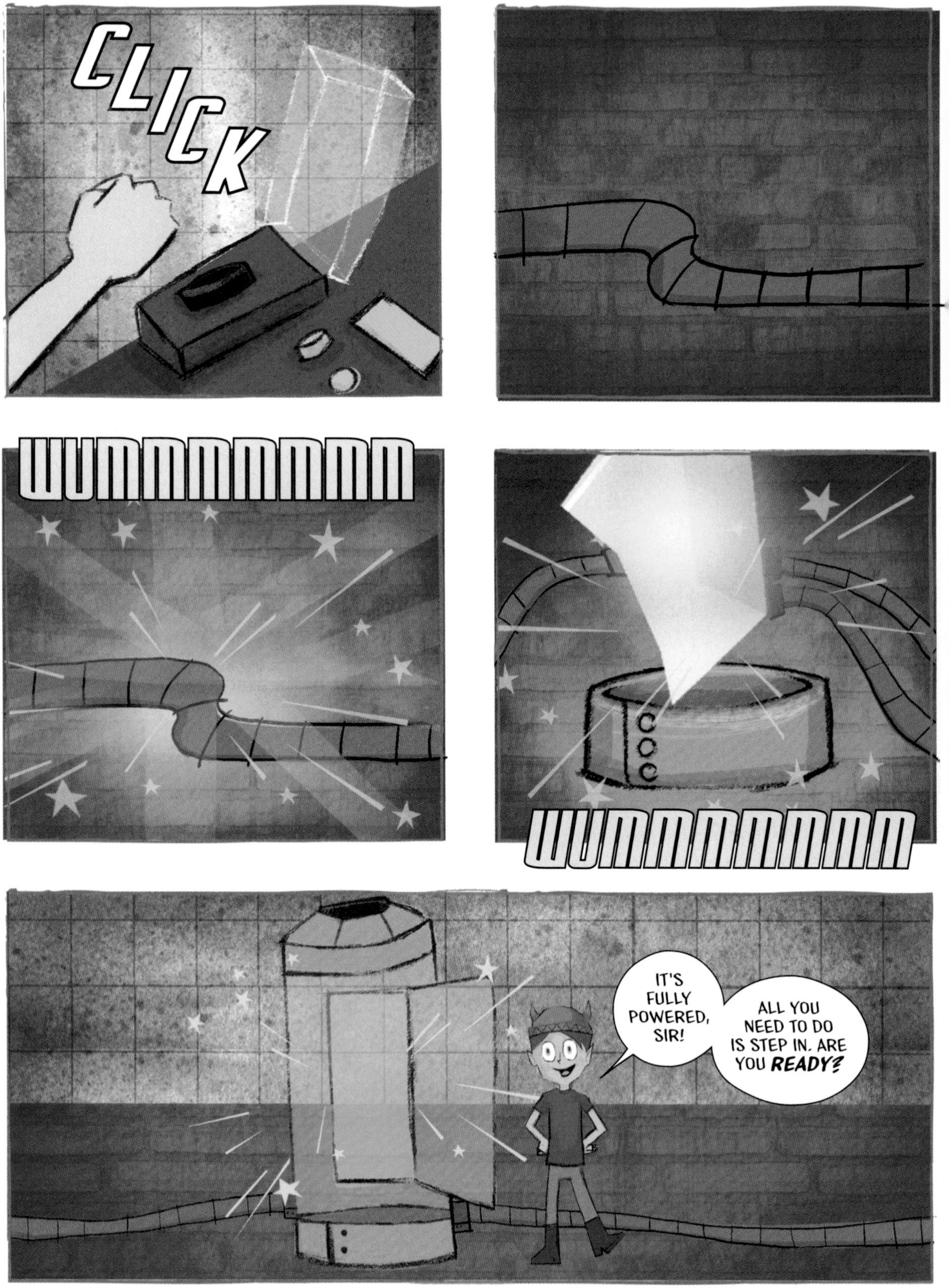
CLICK
WUMMMMMMM
WUMMMMMMMM
IT'S FULLY POWERED, SIR!
ALL YOU NEED TO DO IS STEP IN. ARE YOU READY?

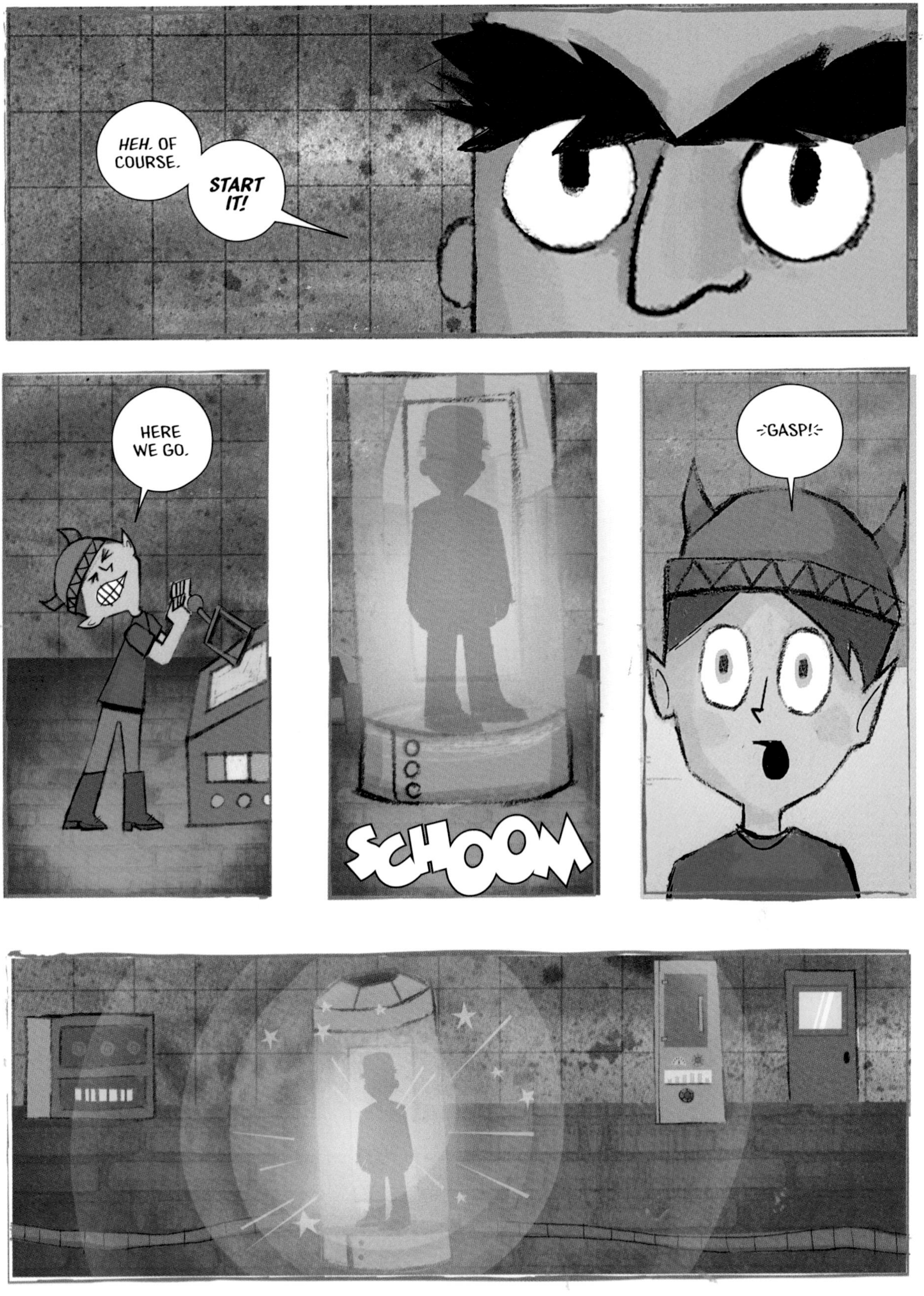
HEH. OF COURSE.
START IT!
HERE WE GO.
SCHOOM
-GASP!-

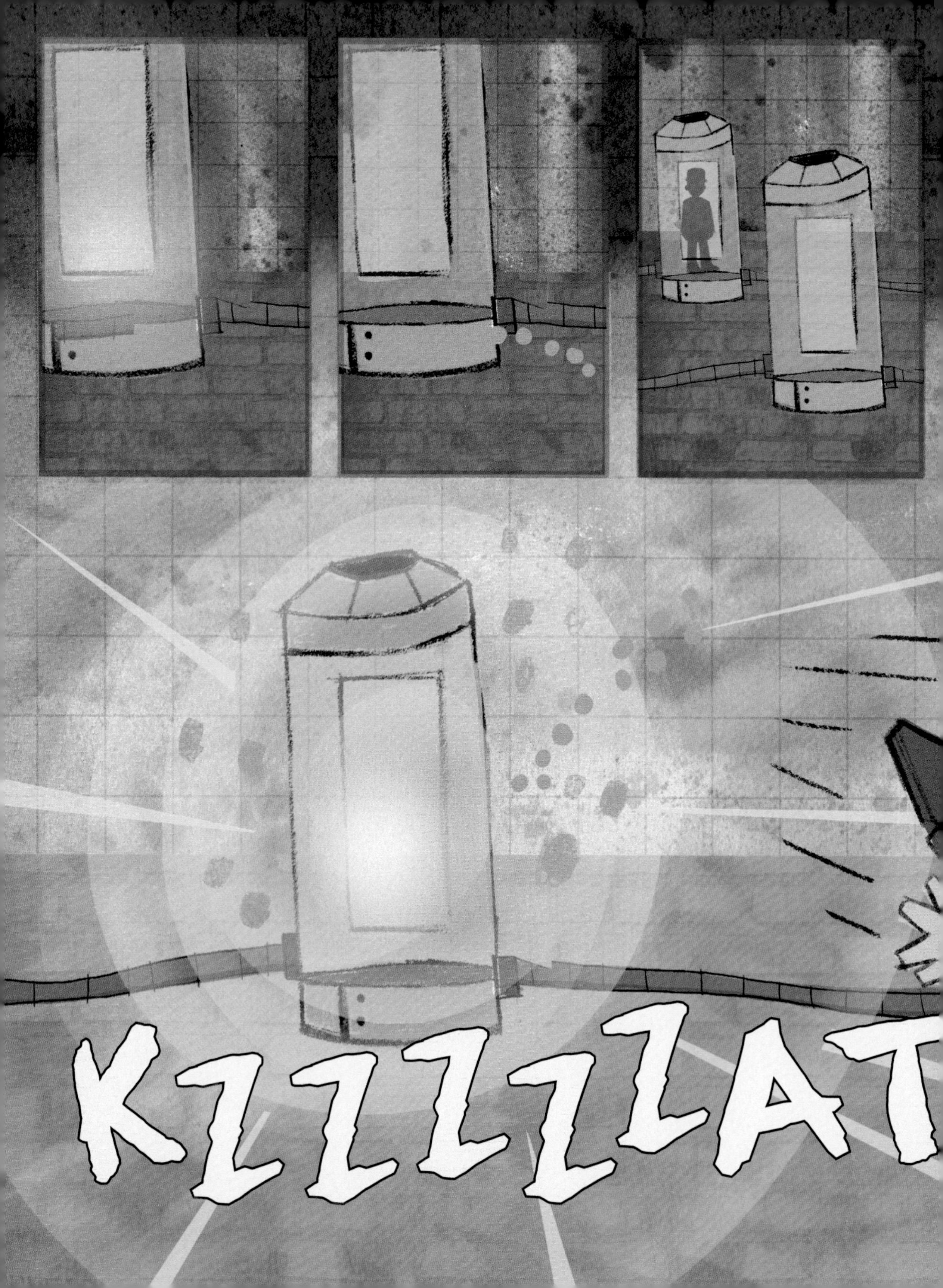
KZZZZZAT

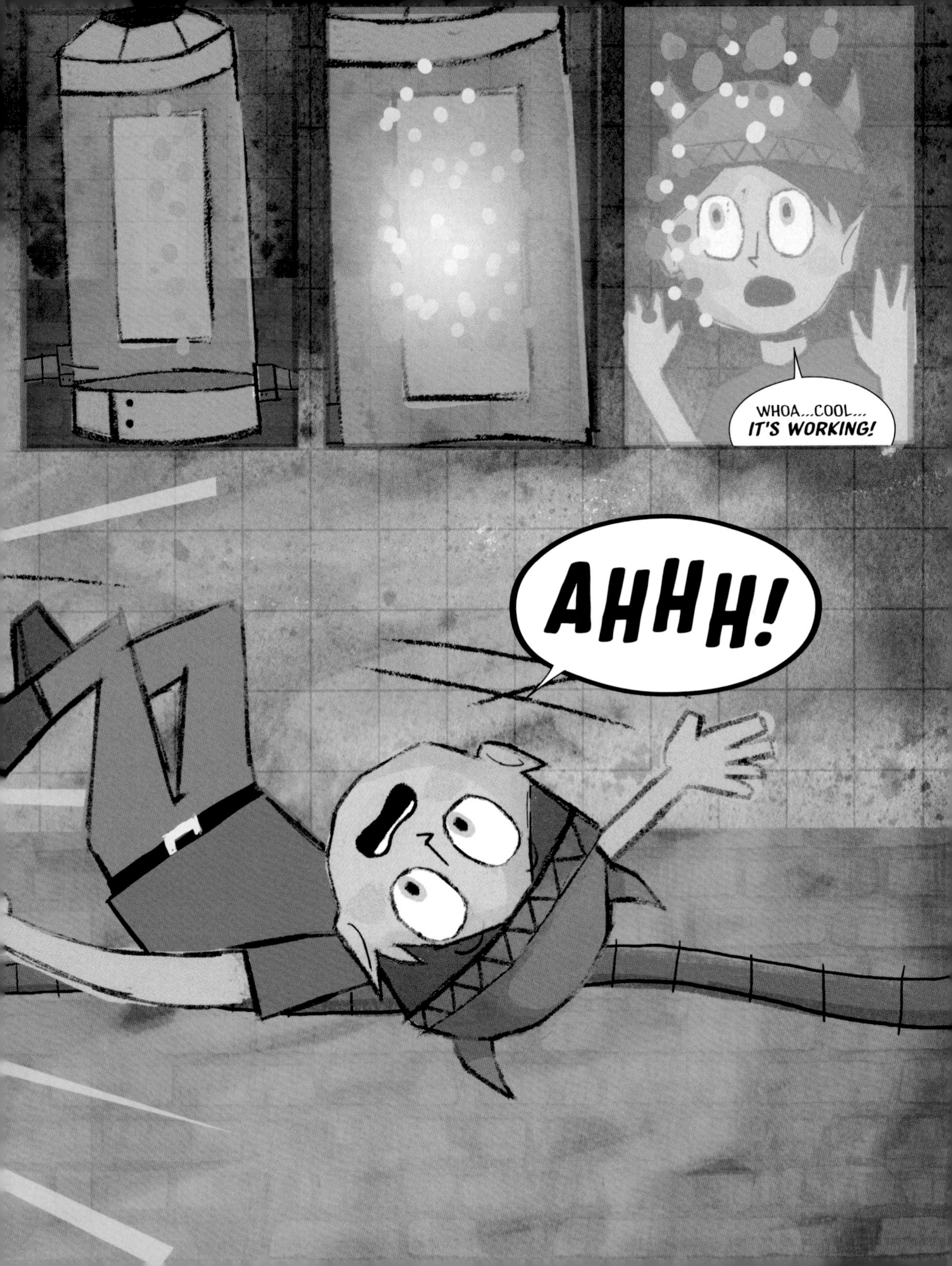
WHOA...COOL...
IT'S WORKING!
AHHH!

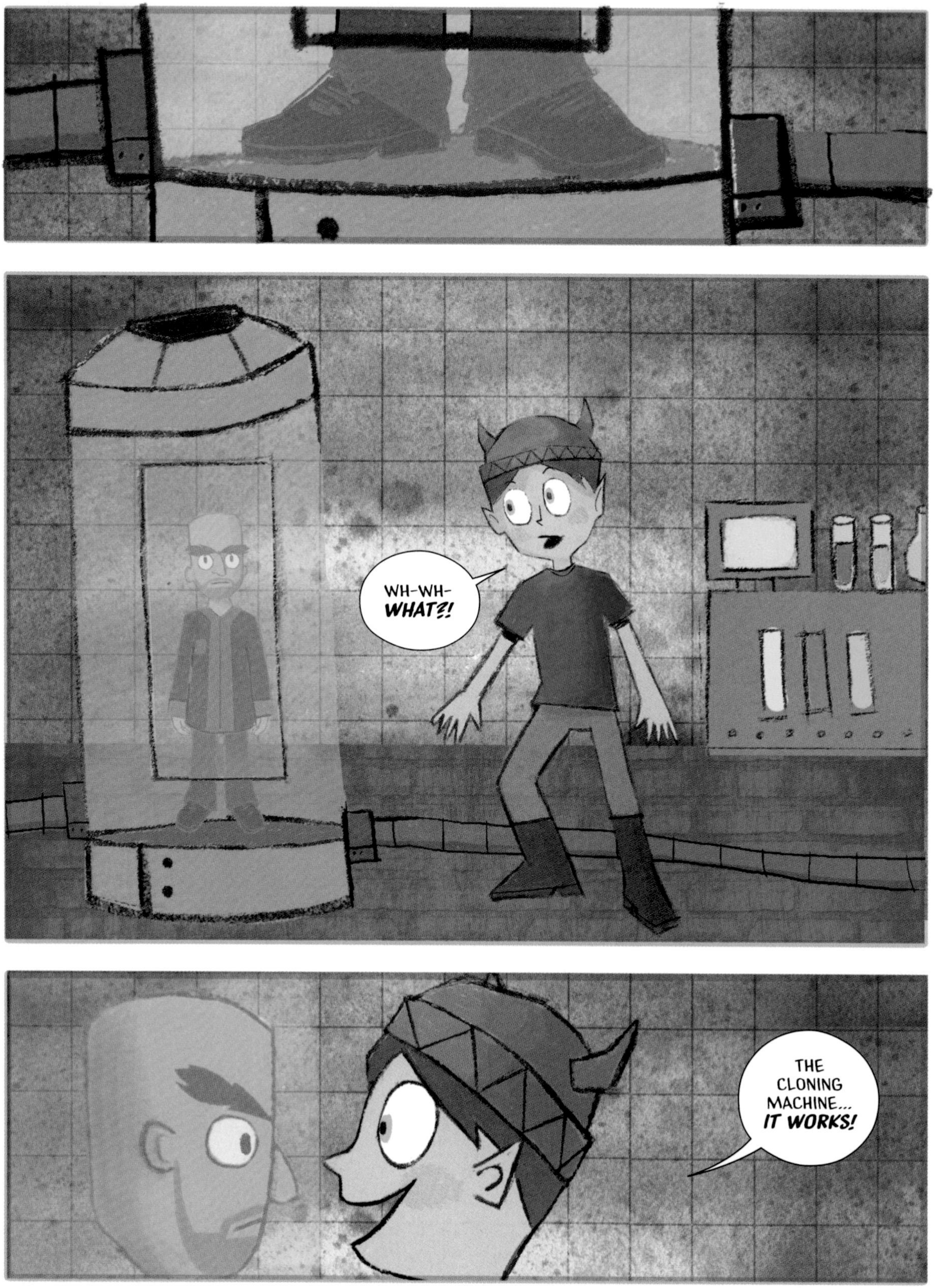
WH-WH-
WHAT?!
THE CLONING MACHINE...
IT WORKS!

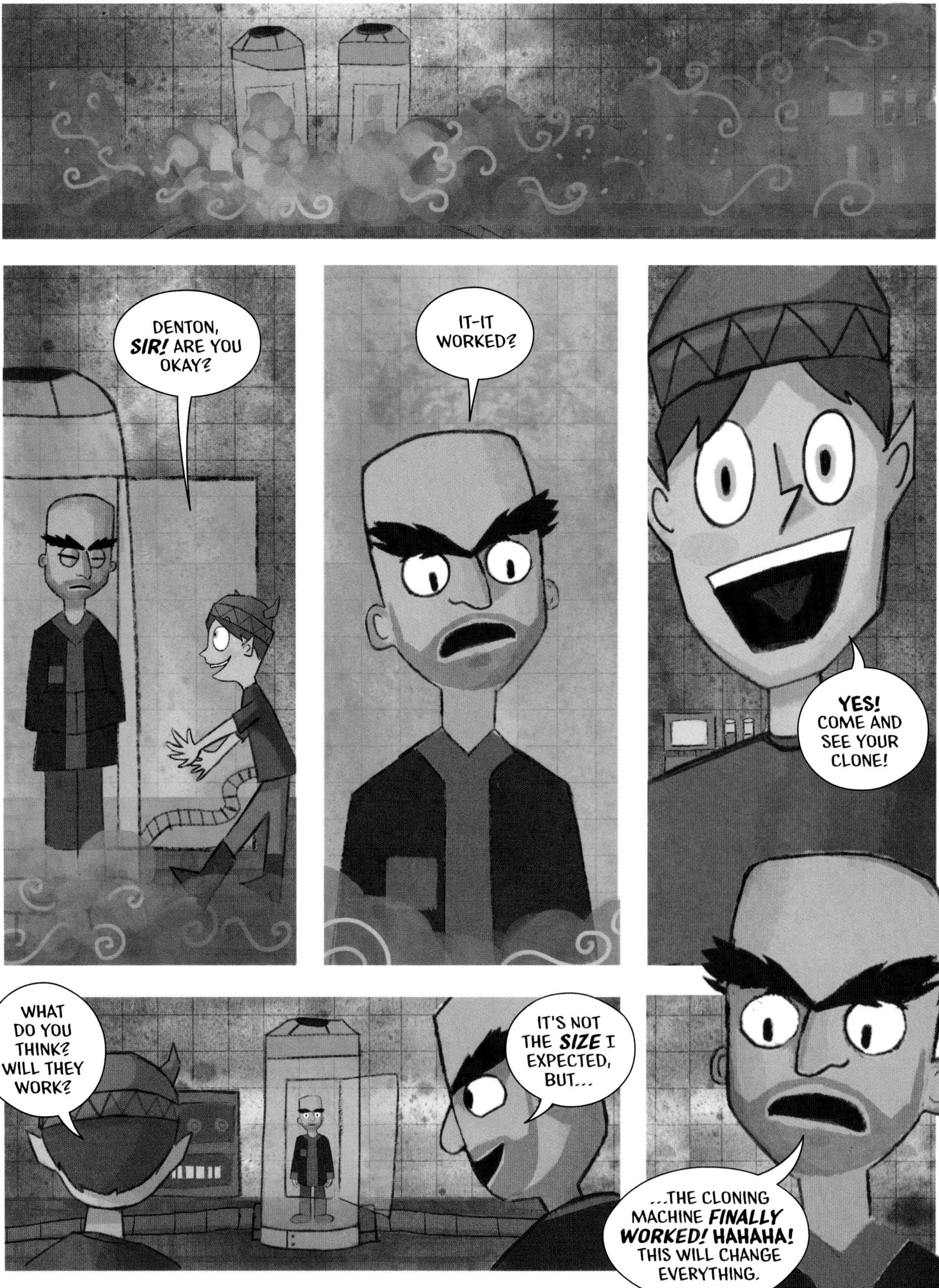
DENTON, SIR! ARE YOU OKAY?
IT-IT WORKED?
YES! COME AND SEE YOUR CLONE!
WHAT DO YOU THINK? WILL THEY WORK?
IT'S NOT THE SIZE I EXPECTED, BUT...
...THE CLONING MACHINE FINALLY WORKED! HAHAHA! THIS WILL CHANGE EVERYTHING.

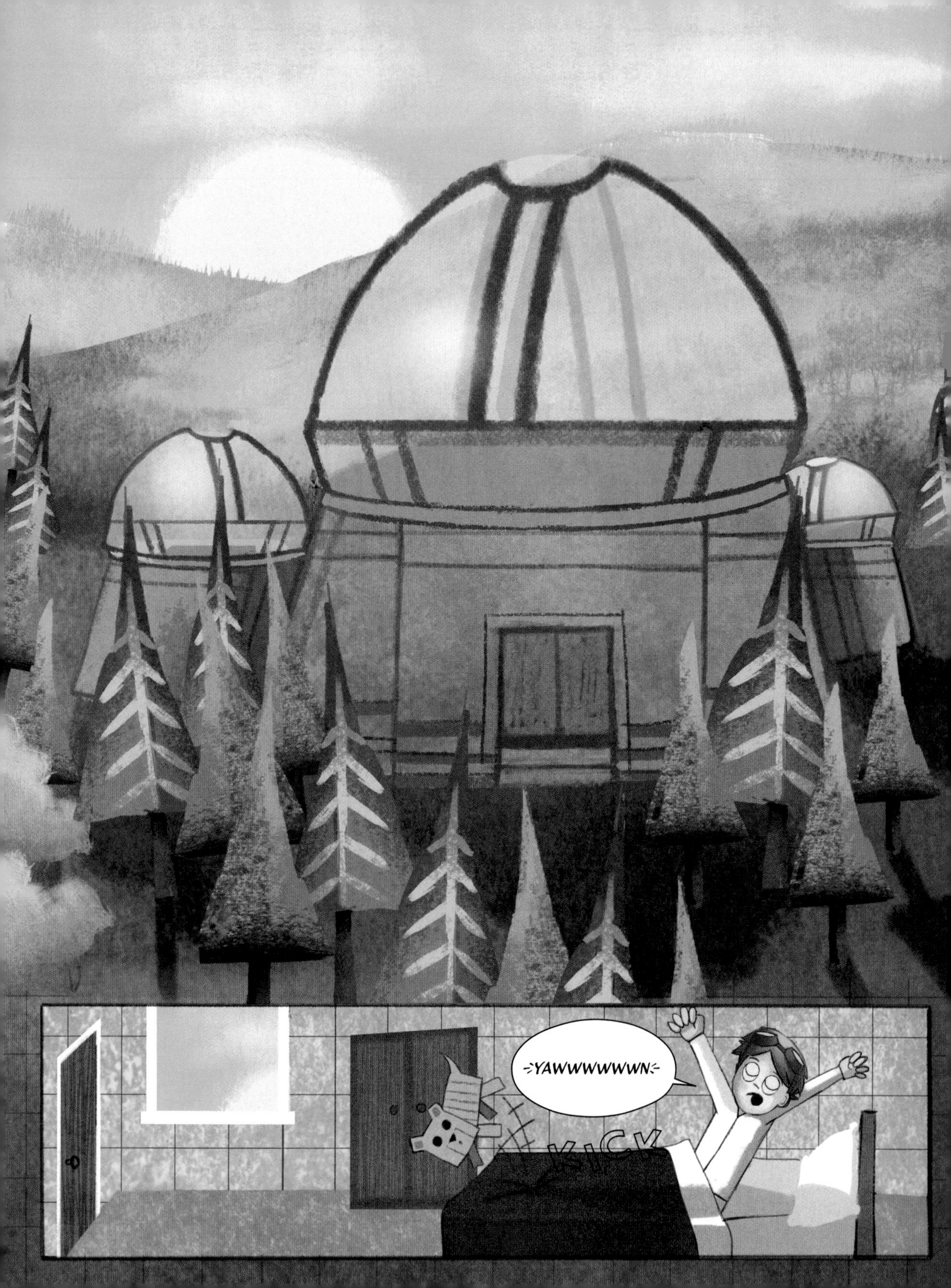
YAWWWWWWN
KICK

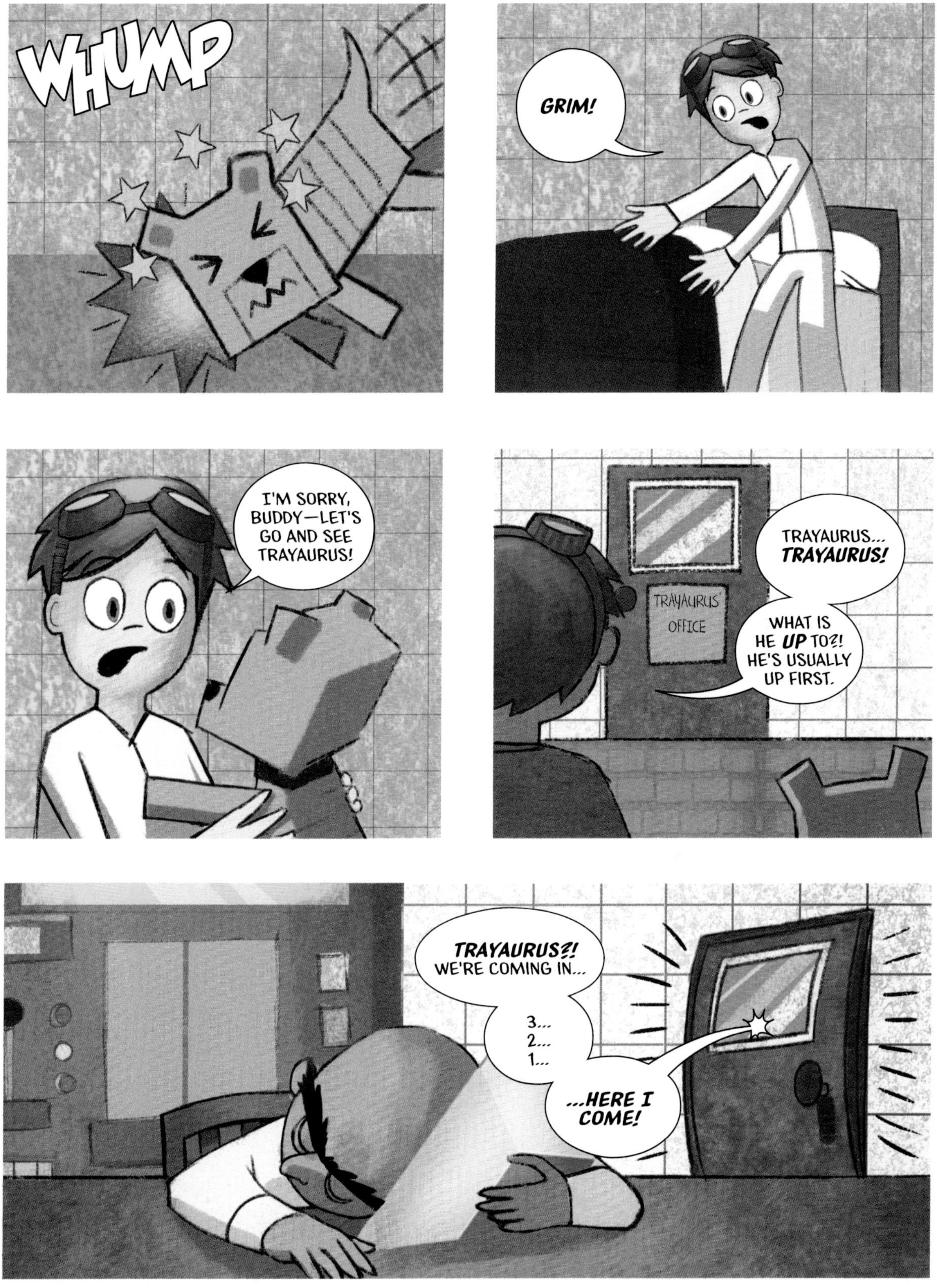
WHUMP
GRIM!
I'M SORRY, BUDDY—LET'S GO AND SEE TRAYAURUS!
TRAYAURUS' OFFICE
TRAYAURUS... TRAYAURUS!
WHAT IS HE UP TO?! HE'S USUALLY UP FIRST.
TRAYAURUS?! WE'RE COMING IN...
3... 2... 1...
...HERE I COME!

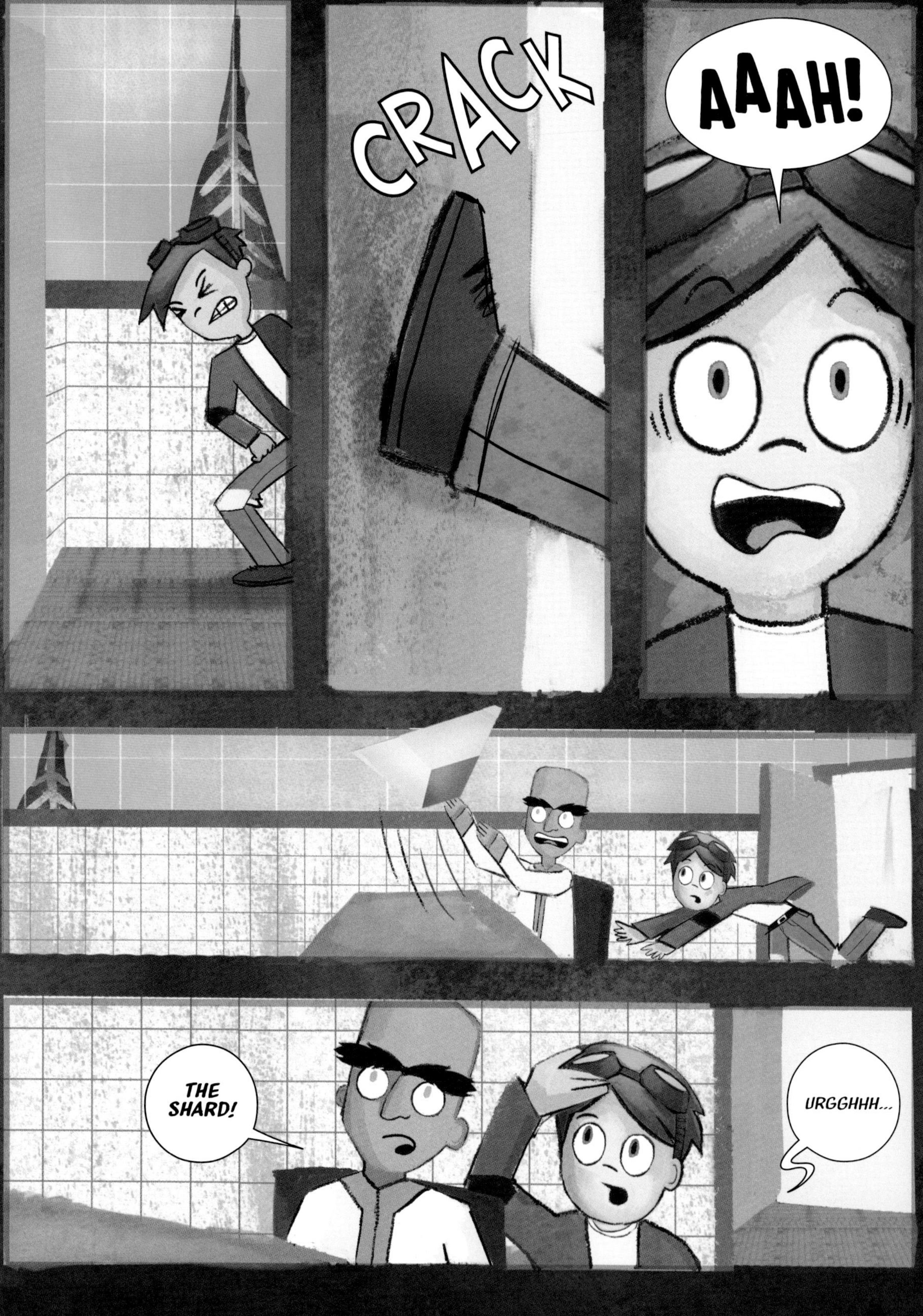
CRACK
AAAH!
THE SHARD!
URGGHHH...

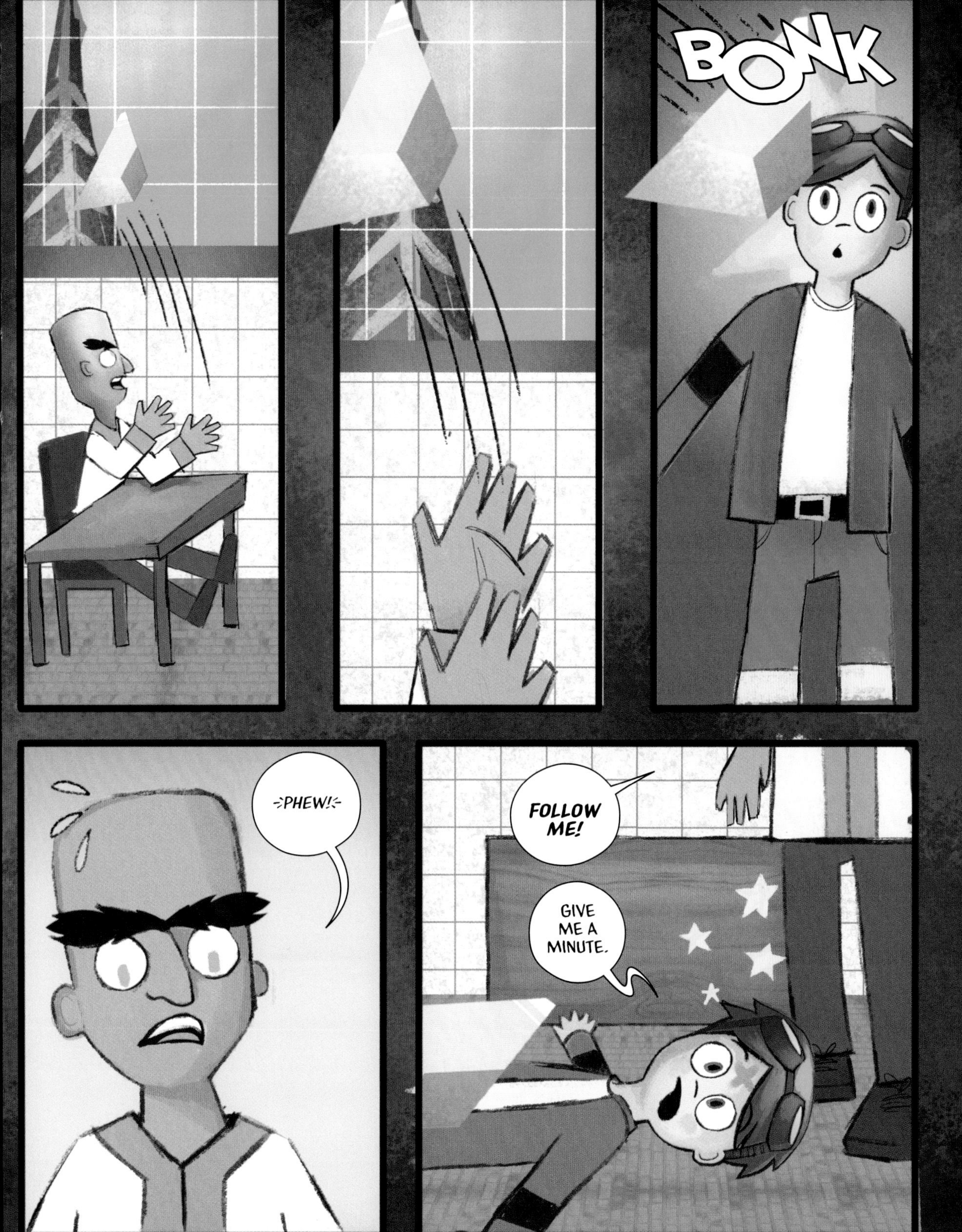
BONK
PHEW!
FOLLOW ME!
GIVE ME A MINUTE.

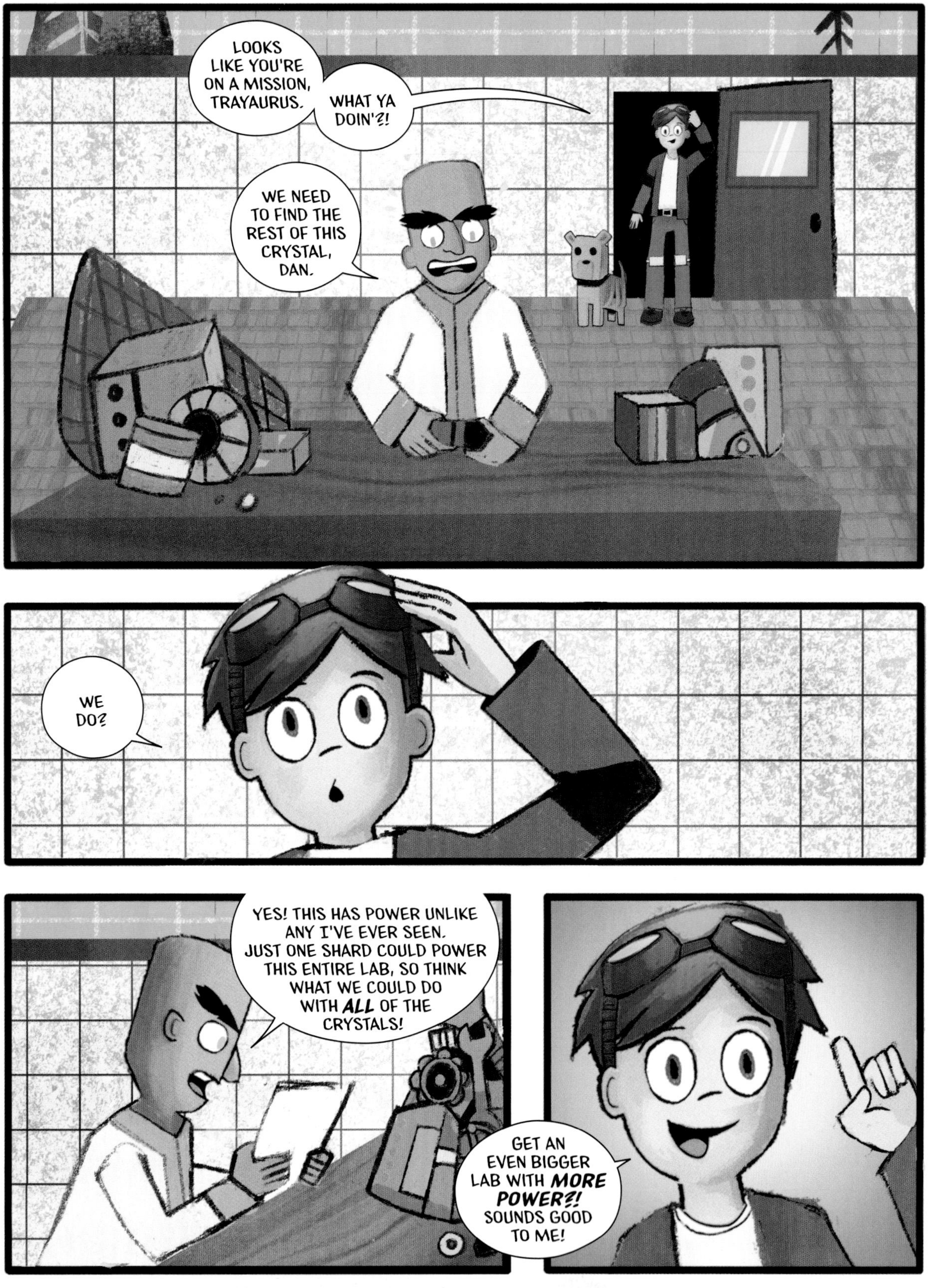
LOOKS LIKE YOU'RE ON A MISSION, TRAYAURUS.
WHAT YA DOIN'?!
WE NEED TO FIND THE REST OF THIS CRYSTAL, DAN.
WE DO?
YES! THIS HAS POWER UNLIKE ANY I'VE EVER SEEN. JUST ONE SHARD COULD POWER THIS ENTIRE LAB, SO THINK WHAT WE COULD DO WITH ALL OF THE CRYSTALS!
GET AN EVEN BIGGER LAB WITH MORE POWER?! SOUNDS GOOD TO ME!

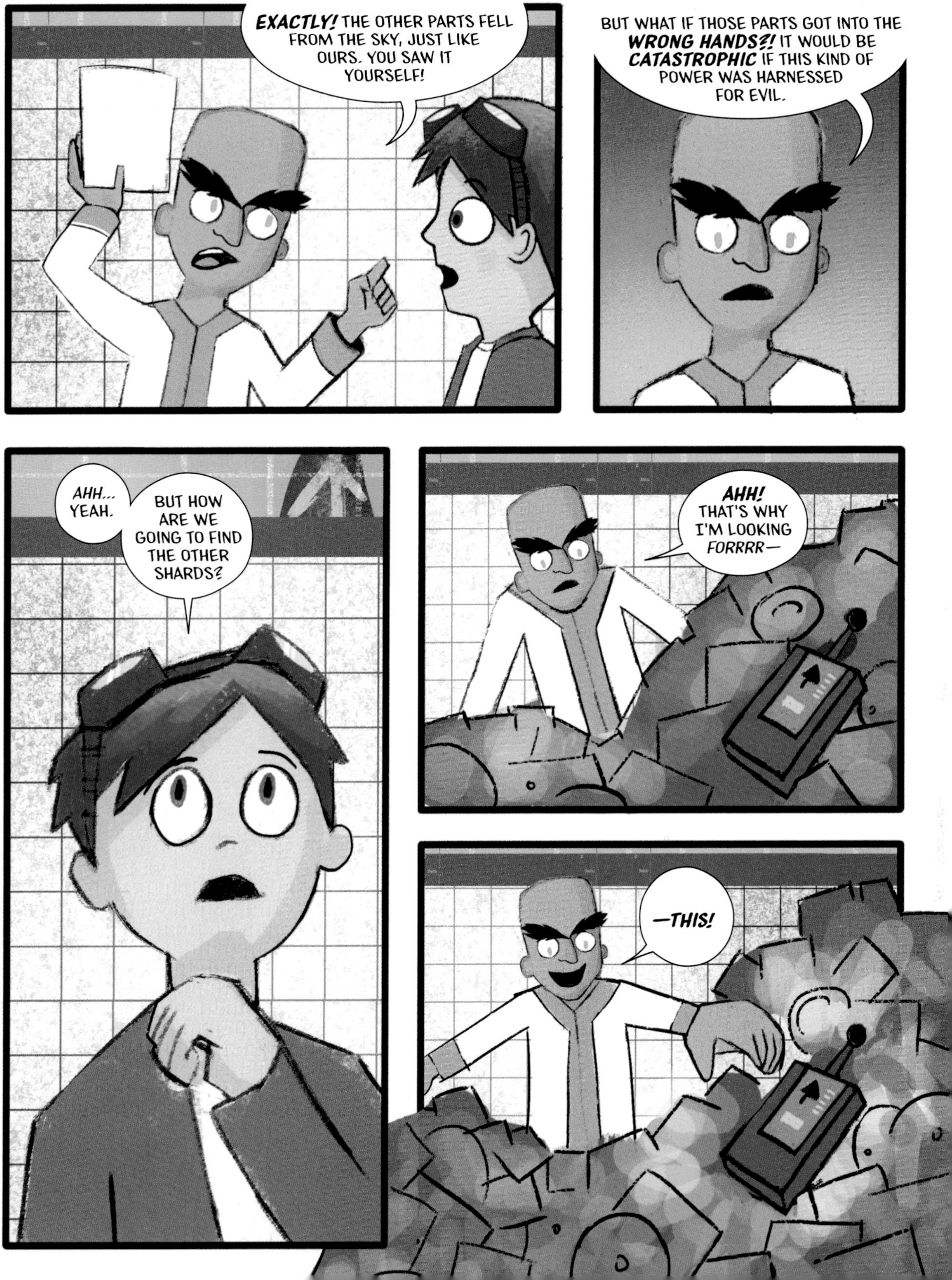
EXACTLY! THE OTHER PARTS FELL FROM THE SKY, JUST LIKE OURS. YOU SAW IT YOURSELF!
BUT WHAT IF THOSE PARTS GOT INTO THE WRONG HANDS?! IT WOULD BE CATASTROPHIC IF THIS KIND OF POWER WAS HARNESSED FOR EVIL.
AHH... YEAH.
BUT HOW ARE WE GOING TO FIND THE OTHER SHARDS?
AHH! THAT'S WHY I'M LOOKING FORRRR—
—THIS!

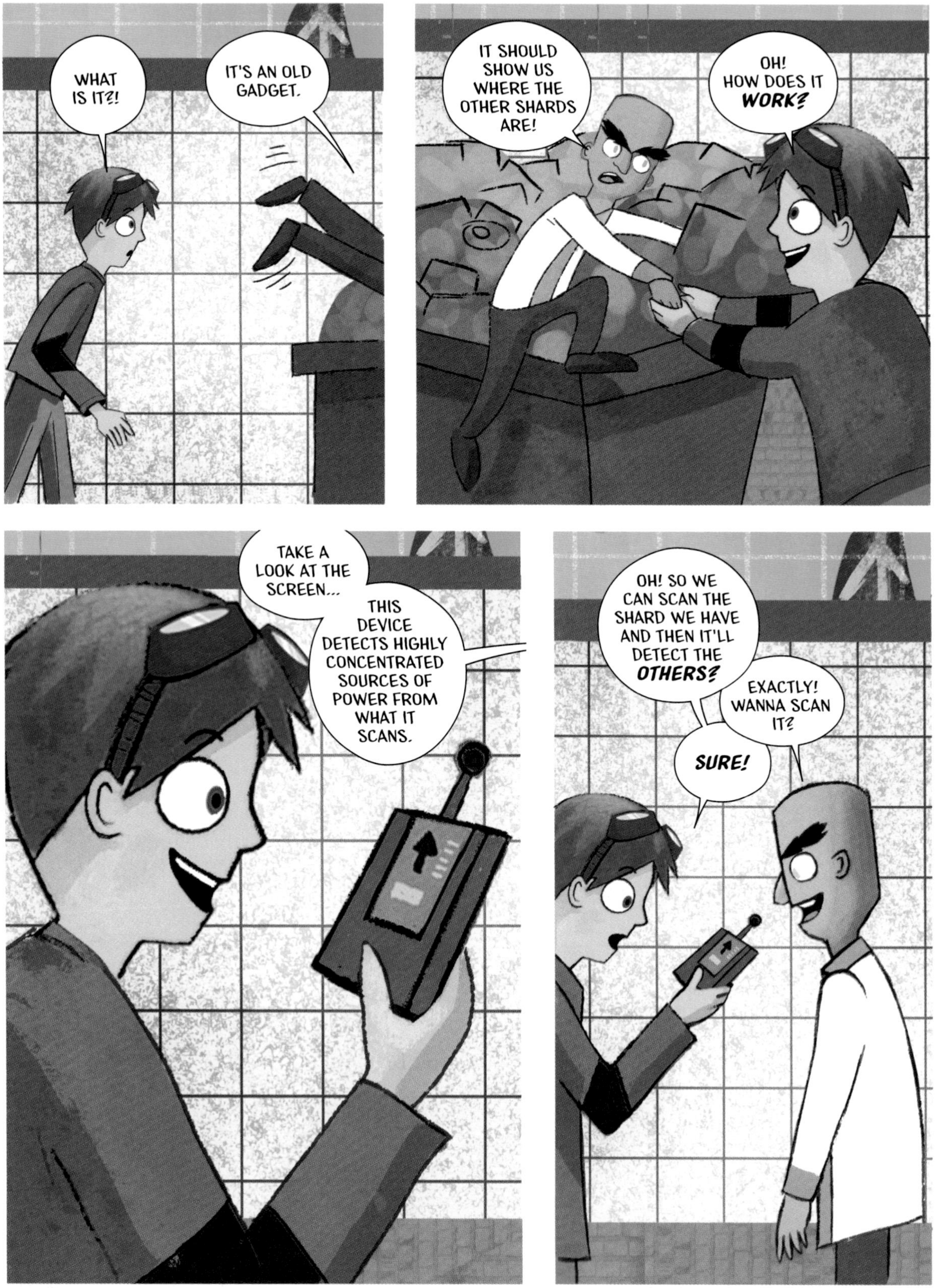
WHAT IS IT?!
IT'S AN OLD GADGET.
IT SHOULD SHOW US WHERE THE OTHER SHARDS ARE!
OH! HOW DOES IT WORK?
TAKE A LOOK AT THE SCREEN...
THIS DEVICE DETECTS HIGHLY CONCENTRATED SOURCES OF POWER FROM WHAT IT SCANS.
OH! SO WE CAN SCAN THE SHARD WE HAVE AND THEN IT'LL DETECT THE OTHERS?
EXACTLY! WANNA SCAN IT?
SURE!

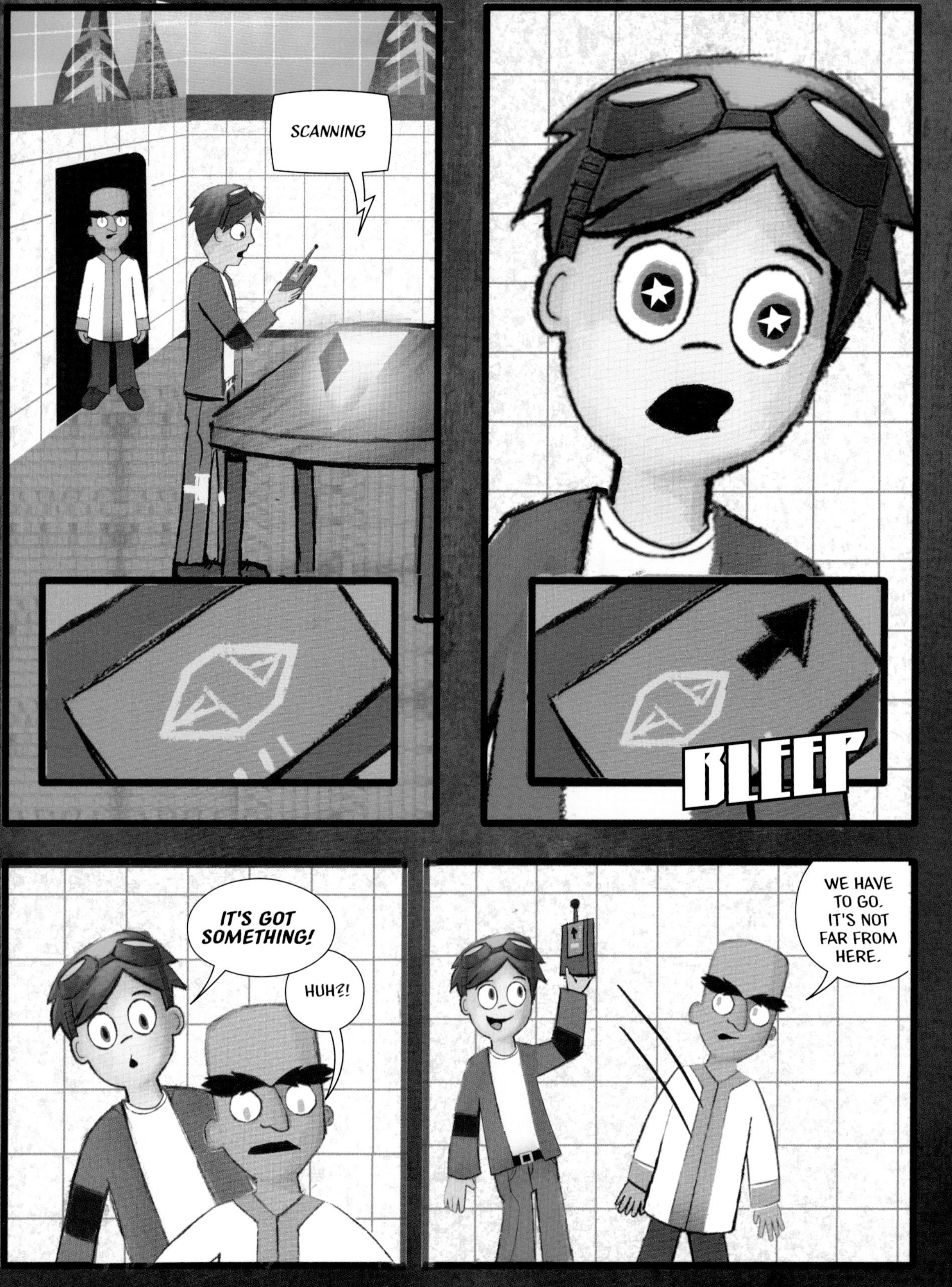
SCANNING
BLEEP
IT'S GOT SOMETHING!
HUH?!
WE HAVE TO GO. IT'S NOT FAR FROM HERE.

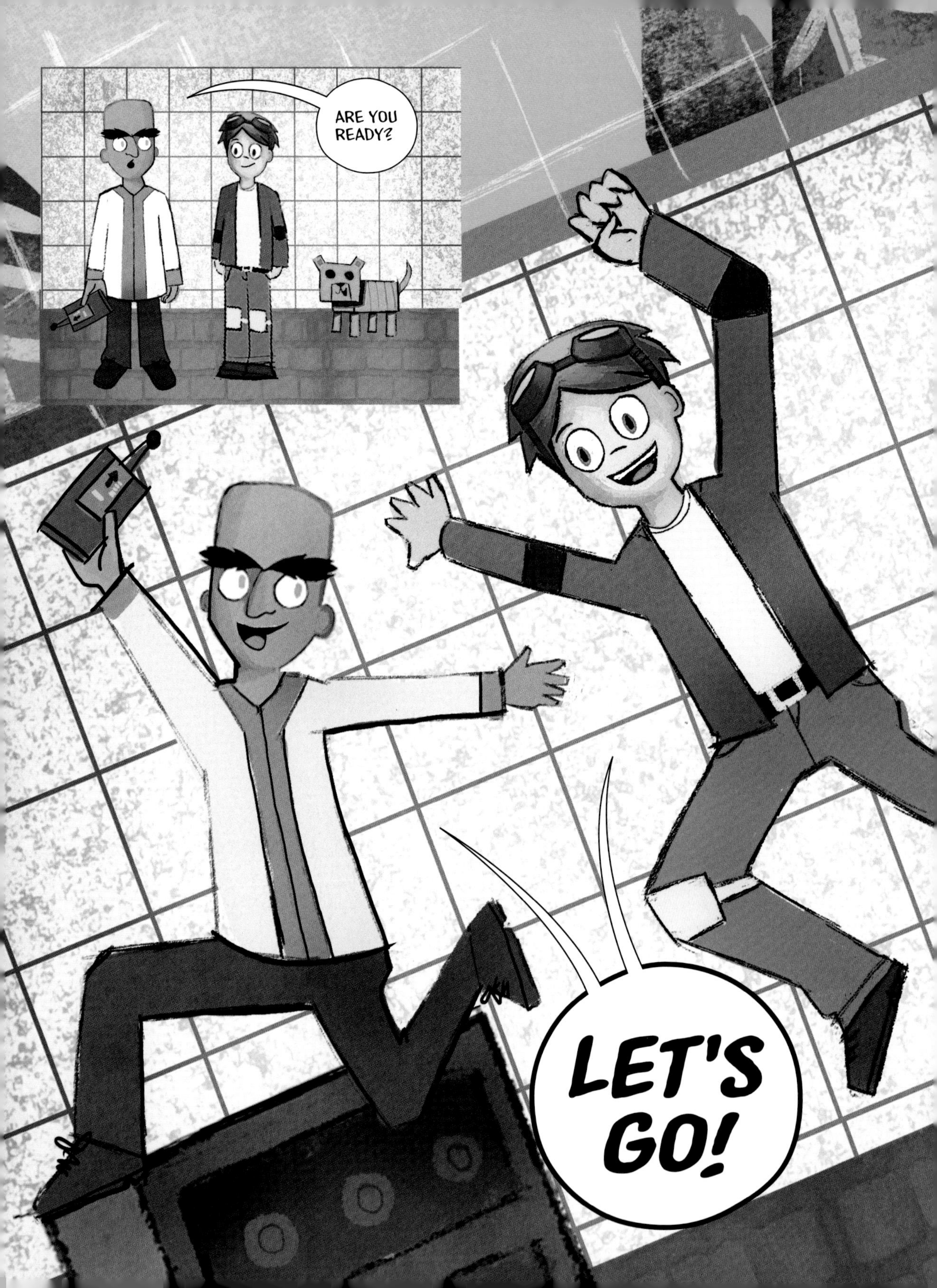
ARE YOU READY?
LET'S GO!

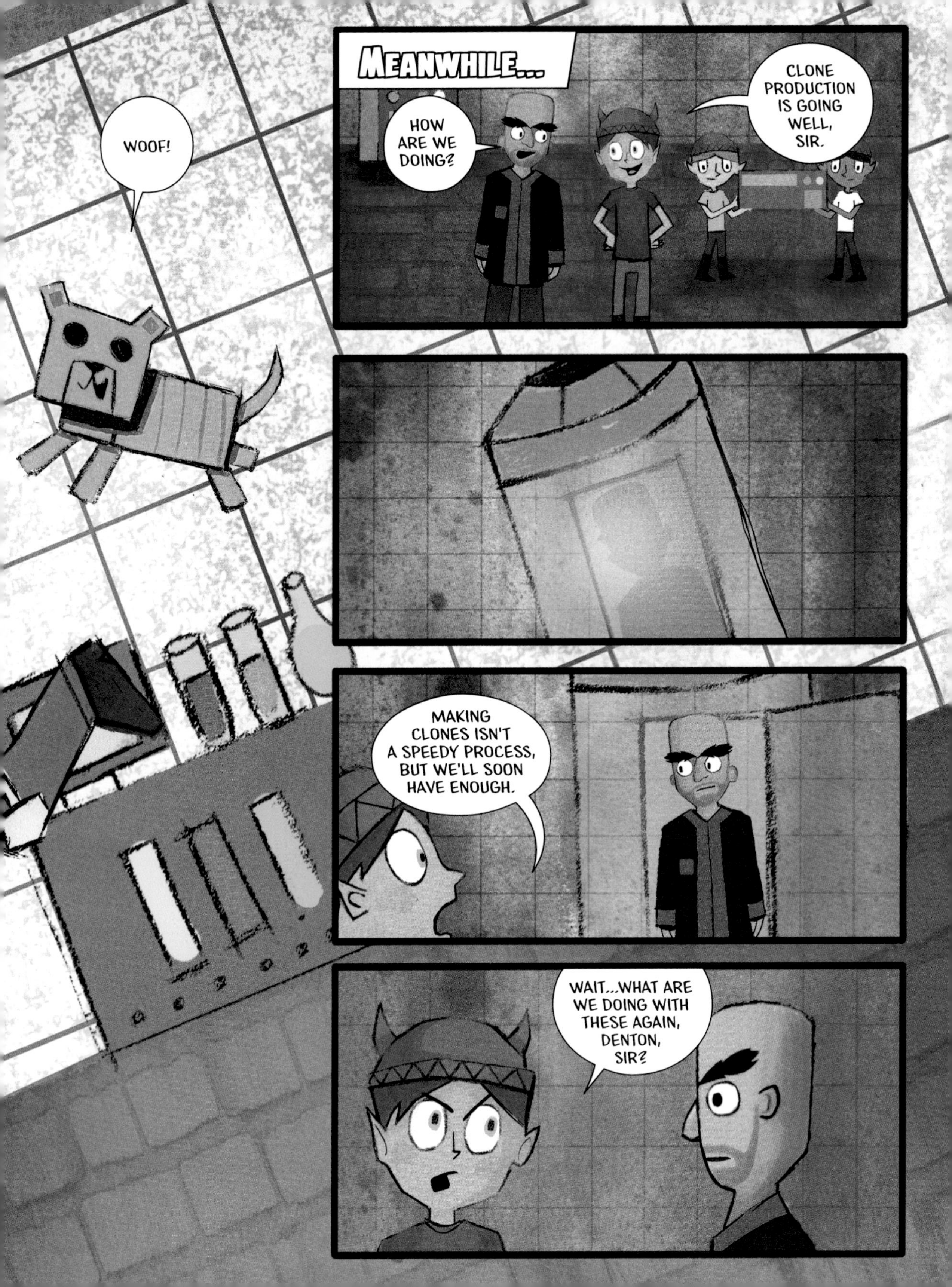
WOOF!
MEANWHILE...
HOW ARE WE DOING?
CLONE PRODUCTION IS GOING WELL, SIR.
MAKING CLONES ISN'T A SPEEDY PROCESS, BUT WE'LL SOON HAVE ENOUGH.
WAIT...WHAT ARE WE DOING WITH THESE AGAIN, DENTON, SIR?

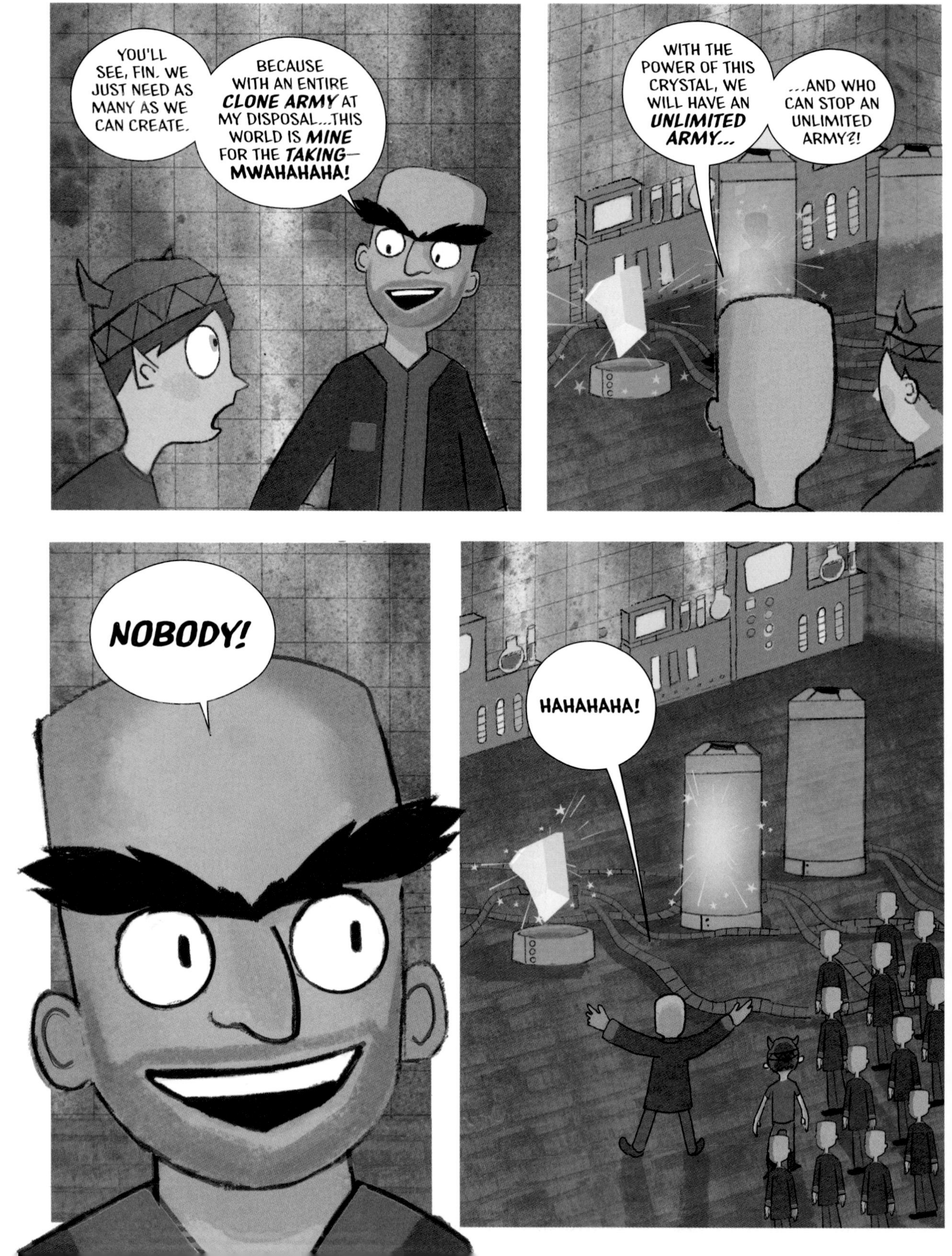
YOU'LL SEE, FIN. WE JUST NEED AS MANY AS WE CAN CREATE.
BECAUSE WITH AN ENTIRE ***CLONE ARMY*** AT MY DISPOSAL...THIS WORLD IS ***MINE*** FOR THE ***TAKING***—MWAHAHAHA!
WITH THE POWER OF THIS CRYSTAL, WE WILL HAVE AN ***UNLIMITED ARMY...***
...AND WHO CAN STOP AN UNLIMITED ARMY?!
NOBODY!
HAHAHAHA!

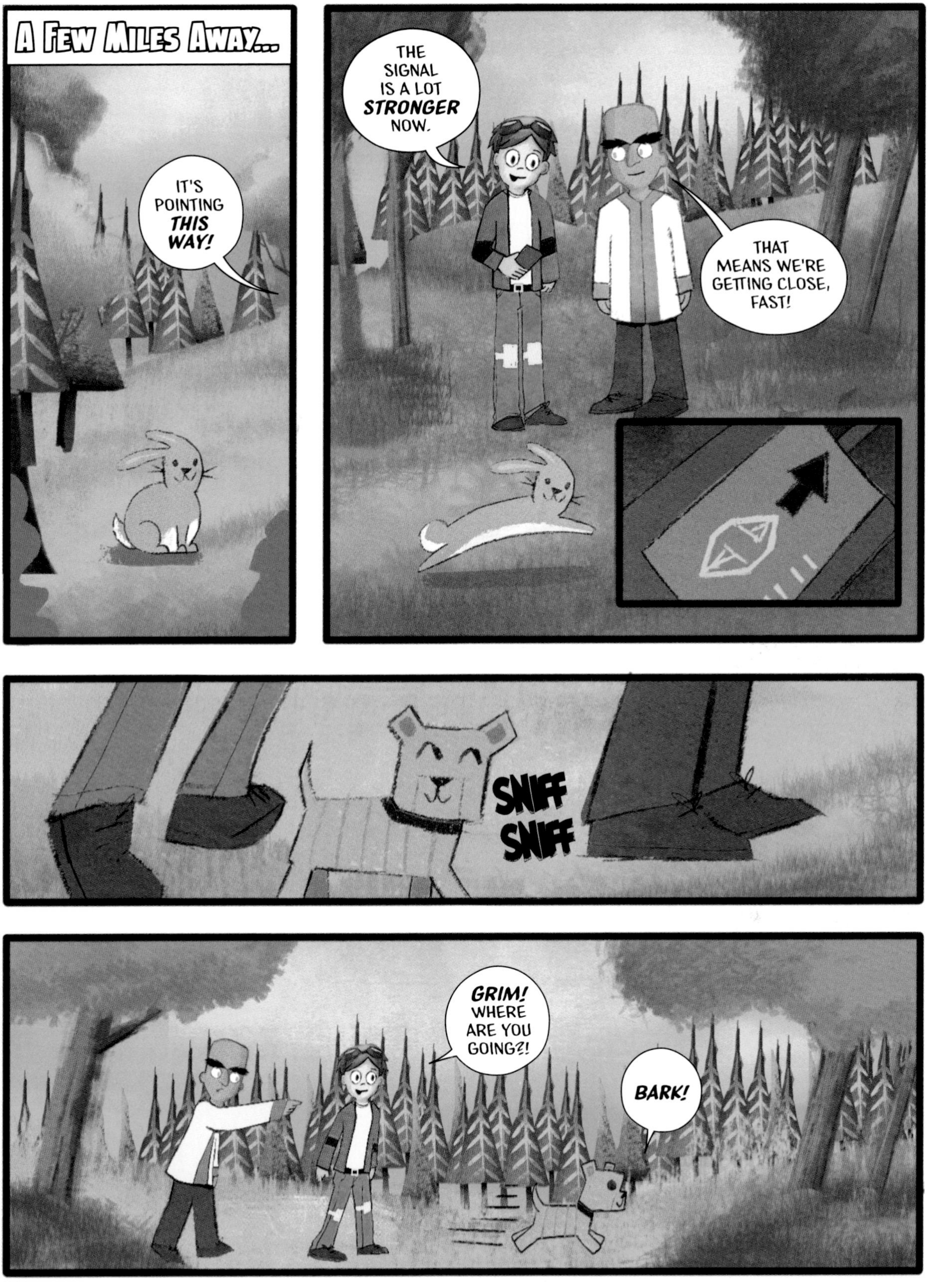
A Few Miles Away...
IT'S POINTING THIS WAY!
THE SIGNAL IS A LOT STRONGER NOW.
THAT MEANS WE'RE GETTING CLOSE, FAST!
SNIFF SNIFF
GRIM! WHERE ARE YOU GOING?!
BARK!

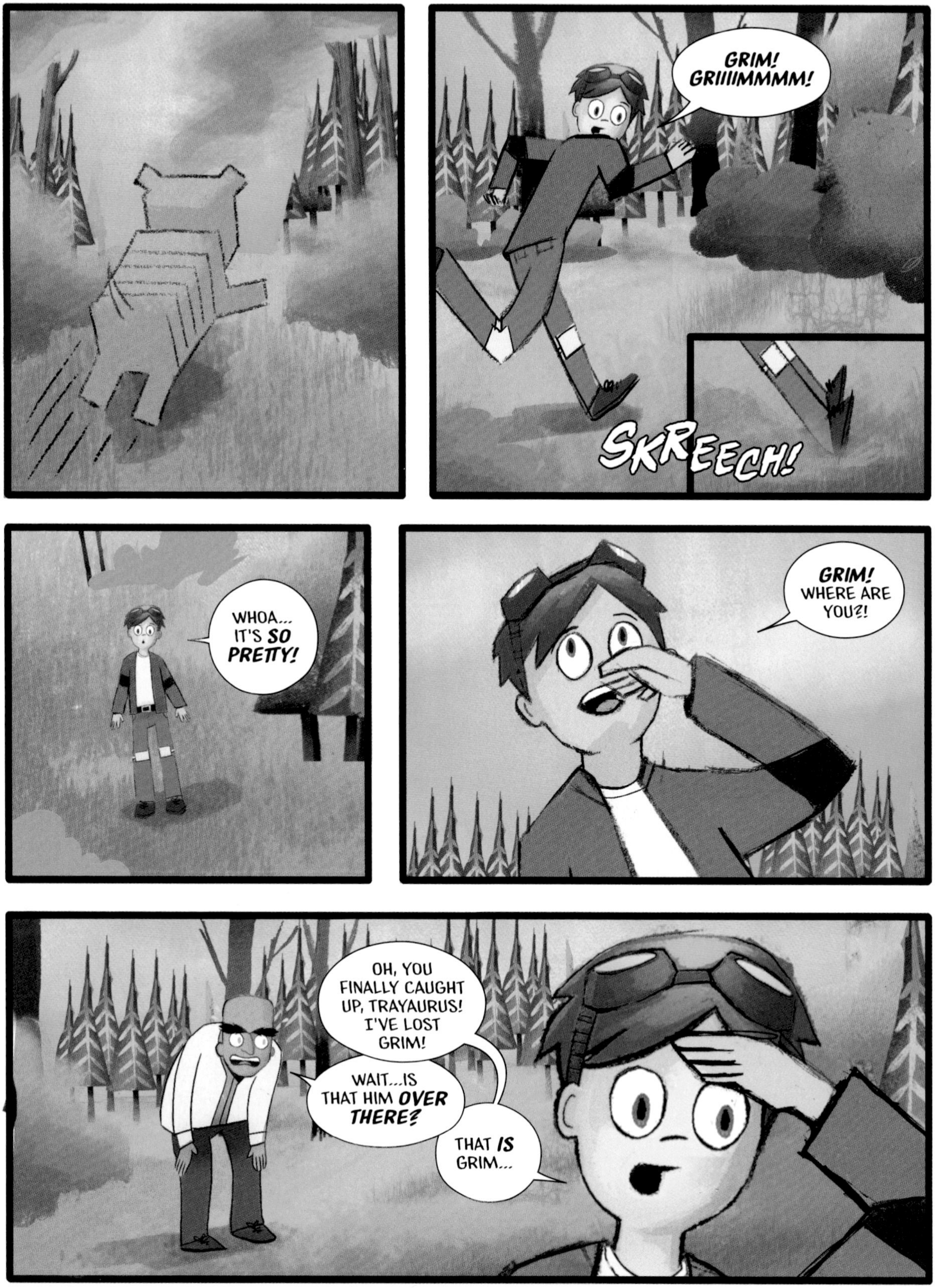
GRIM! GRIIIIMMMM!
SKREECH!
WHOA... IT'S SO PRETTY!
GRIM! WHERE ARE YOU?!
OH, YOU FINALLY CAUGHT UP, TRAYAURUS! I'VE LOST GRIM!
WAIT...IS THAT HIM OVER THERE?
THAT IS GRIM...

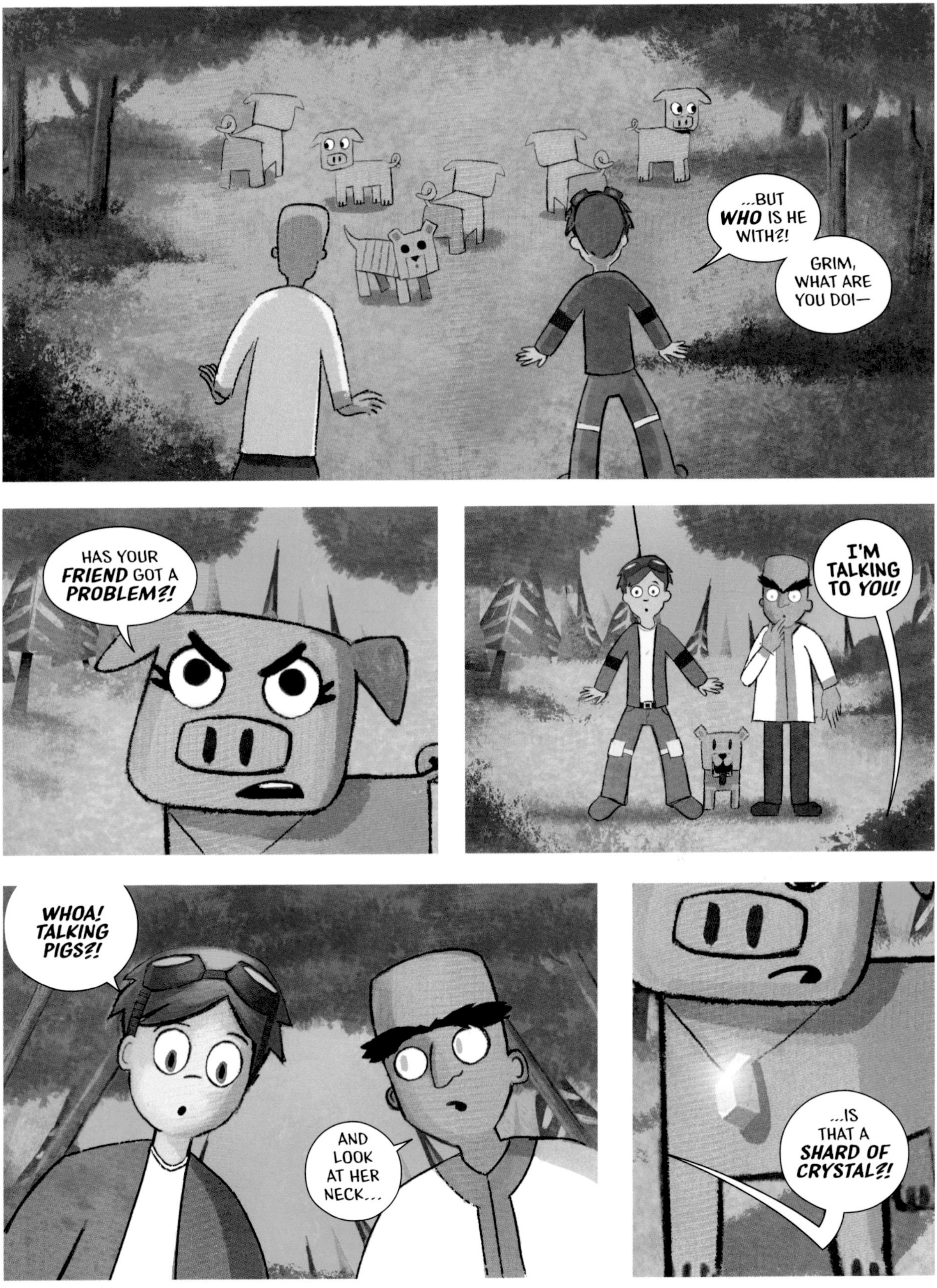
...BUT WHO IS HE WITH?!
GRIM, WHAT ARE YOU DOI—
HAS YOUR FRIEND GOT A PROBLEM?!
I'M TALKING TO YOU!
WHOA! TALKING PIGS?!
AND LOOK AT HER NECK...
...IS THAT A SHARD OF CRYSTAL?!

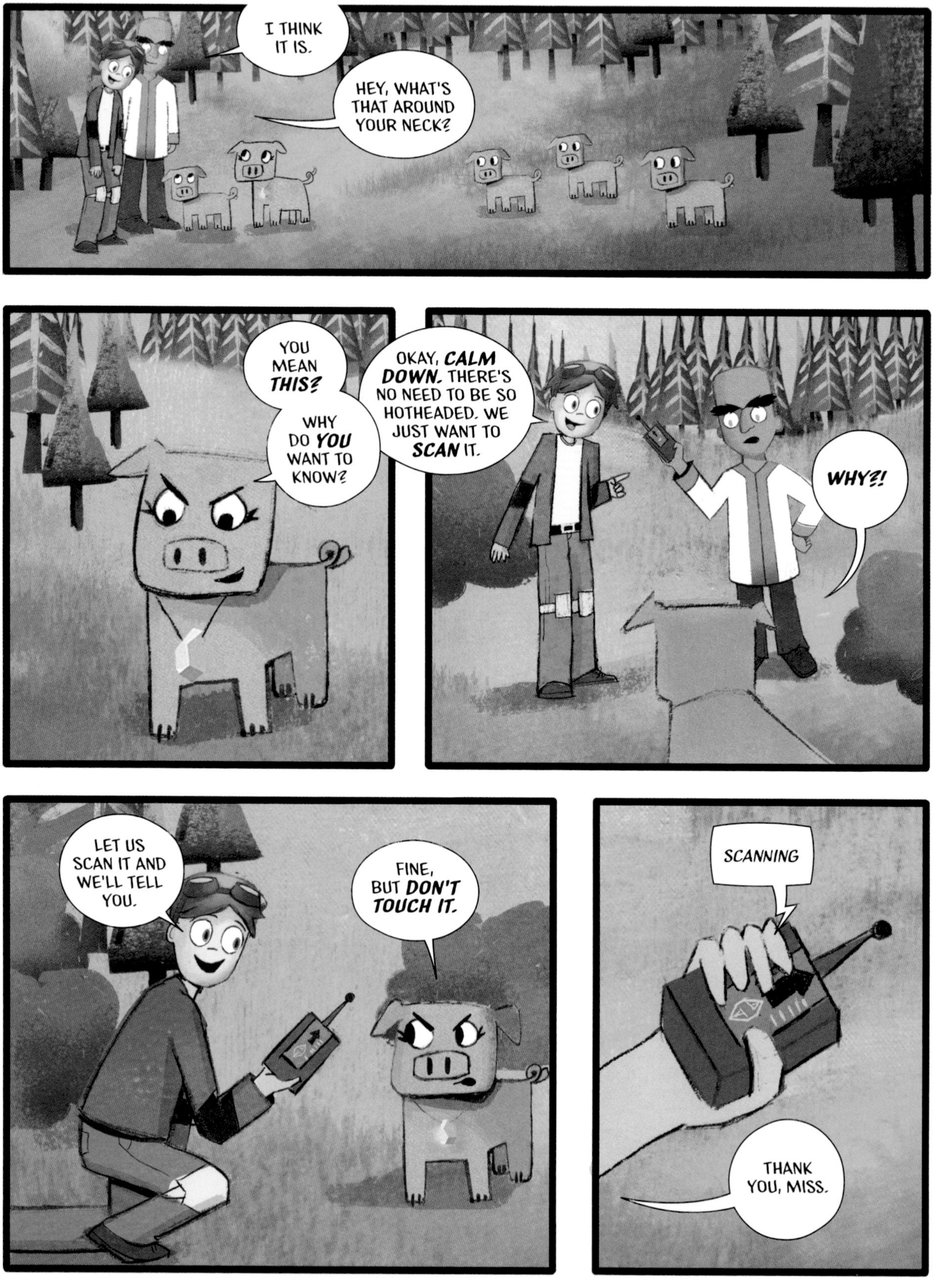
I THINK IT IS.
HEY, WHAT'S THAT AROUND YOUR NECK?
YOU MEAN **THIS?**
WHY DO ***YOU*** WANT TO KNOW?
OKAY, ***CALM DOWN.*** THERE'S NO NEED TO BE SO HOTHEADED. WE JUST WANT TO ***SCAN*** IT.
WHY?!
LET US SCAN IT AND WE'LL TELL YOU.
FINE, BUT ***DON'T TOUCH IT.***
SCANNING
THANK YOU, MISS.

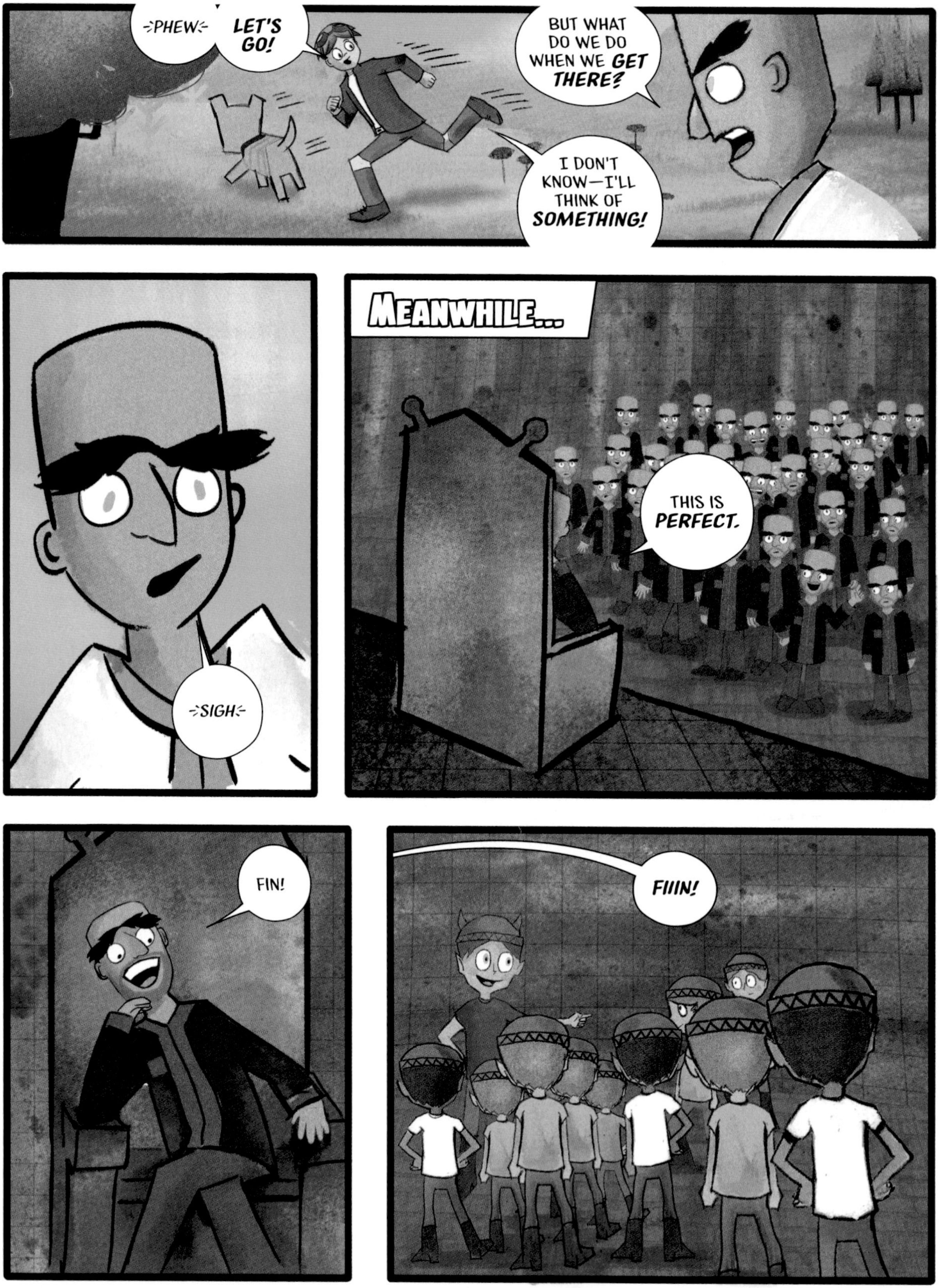

PHEW
LET'S GO!
BUT WHAT DO WE DO WHEN WE GET THERE?
I DON'T KNOW—I'LL THINK OF SOMETHING!
SIGH
MEANWHILE...
THIS IS PERFECT.
FIN!
FIIIN!

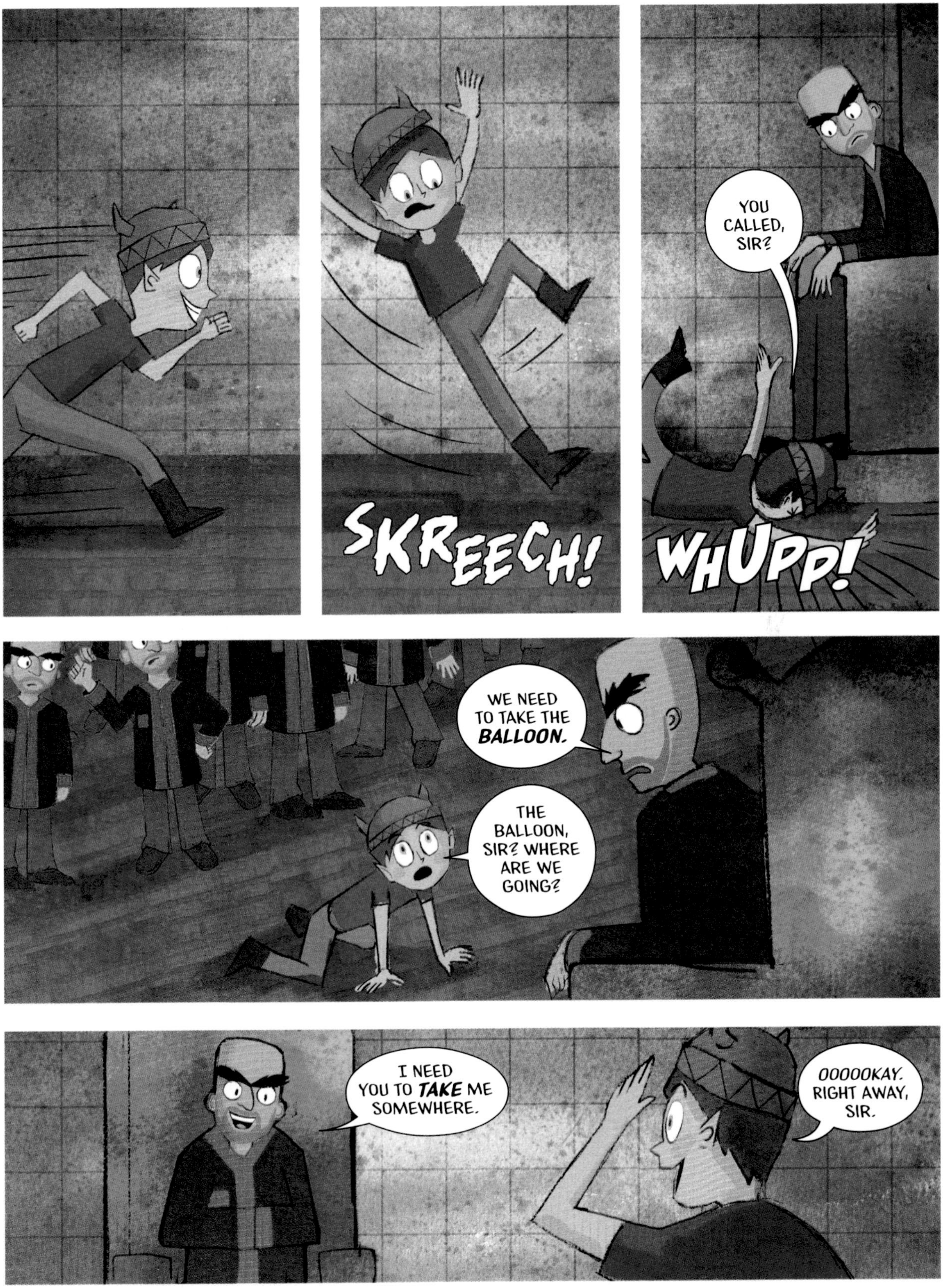
SKREECH!
YOU CALLED, SIR?
WHUPP!
WE NEED TO TAKE THE *BALLOON.*
THE BALLOON, SIR? WHERE ARE WE GOING?
I NEED YOU TO *TAKE* ME SOMEWHERE.
OOOOOKAY. RIGHT AWAY, SIR.

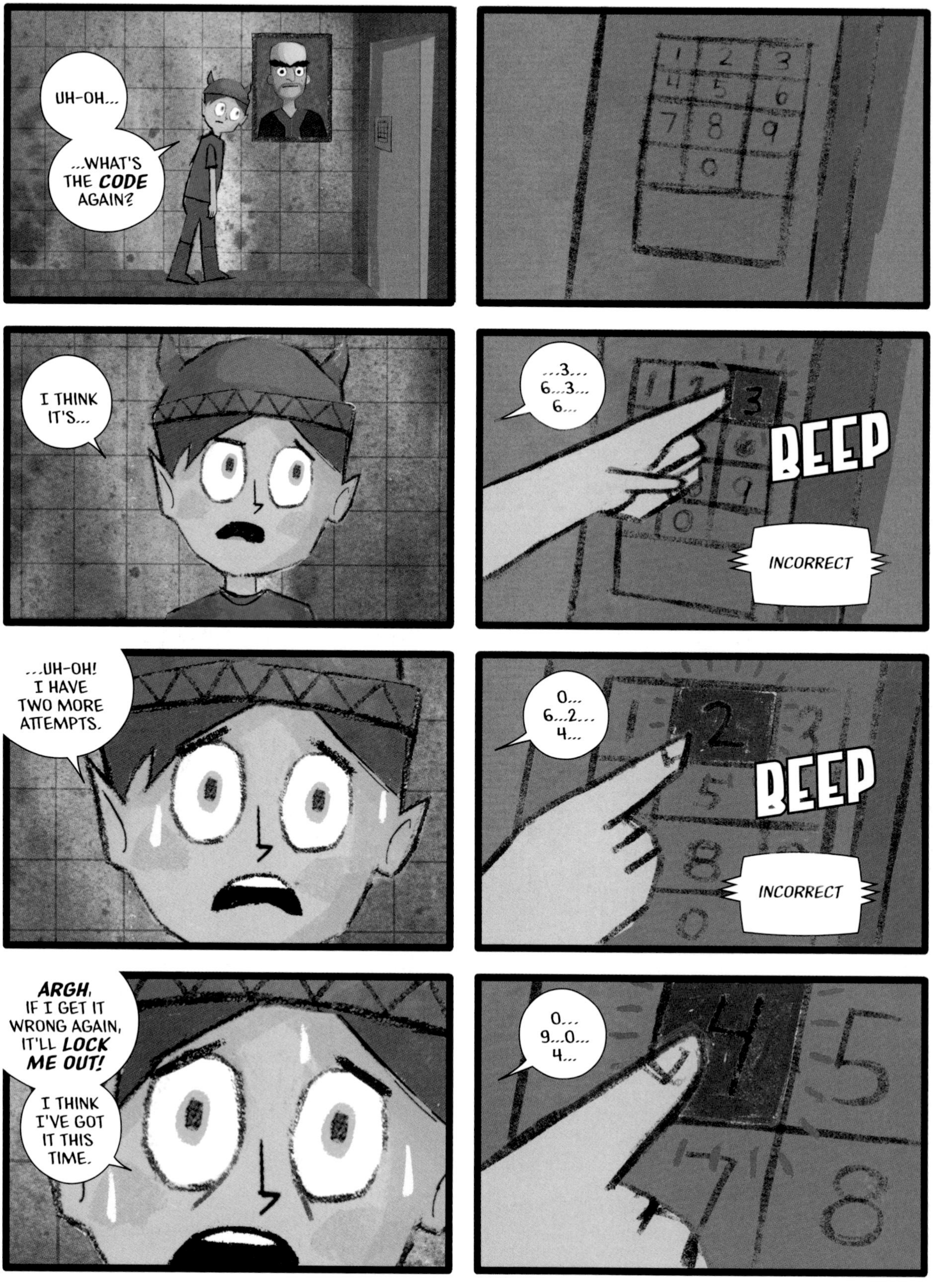

UH-OH...
...WHAT'S THE CODE AGAIN?
I THINK IT'S...
...3... 6...3... 6...
BEEP
INCORRECT
...UH-OH! I HAVE TWO MORE ATTEMPTS.
0... 6...2... 4...
BEEP
INCORRECT
ARGH, IF I GET IT WRONG AGAIN, IT'LL LOCK ME OUT!
I THINK I'VE GOT IT THIS TIME.
0... 9...0... 4...

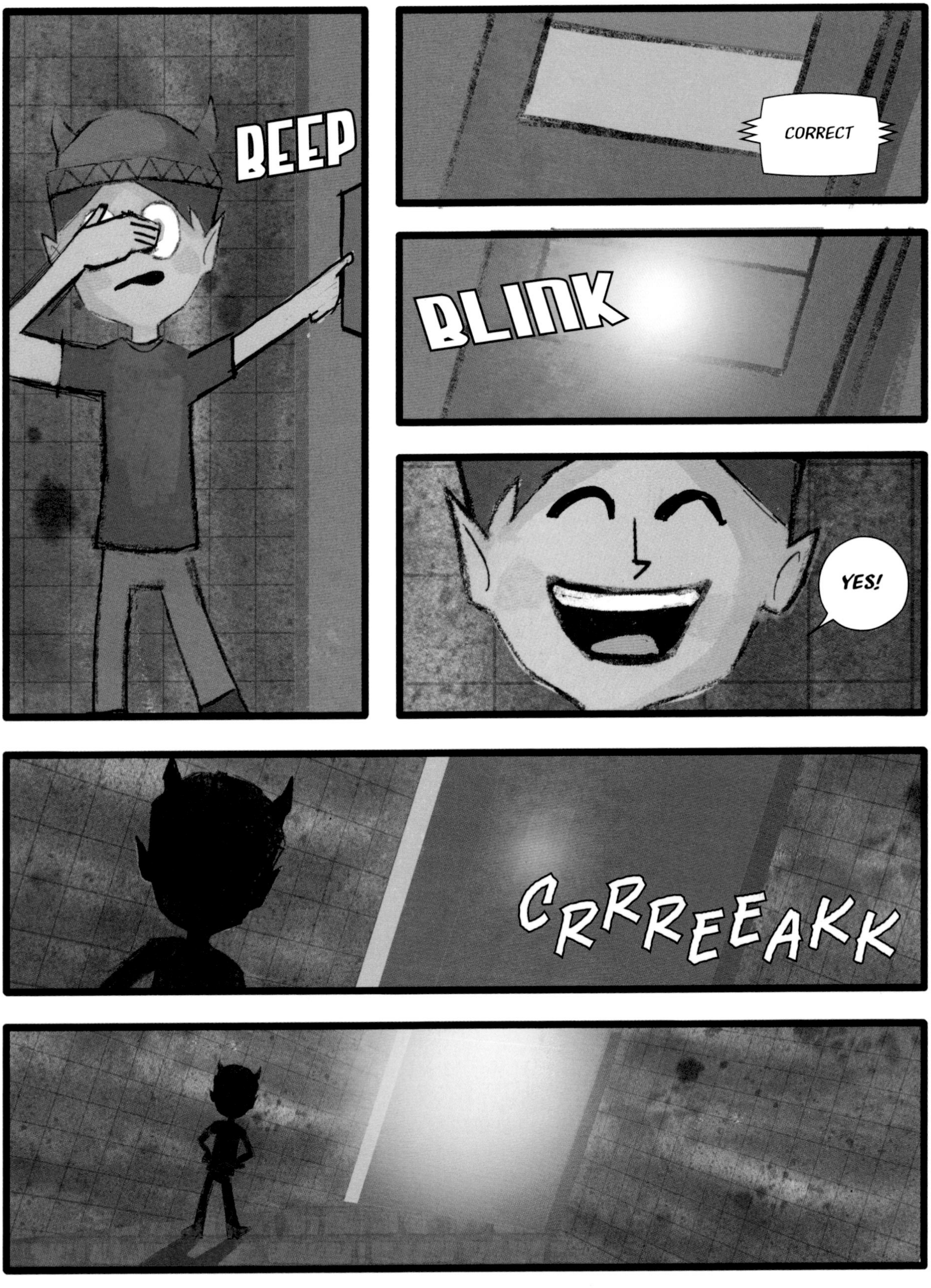
BEEP
CORRECT
BLINK
YES!
CRRREEAKK

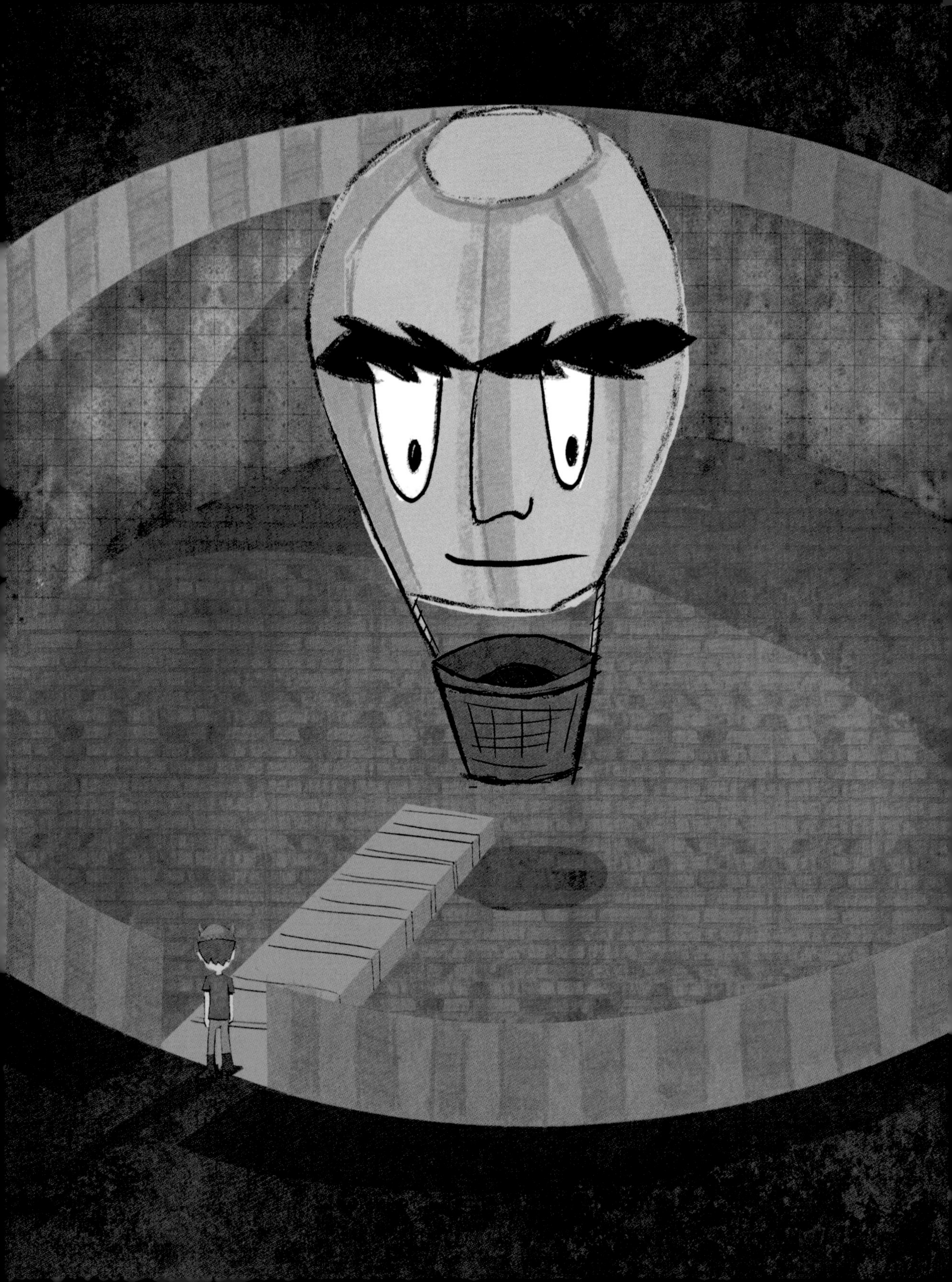

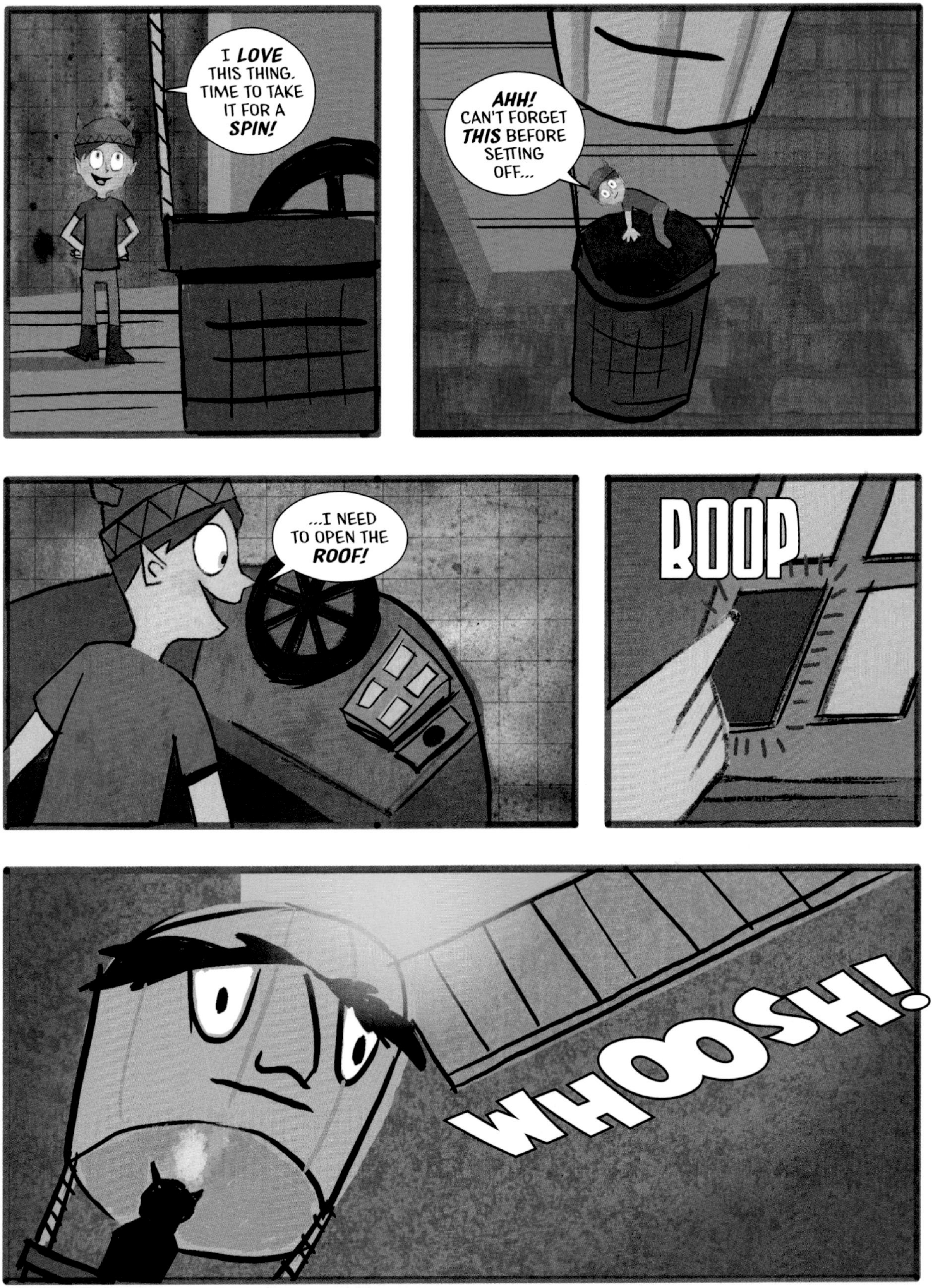
I LOVE THIS THING. TIME TO TAKE IT FOR A SPIN!
AHH! CAN'T FORGET THIS BEFORE SETTING OFF...
...I NEED TO OPEN THE ROOF!
BOOP
WHOOSH!

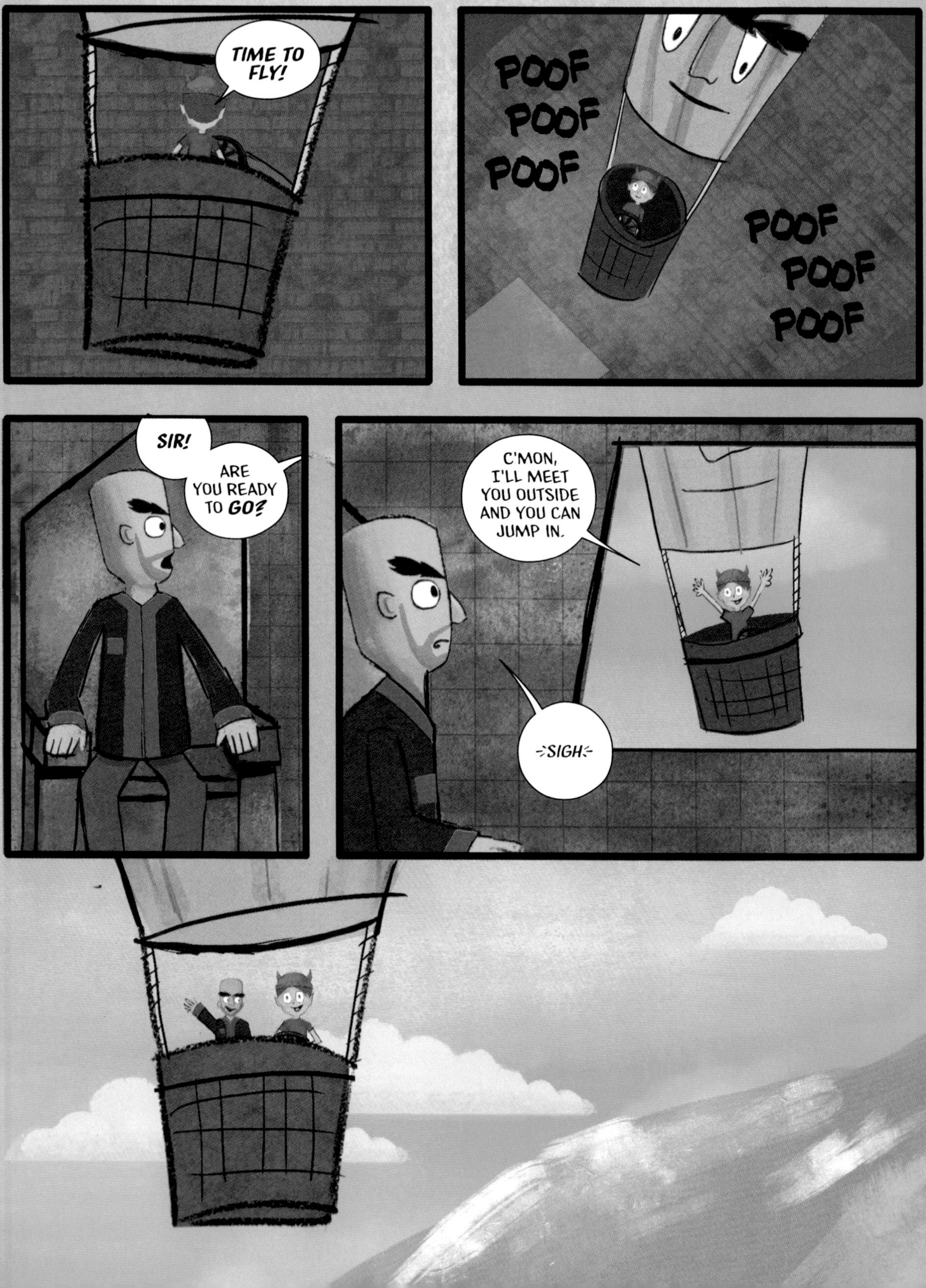
TIME TO FLY!
POOF POOF POOF
POOF POOF POOF
SIR!
ARE YOU READY TO GO?
C'MON, I'LL MEET YOU OUTSIDE AND YOU CAN JUMP IN.
-SIGH-

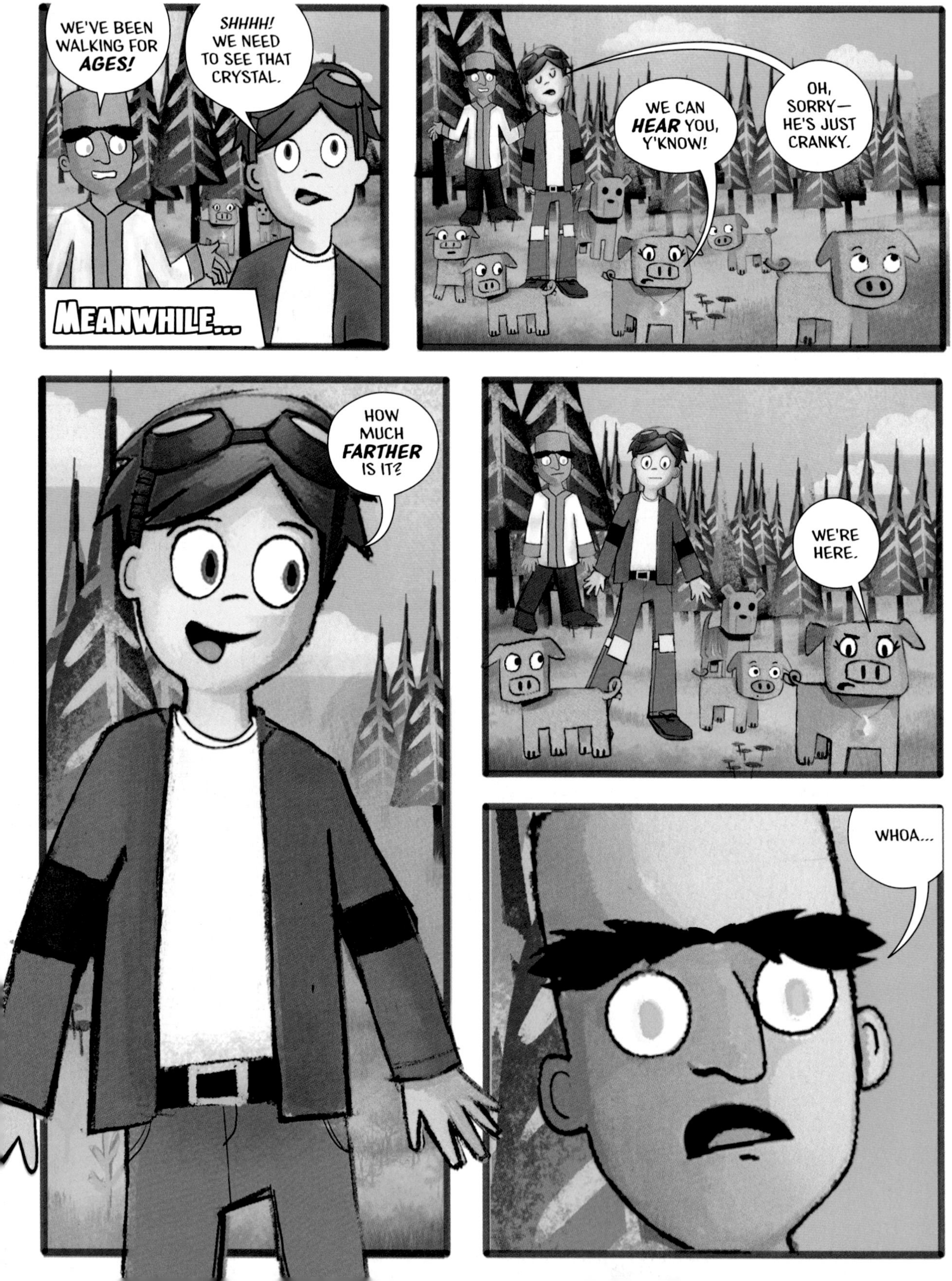
MEANWHILE...
WE'VE BEEN WALKING FOR *AGES!*
SHHHH! WE NEED TO SEE THAT CRYSTAL.
OH, SORRY— HE'S JUST CRANKY.
WE CAN *HEAR* YOU, Y'KNOW!
HOW MUCH *FARTHER* IS IT?
WE'RE HERE.
WHOA...

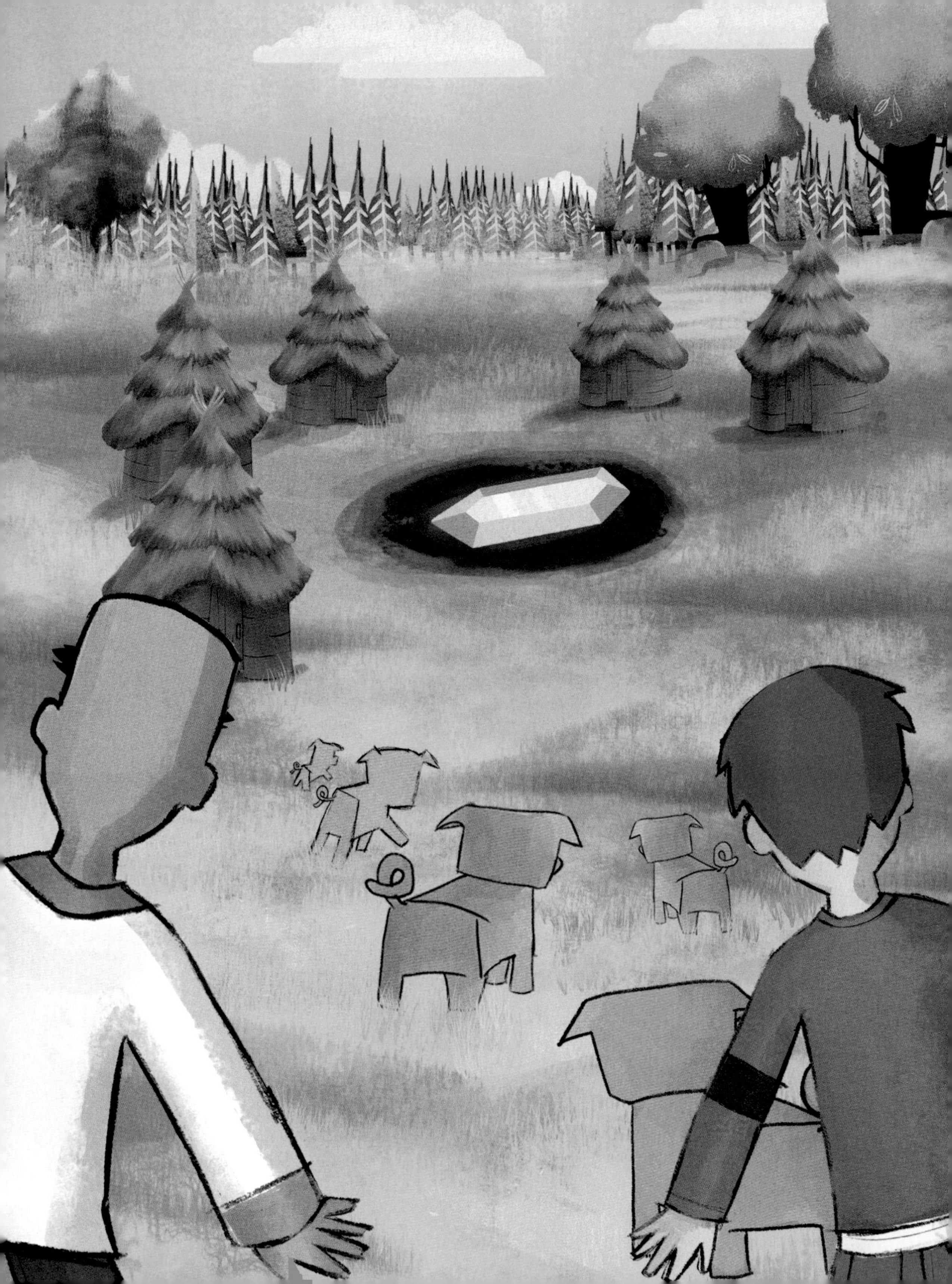

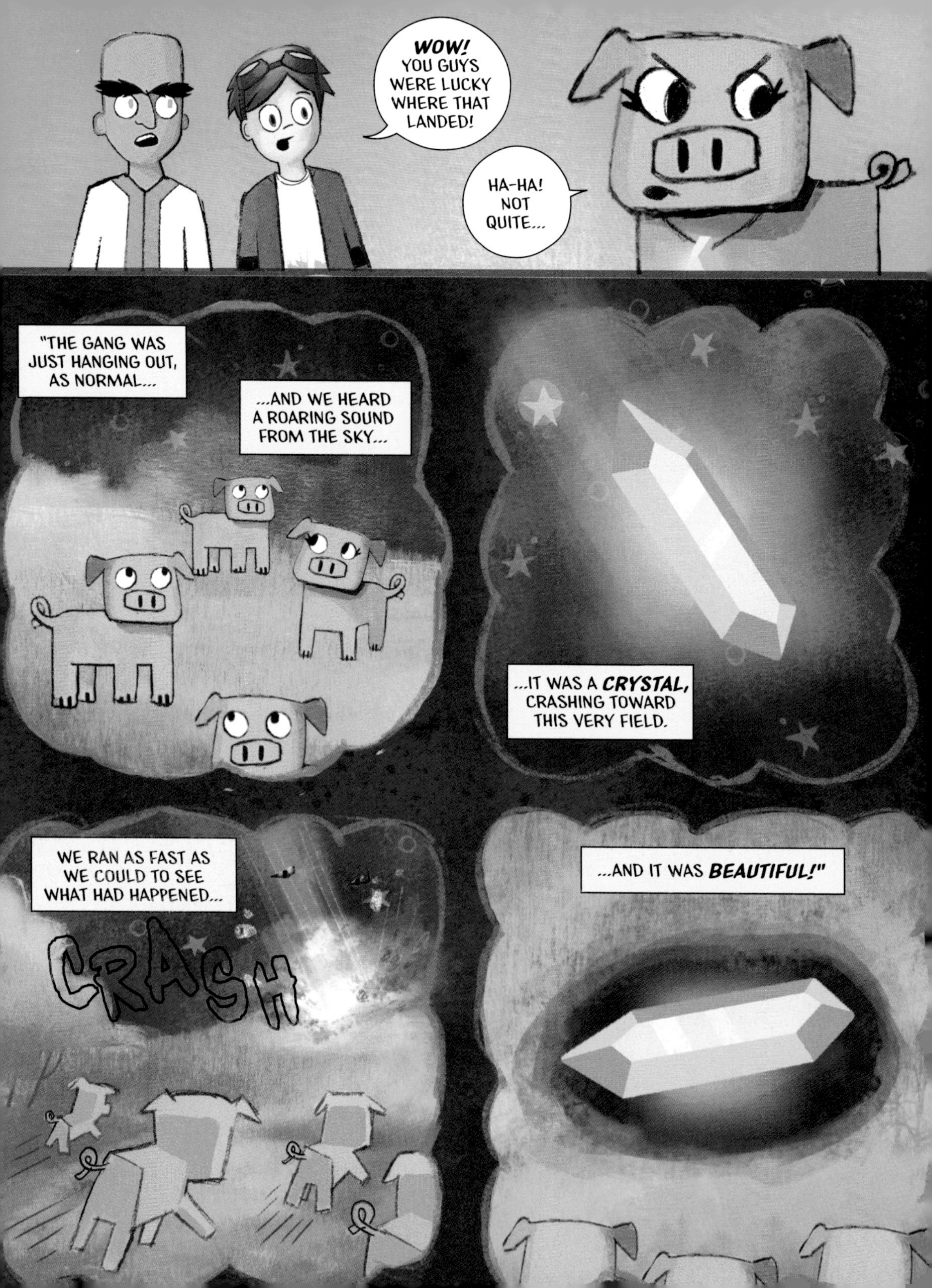
WOW! YOU GUYS WERE LUCKY WHERE THAT LANDED!
HA-HA! NOT QUITE...
"THE GANG WAS JUST HANGING OUT, AS NORMAL...
...AND WE HEARD A ROARING SOUND FROM THE SKY...
...IT WAS A CRYSTAL, CRASHING TOWARD THIS VERY FIELD.
WE RAN AS FAST AS WE COULD TO SEE WHAT HAD HAPPENED...
CRASH
...AND IT WAS BEAUTIFUL!"

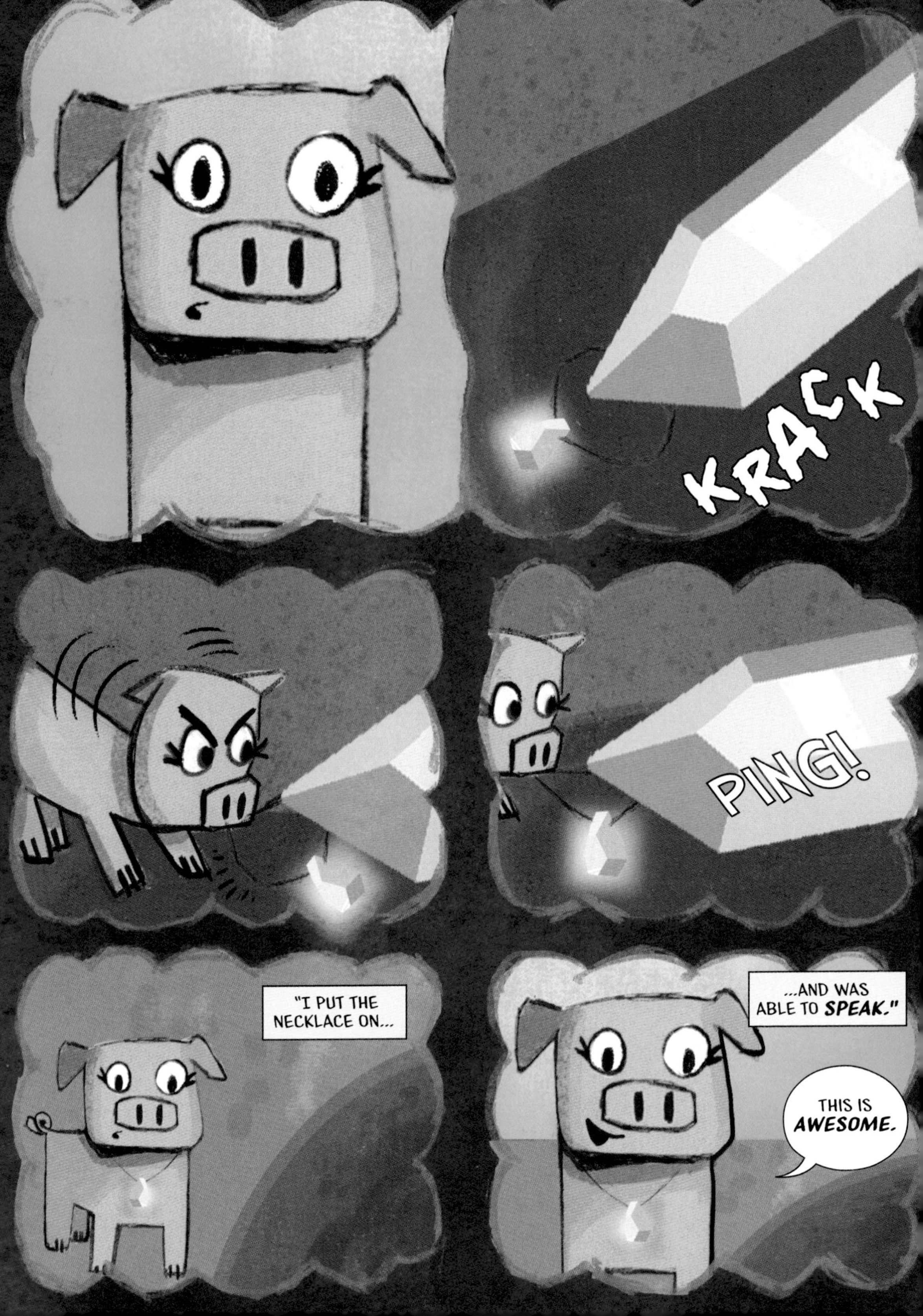
KRACK
PING!
"I PUT THE NECKLACE ON...
...AND WAS ABLE TO SPEAK."
THIS IS AWESOME.

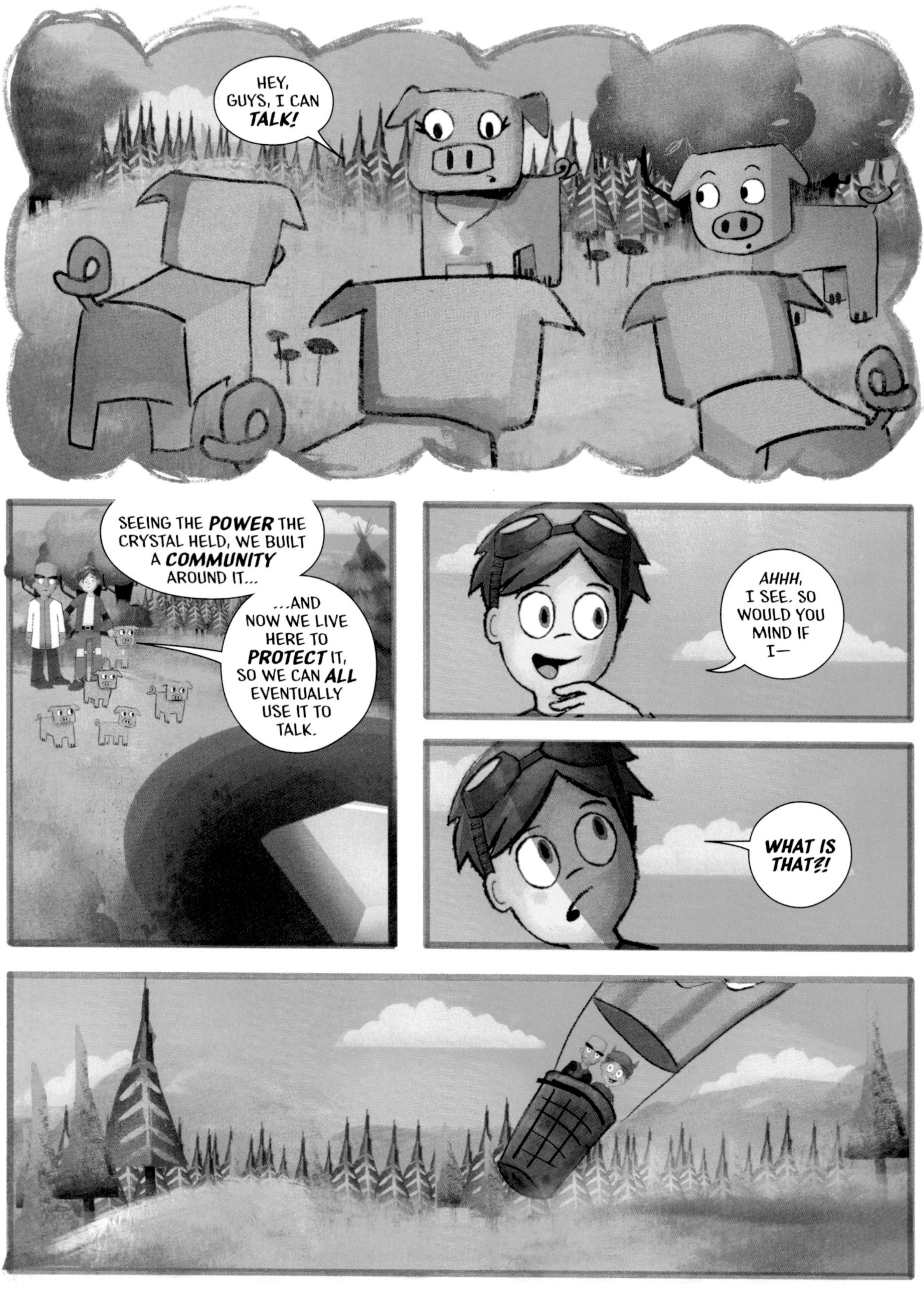
HEY, GUYS, I CAN TALK!
SEEING THE POWER THE CRYSTAL HELD, WE BUILT A COMMUNITY AROUND IT...
...AND NOW WE LIVE HERE TO PROTECT IT, SO WE CAN ALL EVENTUALLY USE IT TO TALK.
AHHH, I SEE. SO WOULD YOU MIND IF I—
WHAT IS THAT?!

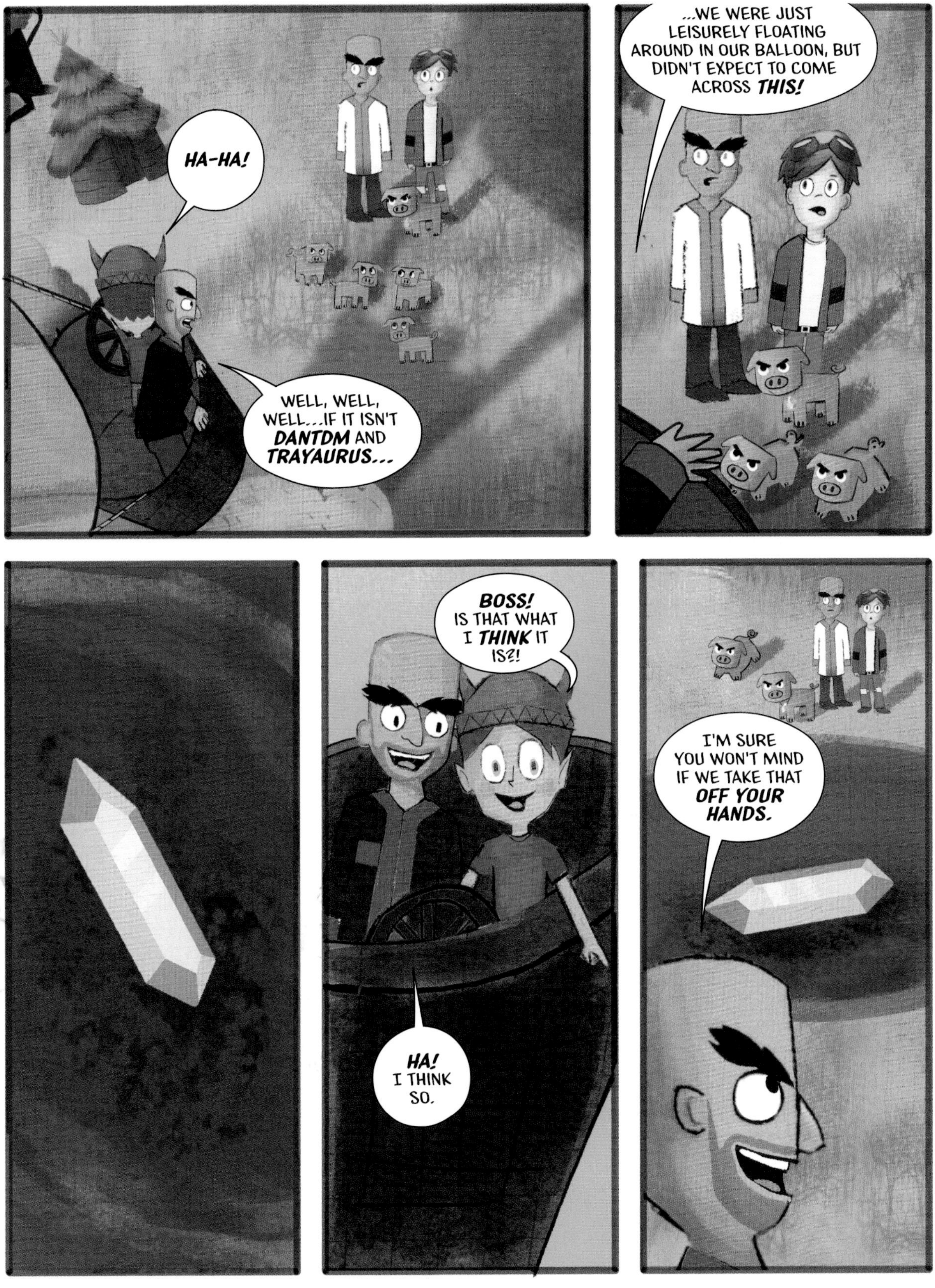
HA-HA!
WELL, WELL, WELL...IF IT ISN'T DANTDM AND TRAYAURUS...
...WE WERE JUST LEISURELY FLOATING AROUND IN OUR BALLOON, BUT DIDN'T EXPECT TO COME ACROSS THIS!
BOSS! IS THAT WHAT I THINK IT IS?!
HA! I THINK SO.
I'M SURE YOU WON'T MIND IF WE TAKE THAT OFF YOUR HANDS.

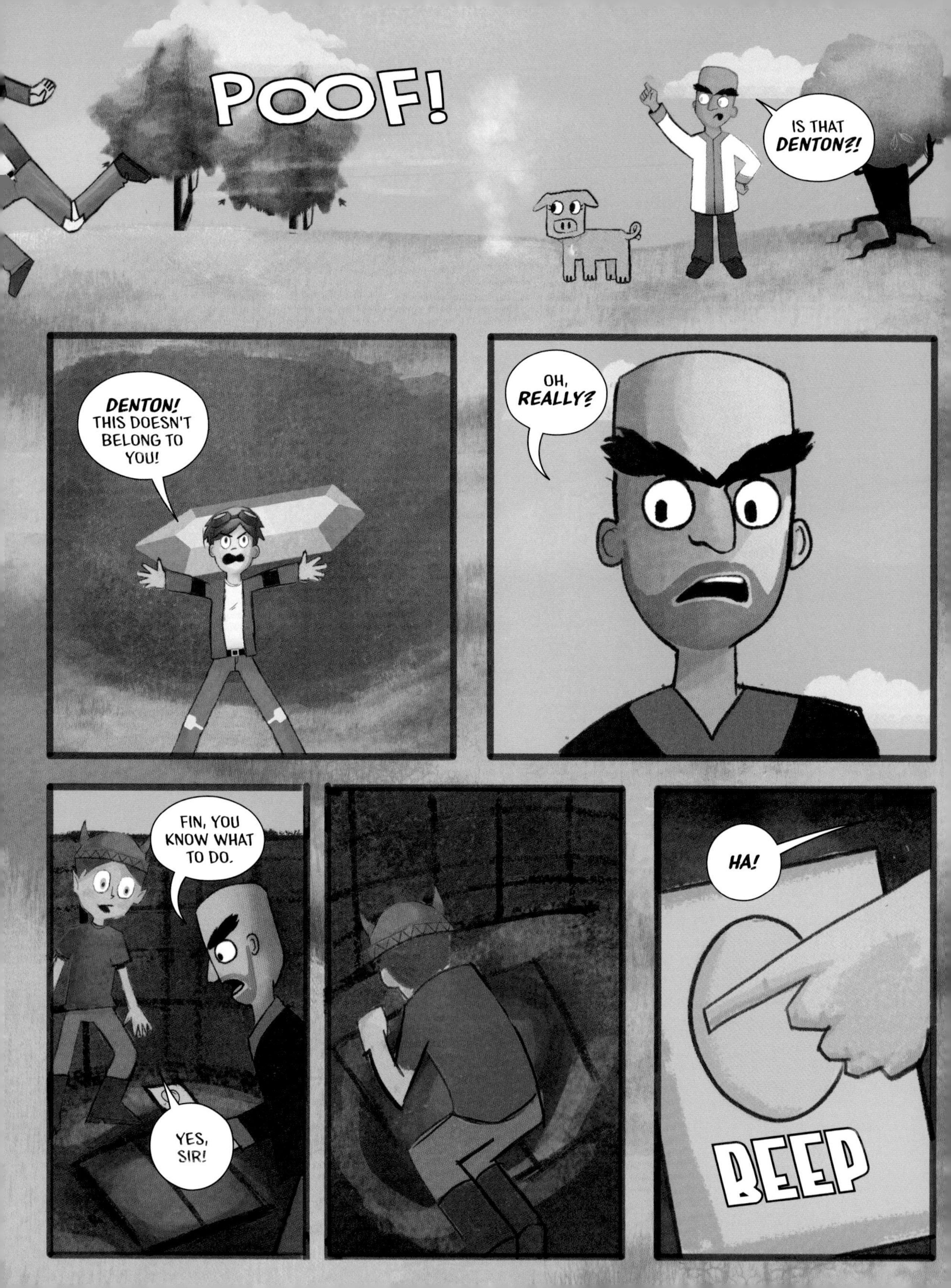
POOF!
IS THAT DENTON?!
DENTON! THIS DOESN'T BELONG TO YOU!
OH, REALLY?
FIN, YOU KNOW WHAT TO DO.
YES, SIR!
HA!
BEEP

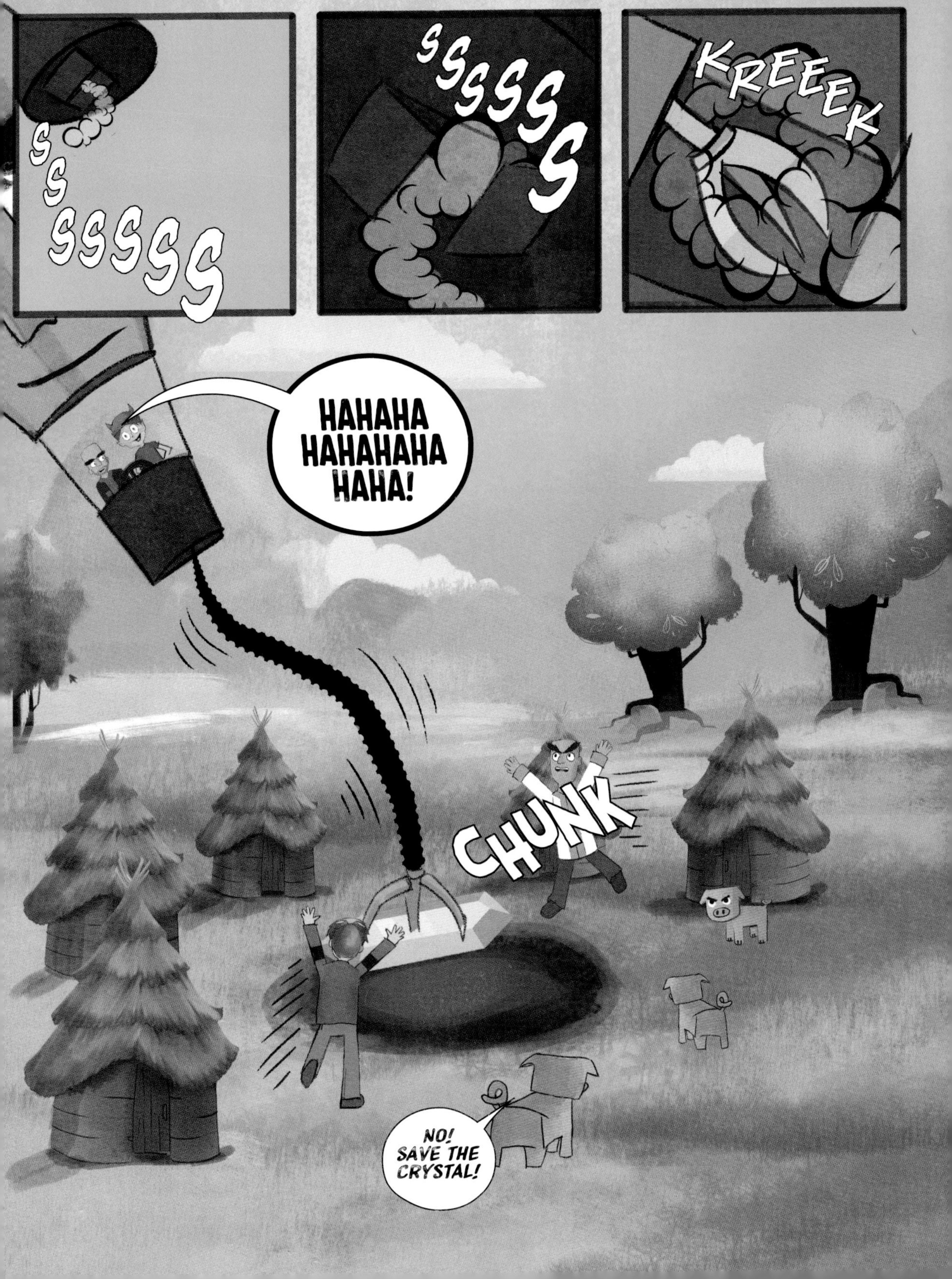
SSSSSSSS
SSSSSSS
KREEEK
HAHAHA HAHAHAHA HAHA!
CHUNK
NO! SAVE THE CRYSTAL!

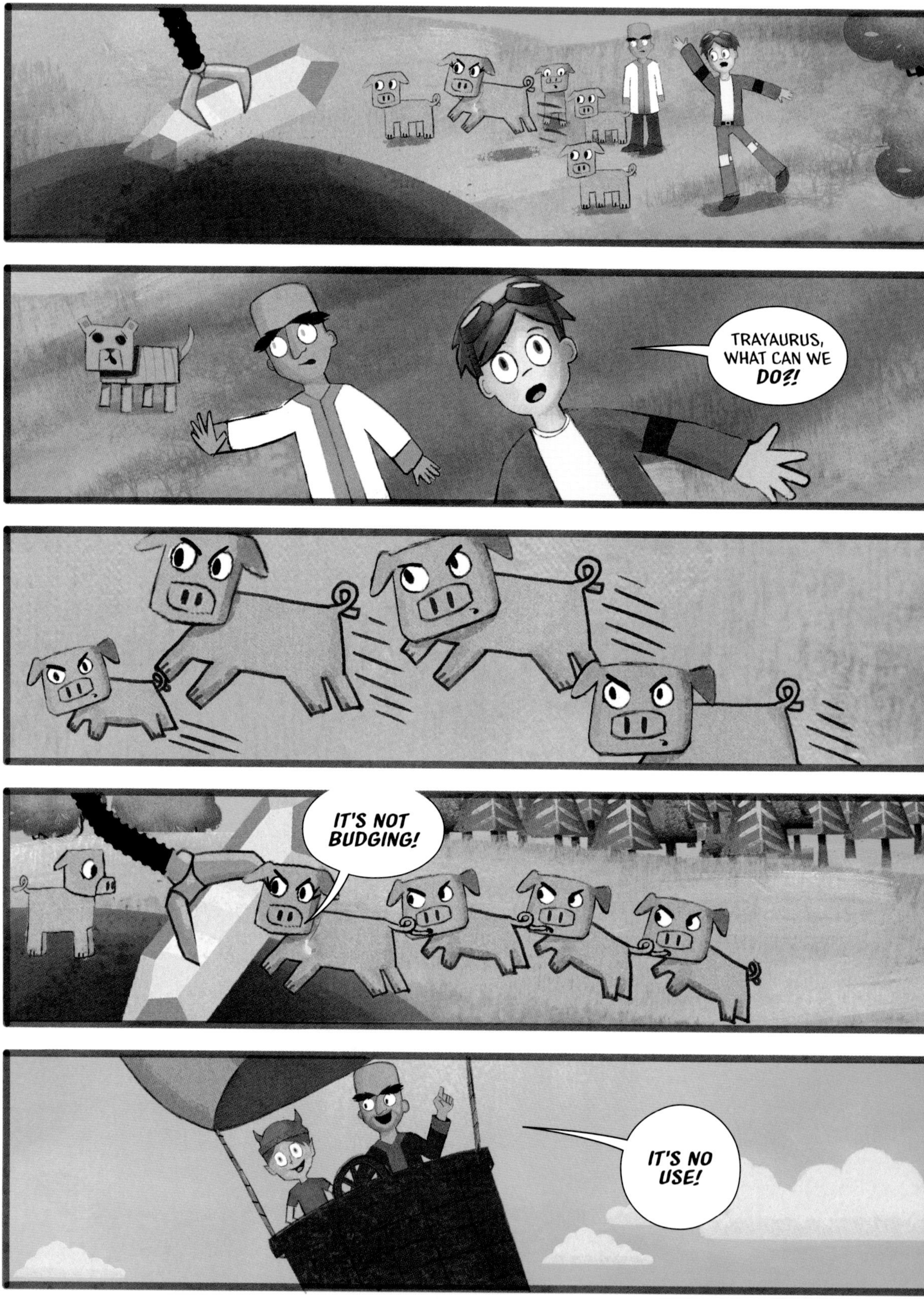

TRAYAURUS, WHAT CAN WE DO?!
IT'S NOT BUDGING!
IT'S NO USE!

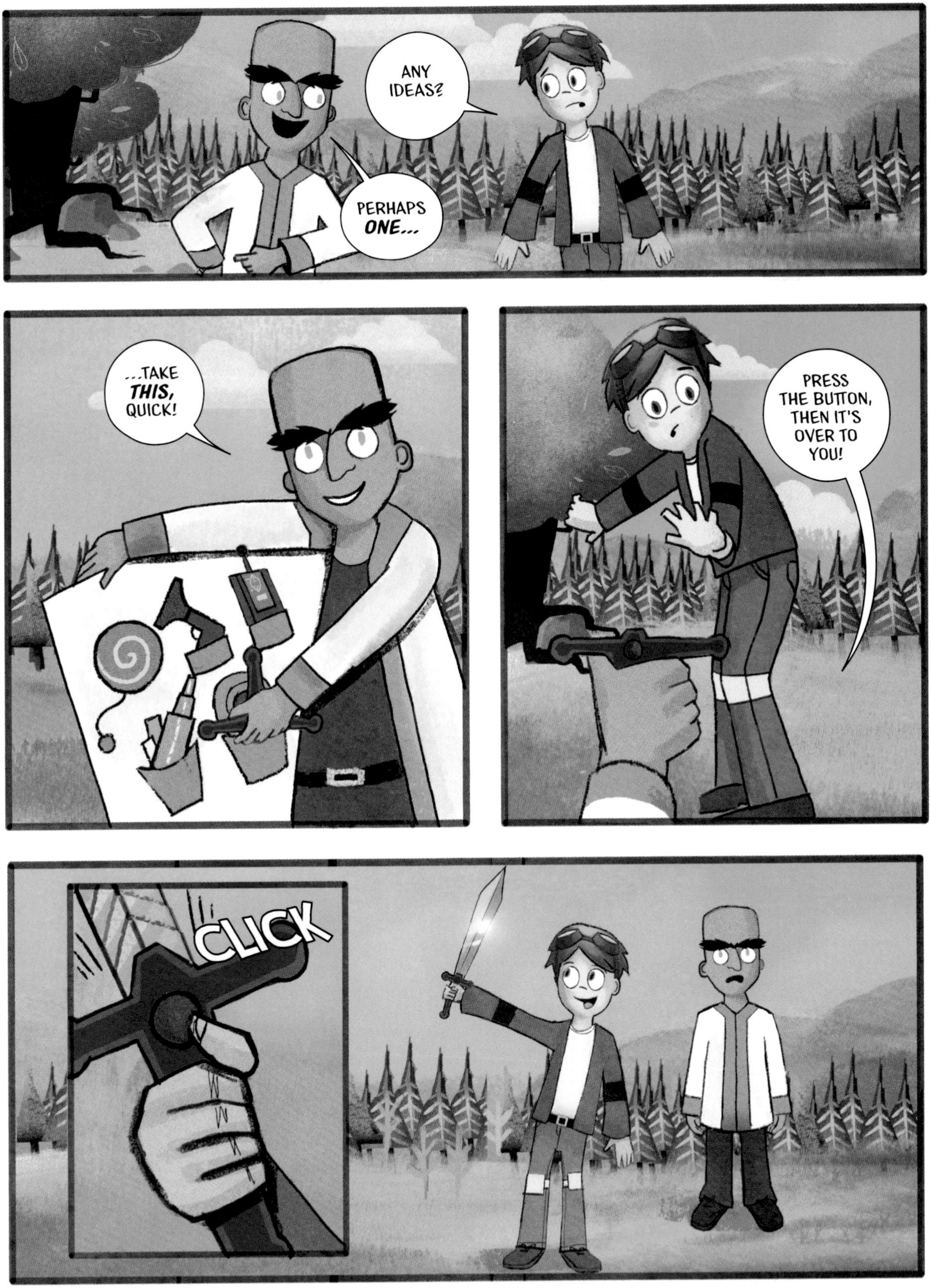
ANY IDEAS?
PERHAPS ONE...
...TAKE THIS, QUICK!
PRESS THE BUTTON, THEN IT'S OVER TO YOU!
CLICK

ZZZ

IING!

CLANG!

TAKE THAT!

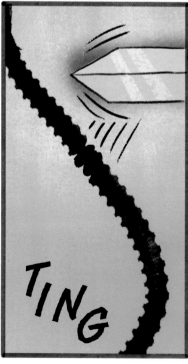

TING

IT JUST BOUNCED RIGHT OFF!

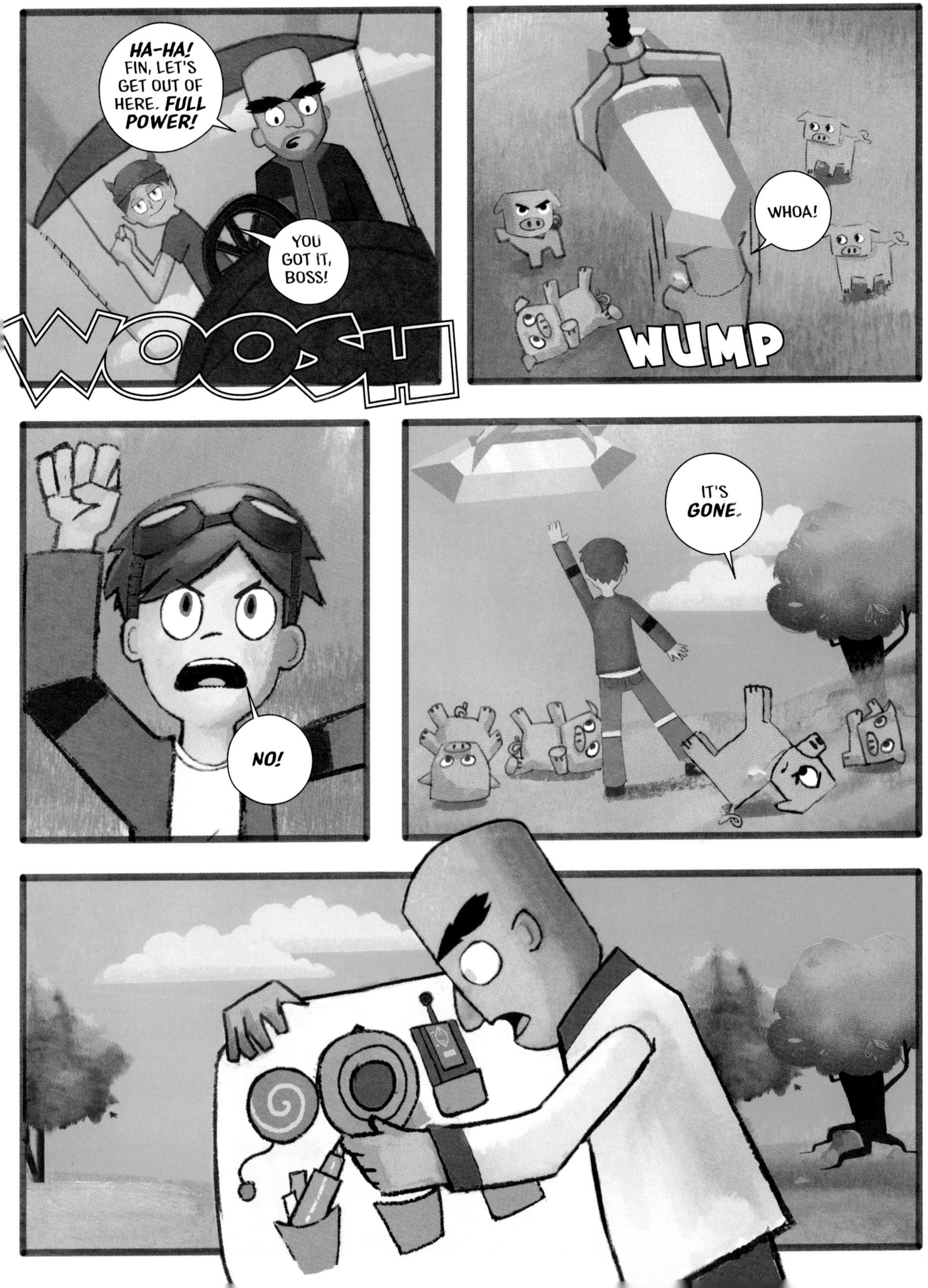
HA-HA! FIN, LET'S GET OUT OF HERE. FULL POWER!
YOU GOT IT, BOSS!
WOOSH
WHOA!
WUMP
NO!
IT'S GONE.

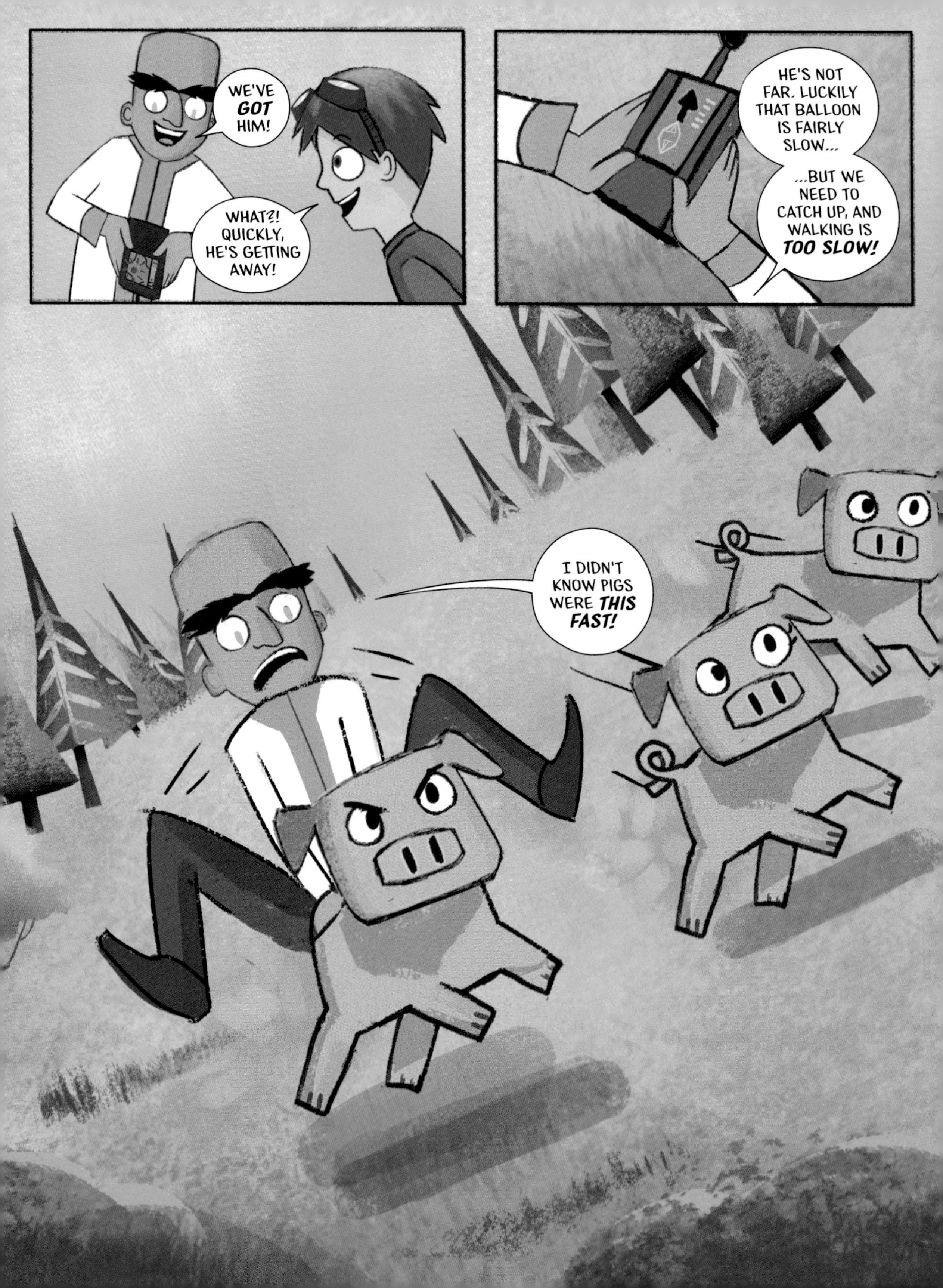
WE'VE GOT HIM!
WHAT?! QUICKLY, HE'S GETTING AWAY!
HE'S NOT FAR. LUCKILY THAT BALLOON IS FAIRLY SLOW...
...BUT WE NEED TO CATCH UP, AND WALKING IS TOO SLOW!
I DIDN'T KNOW PIGS WERE THIS FAST!

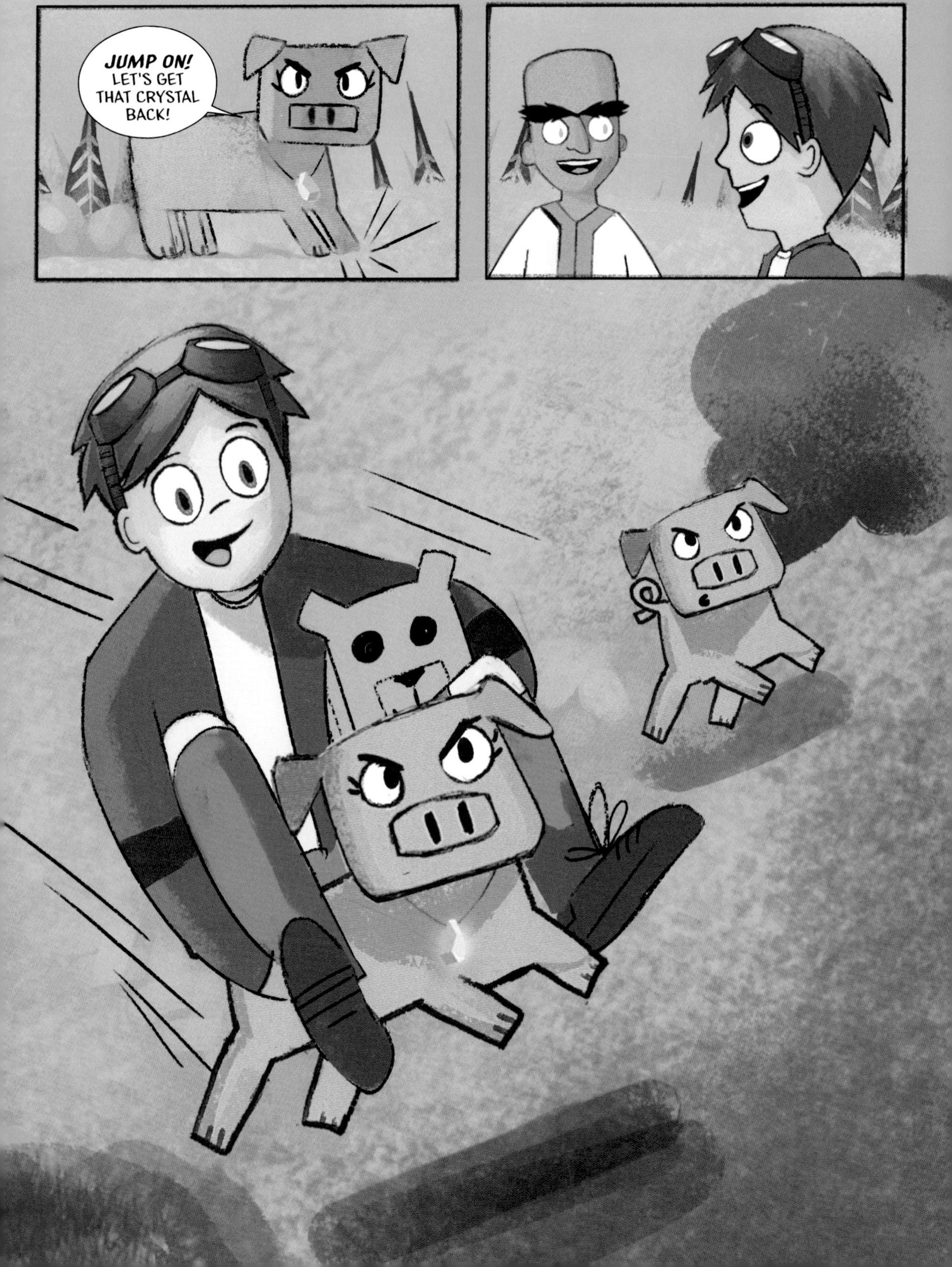
JUMP ON!
LET'S GET THAT CRYSTAL BACK!

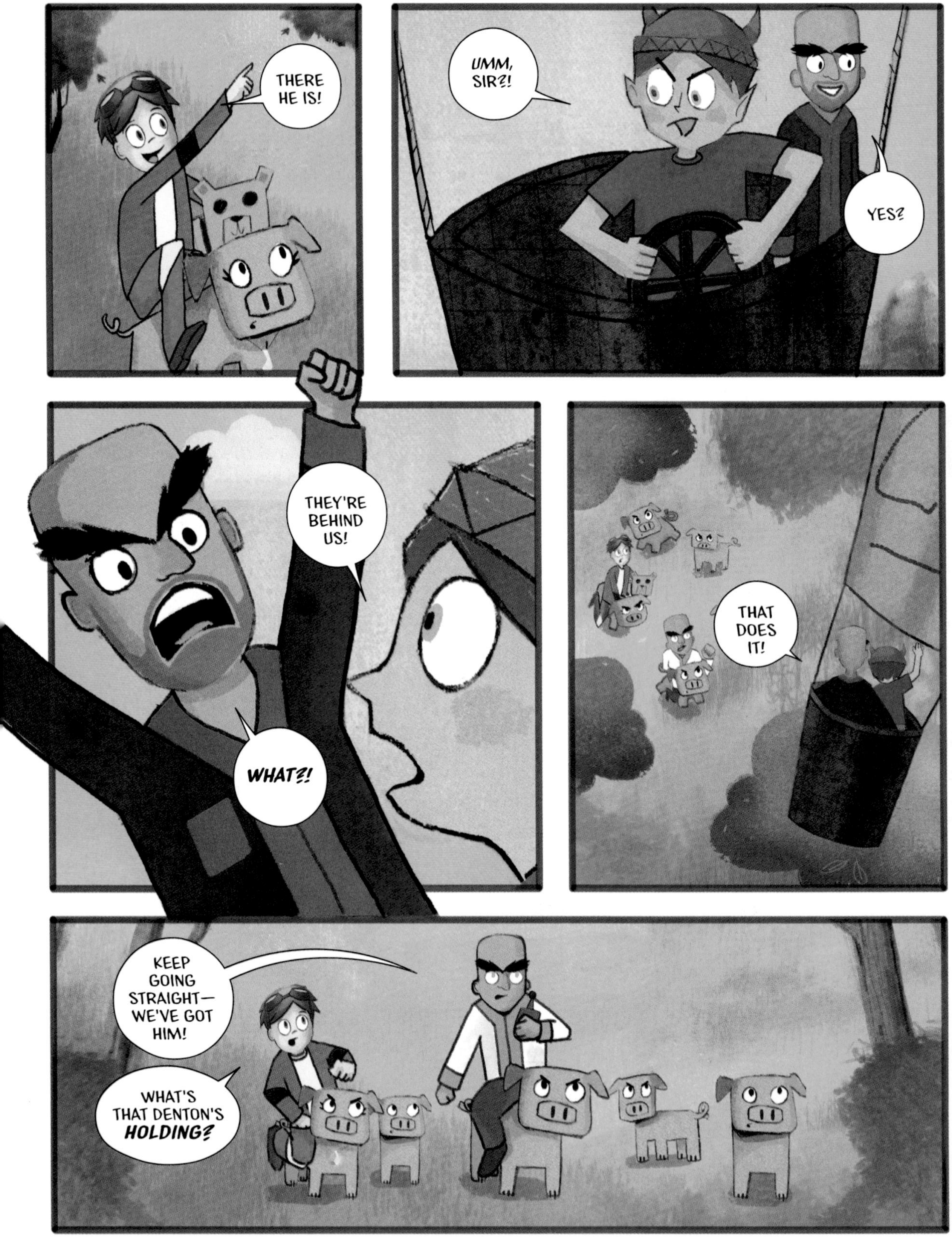
THERE HE IS!
UMM, SIR?!
YES?
THEY'RE BEHIND US!
WHAT?!
THAT DOES IT!
KEEP GOING STRAIGHT— WE'VE GOT HIM!
WHAT'S THAT DENTON'S HOLDING?

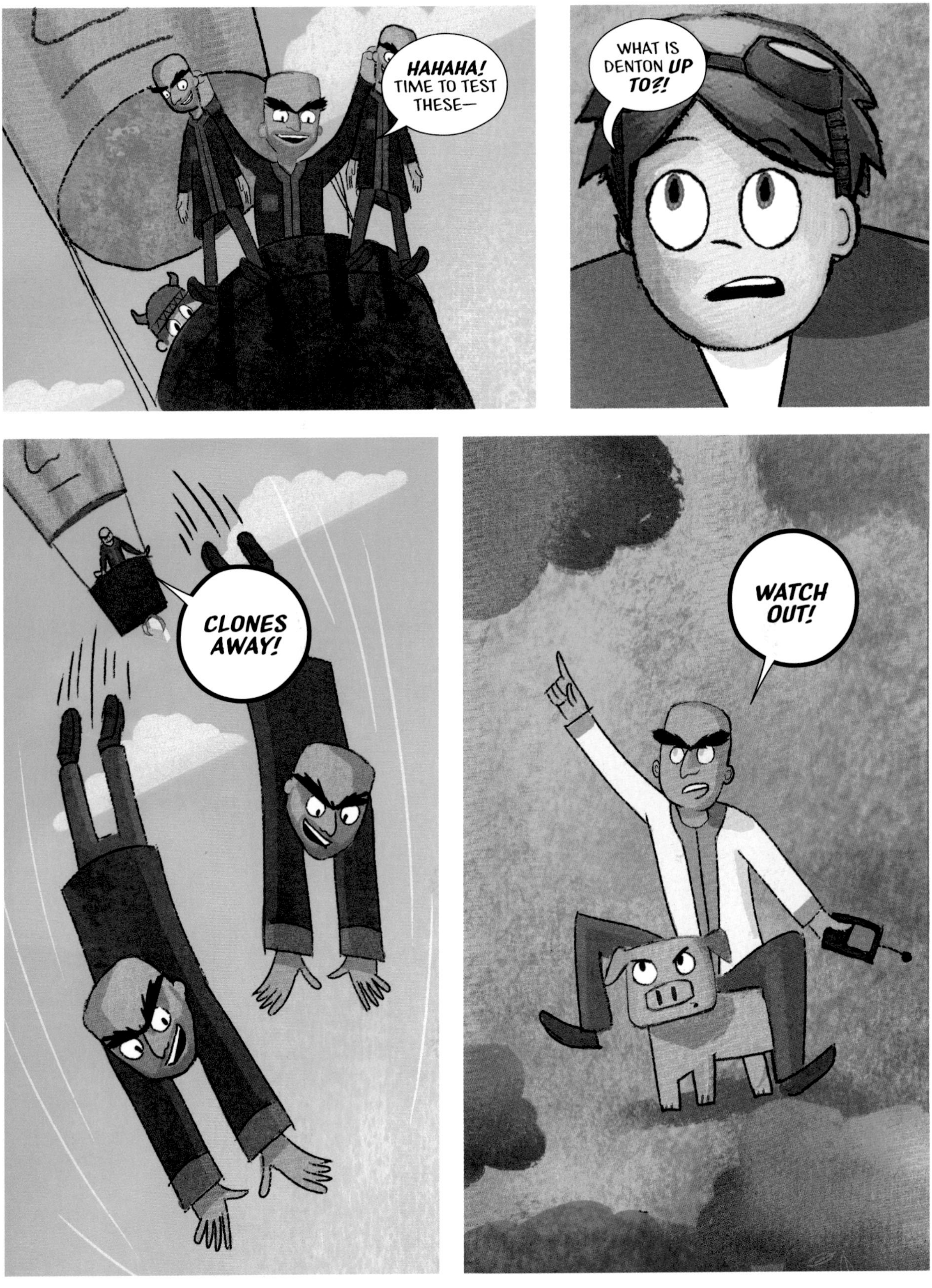
HAHAHA! TIME TO TEST THESE—
WHAT IS DENTON UP TO?!
CLONES AWAY!
WATCH OUT!

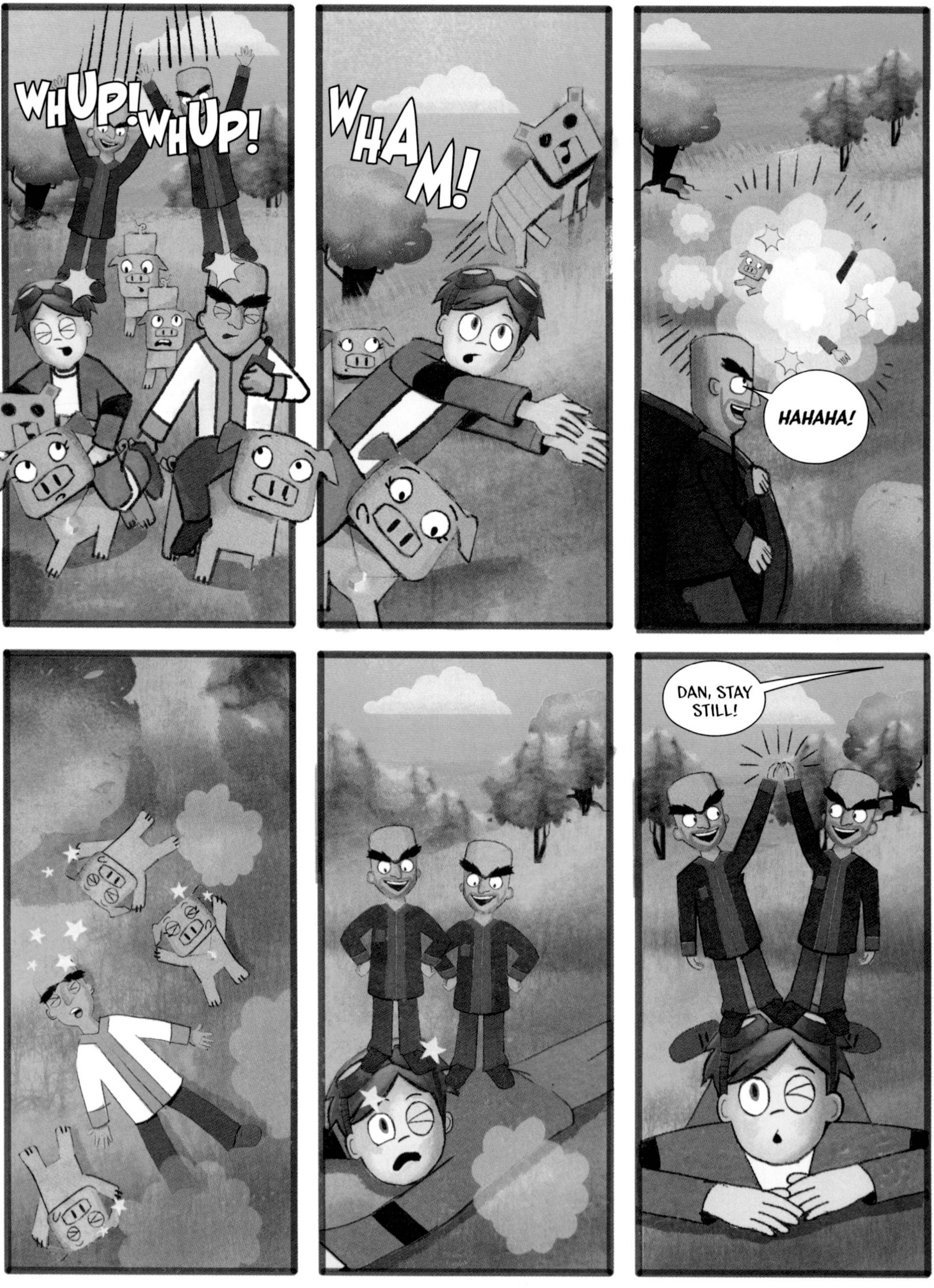
WHUP! WHUP!
WHAM!
HAHAHA!
DAN, STAY STILL!

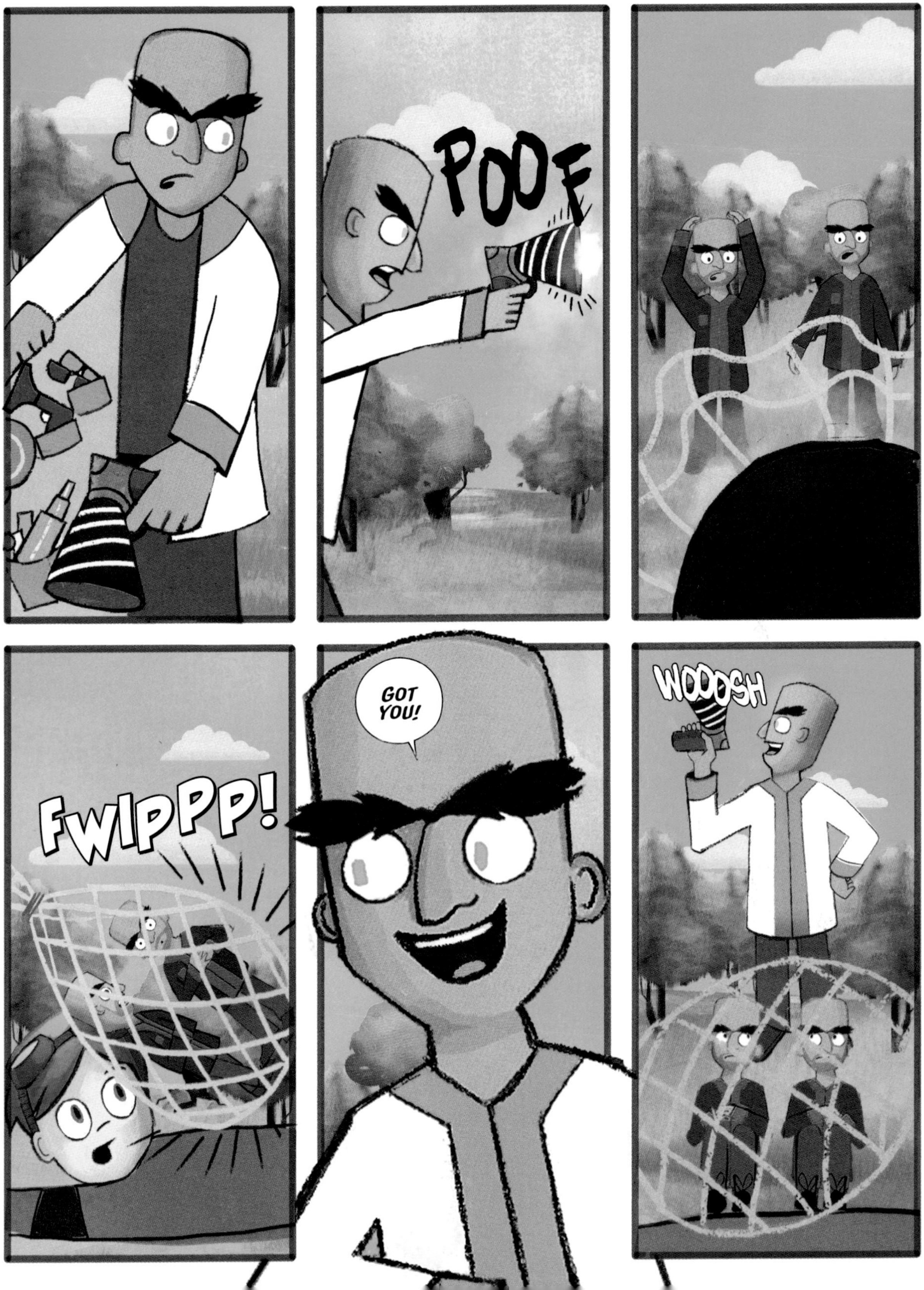
POOF
FWIPPP!
GOT YOU!
WOOOSH

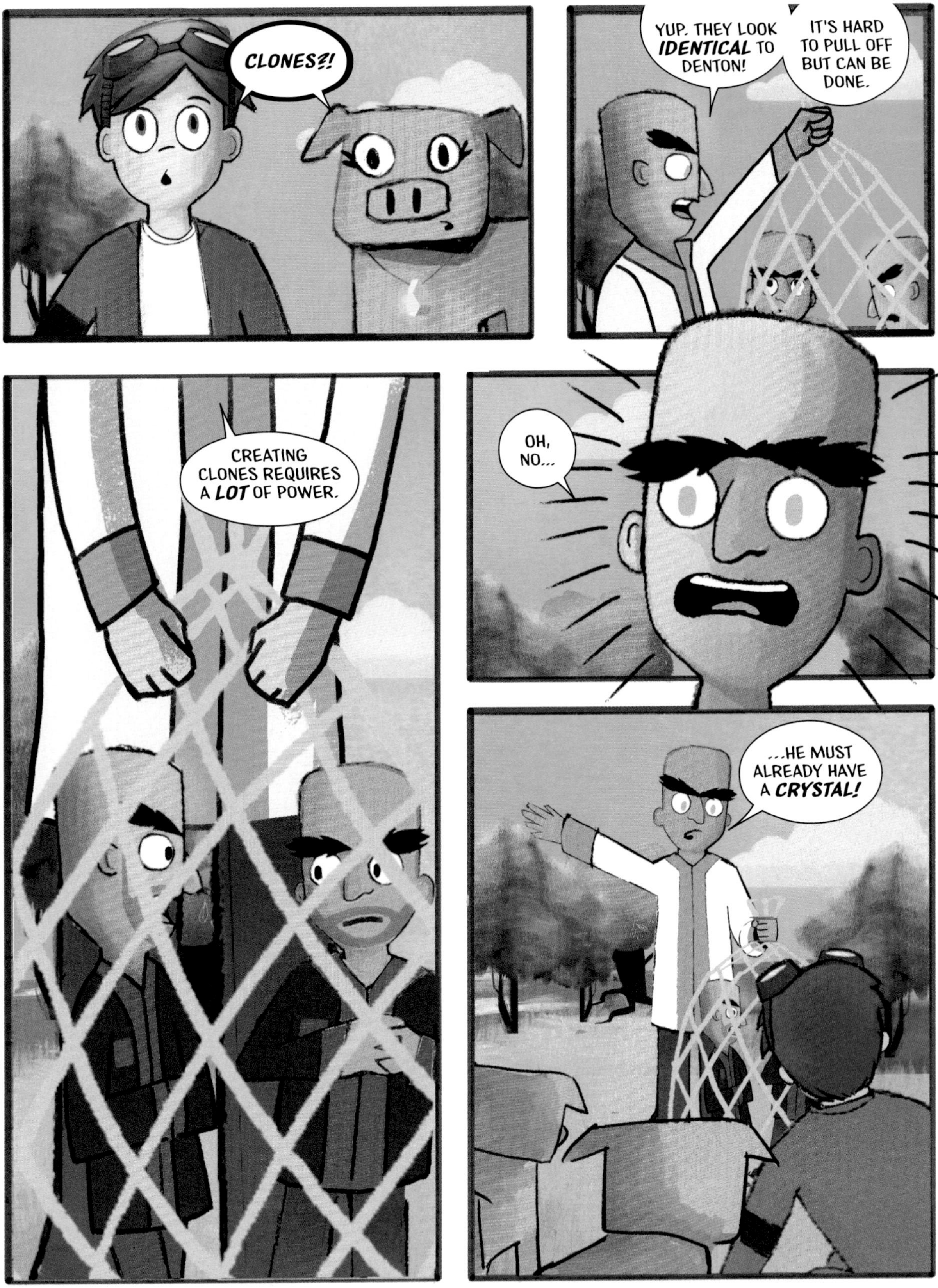
CLONES?!
YUP. THEY LOOK IDENTICAL TO DENTON!
IT'S HARD TO PULL OFF BUT CAN BE DONE.
CREATING CLONES REQUIRES A LOT OF POWER.
OH, NO...
...HE MUST ALREADY HAVE A CRYSTAL!

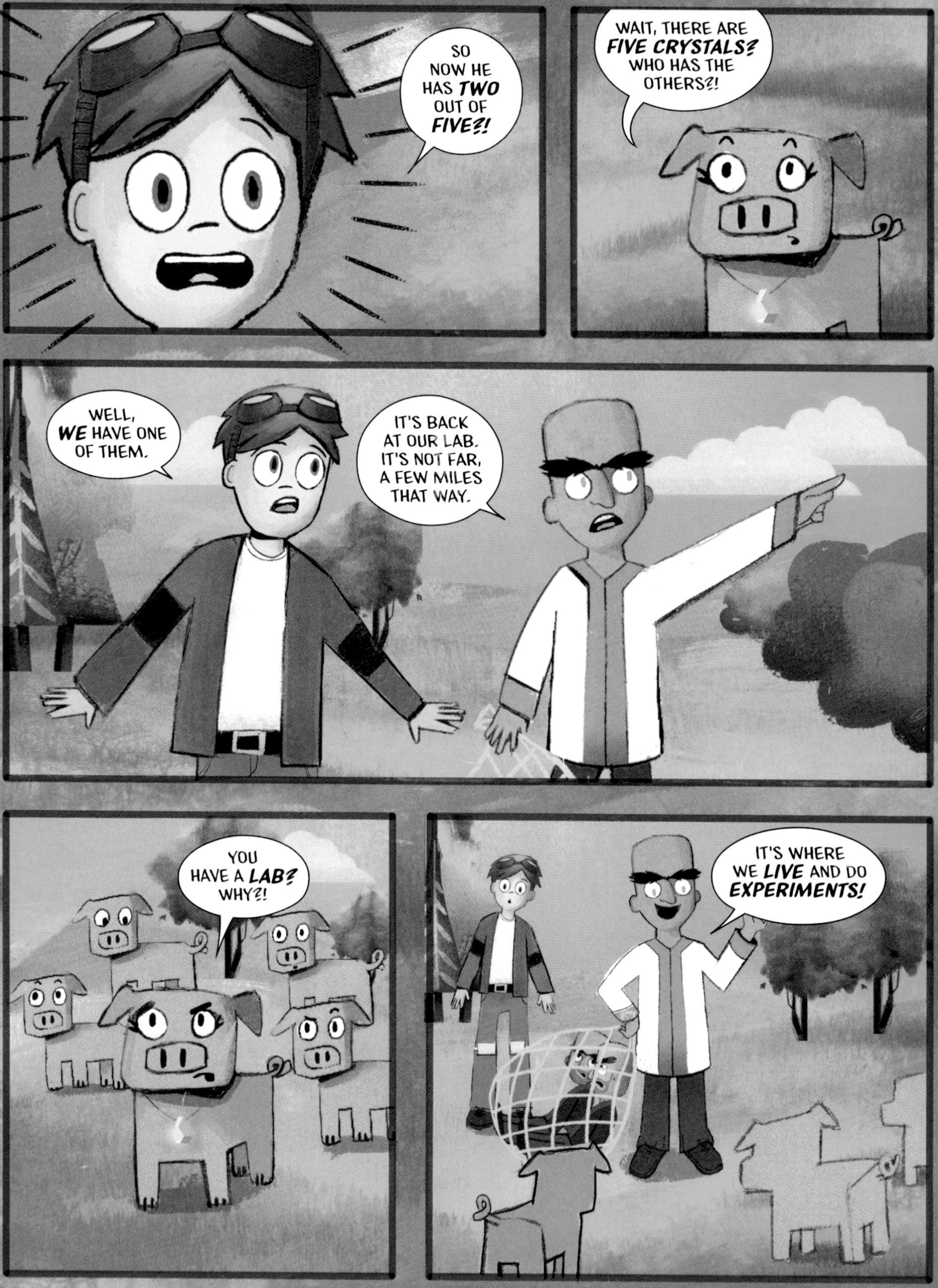
SO NOW HE HAS TWO OUT OF FIVE?!
WAIT, THERE ARE FIVE CRYSTALS? WHO HAS THE OTHERS?!
WELL, WE HAVE ONE OF THEM.
IT'S BACK AT OUR LAB. IT'S NOT FAR, A FEW MILES THAT WAY.
YOU HAVE A LAB? WHY?!
IT'S WHERE WE LIVE AND DO EXPERIMENTS!

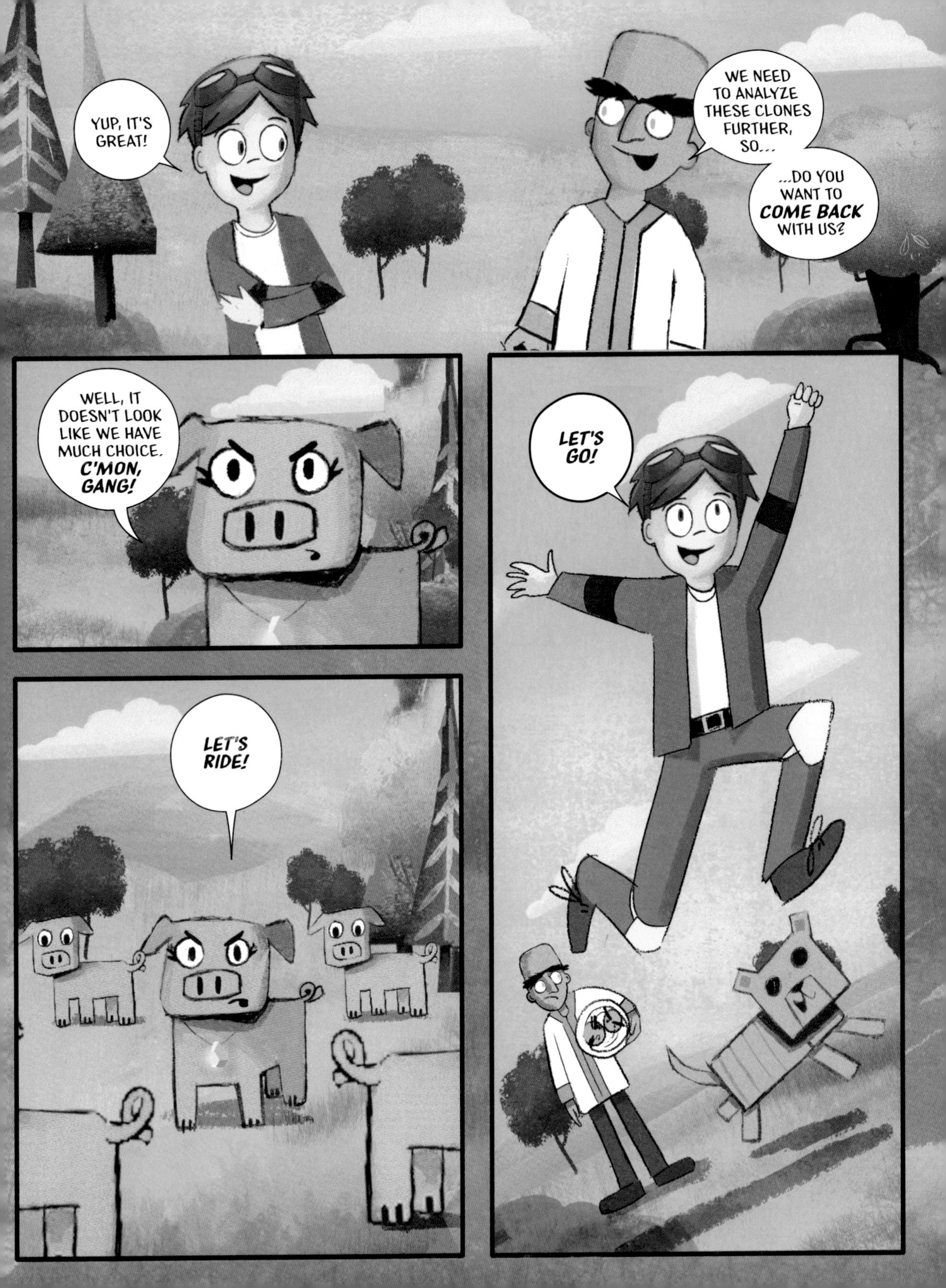
YUP, IT'S GREAT!
WE NEED TO ANALYZE THESE CLONES FURTHER, SO...
...DO YOU WANT TO COME BACK WITH US?
WELL, IT DOESN'T LOOK LIKE WE HAVE MUCH CHOICE. C'MON, GANG!
LET'S RIDE!
LET'S GO!

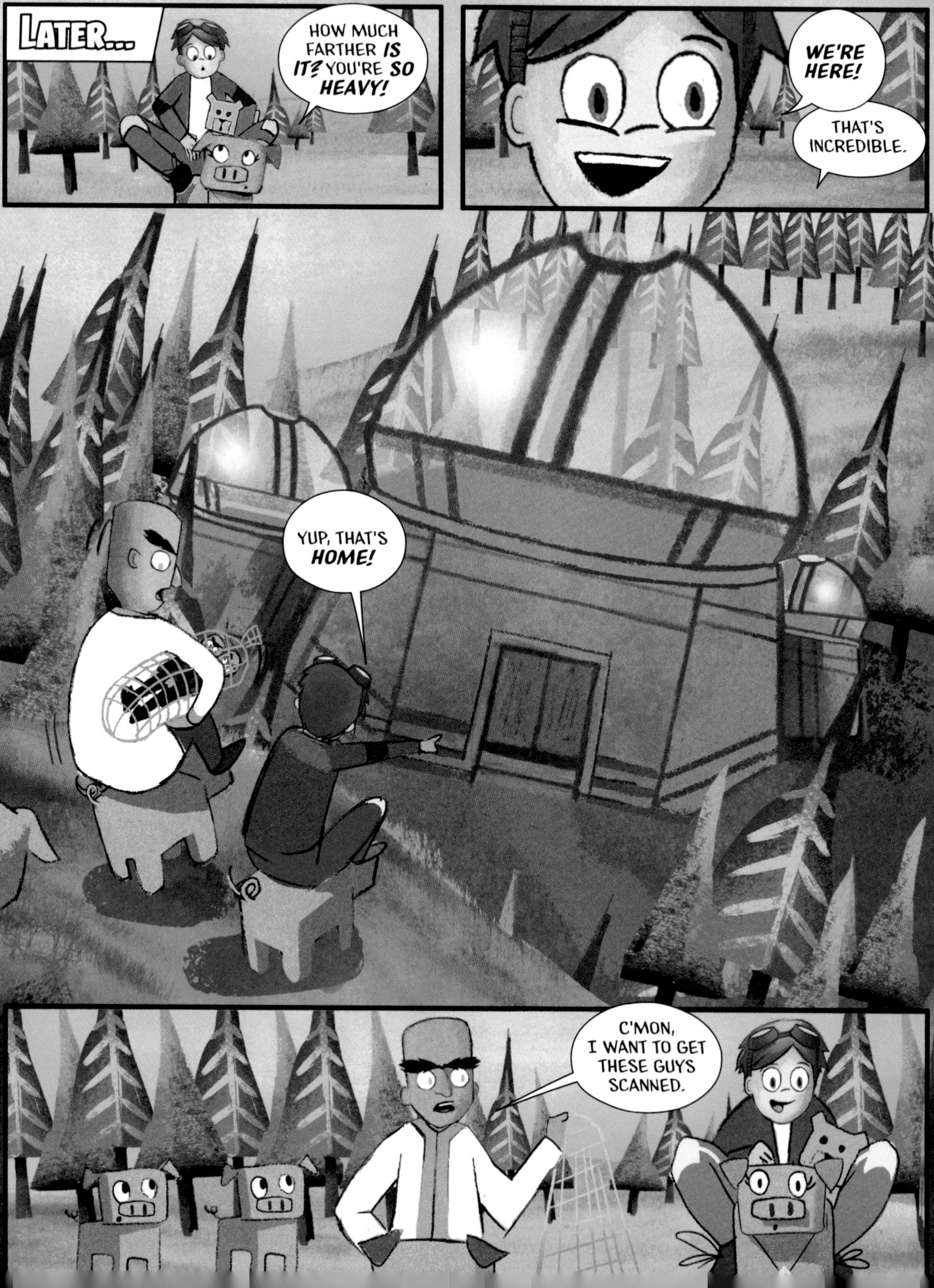
LATER...
HOW MUCH FARTHER IS IT? YOU'RE SO HEAVY!
WE'RE HERE!
THAT'S INCREDIBLE.
YUP, THAT'S HOME!
C'MON, I WANT TO GET THESE GUYS SCANNED.

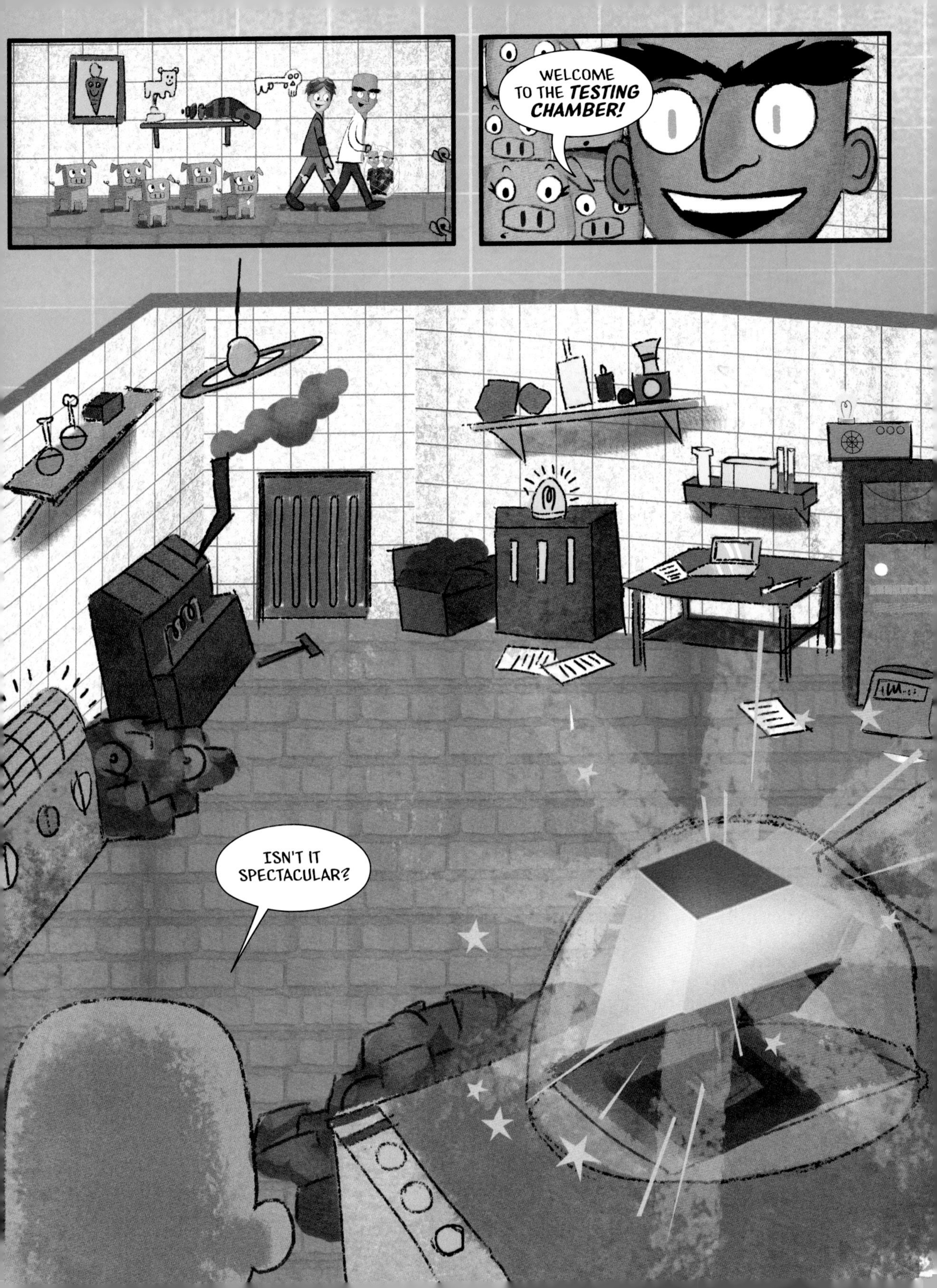
WELCOME TO THE TESTING CHAMBER!
ISN'T IT SPECTACULAR?

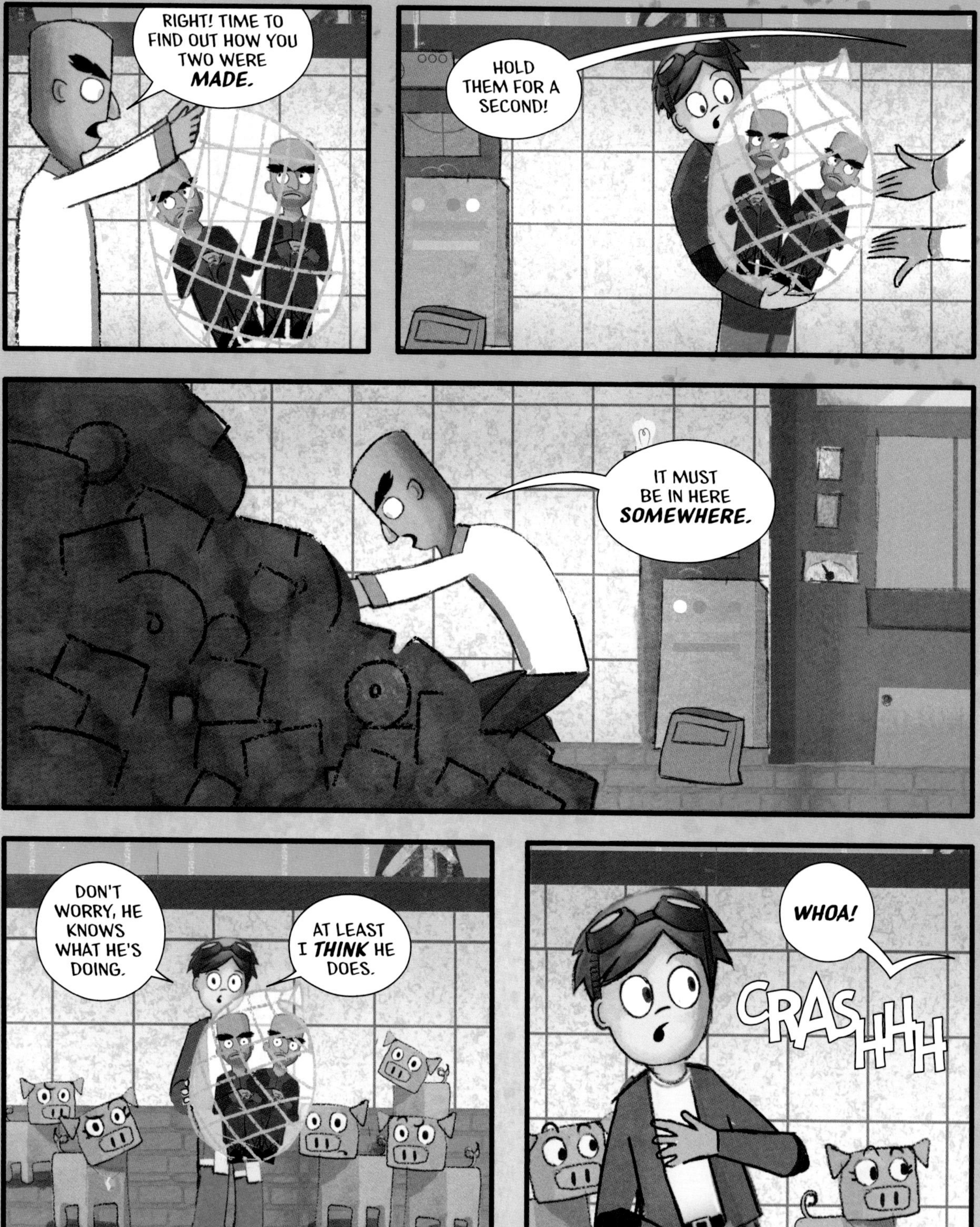
RIGHT! TIME TO FIND OUT HOW YOU TWO WERE *MADE.*
HOLD THEM FOR A SECOND!
IT MUST BE IN HERE *SOMEWHERE.*
DON'T WORRY, HE KNOWS WHAT HE'S DOING.
AT LEAST I *THINK* HE DOES.
WHOA!
CRASHHHH

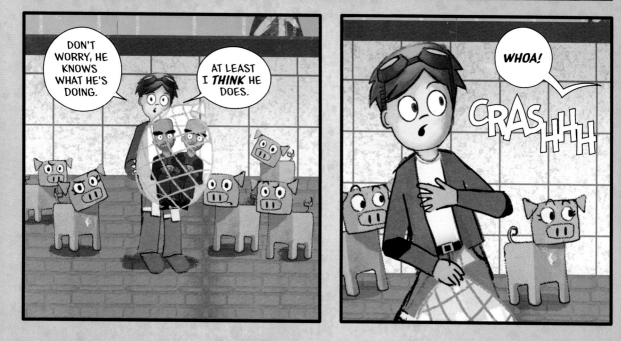

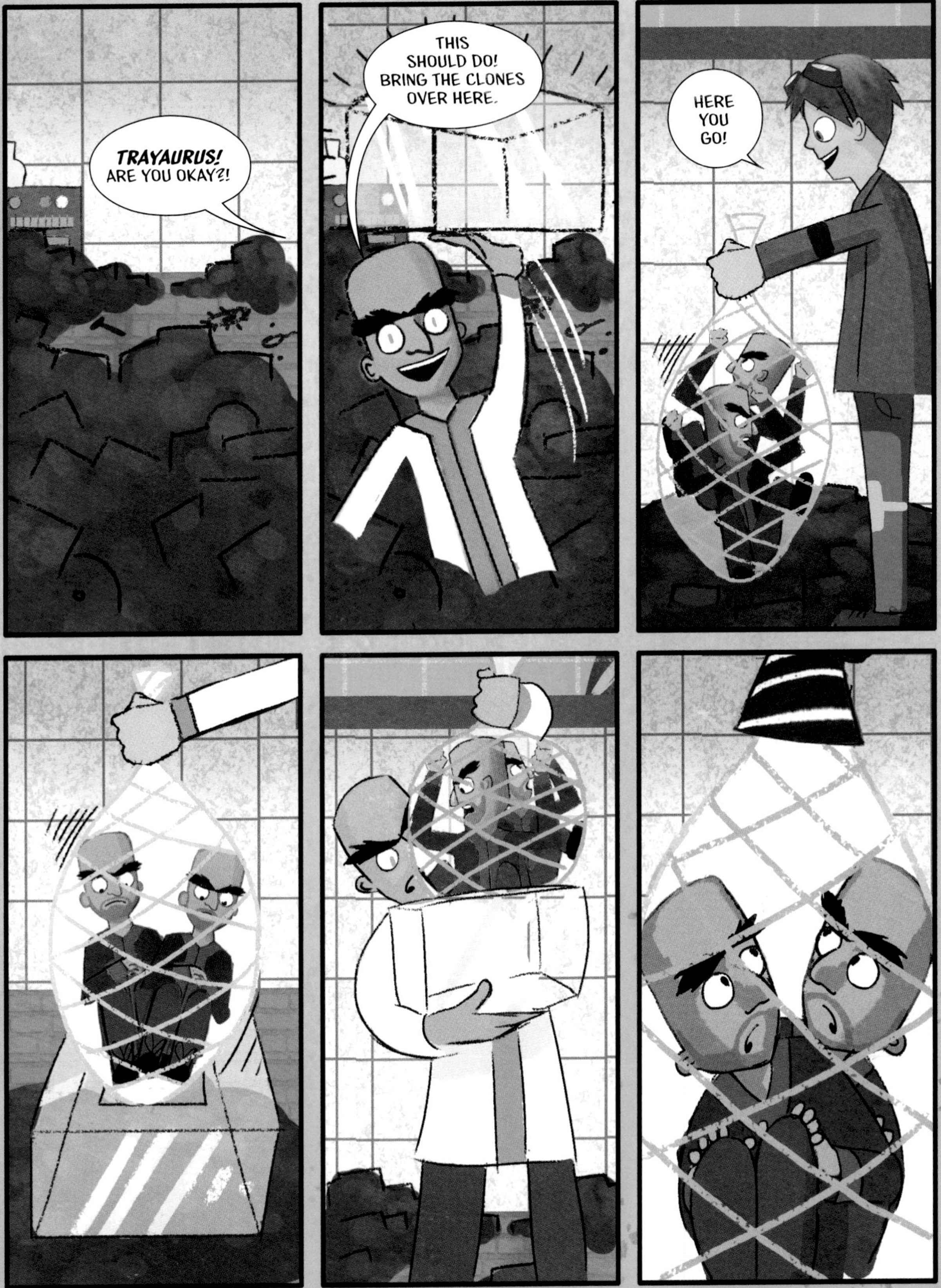
TRAYAURUS! ARE YOU OKAY?!
THIS SHOULD DO! BRING THE CLONES OVER HERE.
HERE YOU GO!

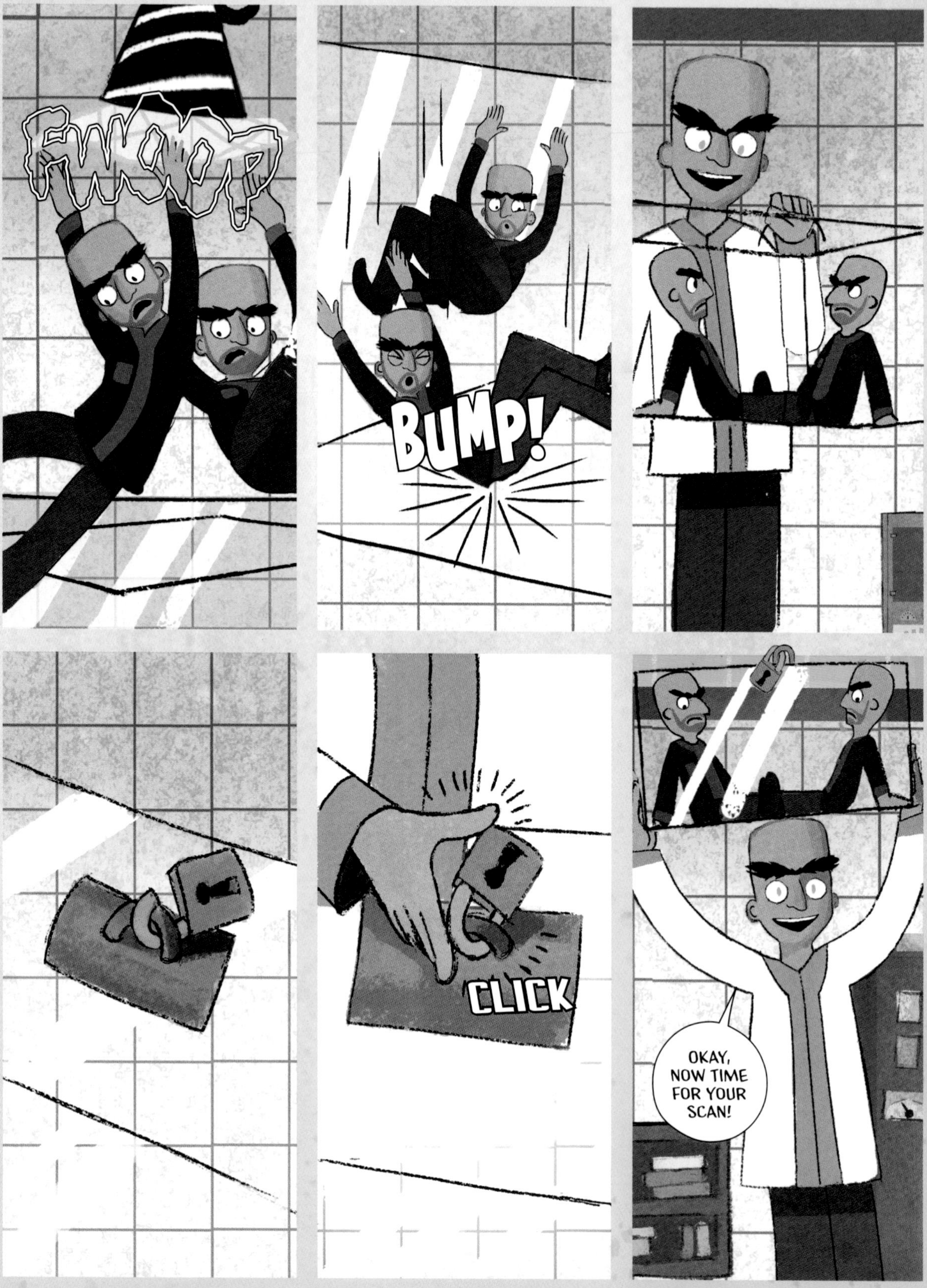
FWOOP
BUMP!
CLICK
OKAY, NOW TIME FOR YOUR SCAN!

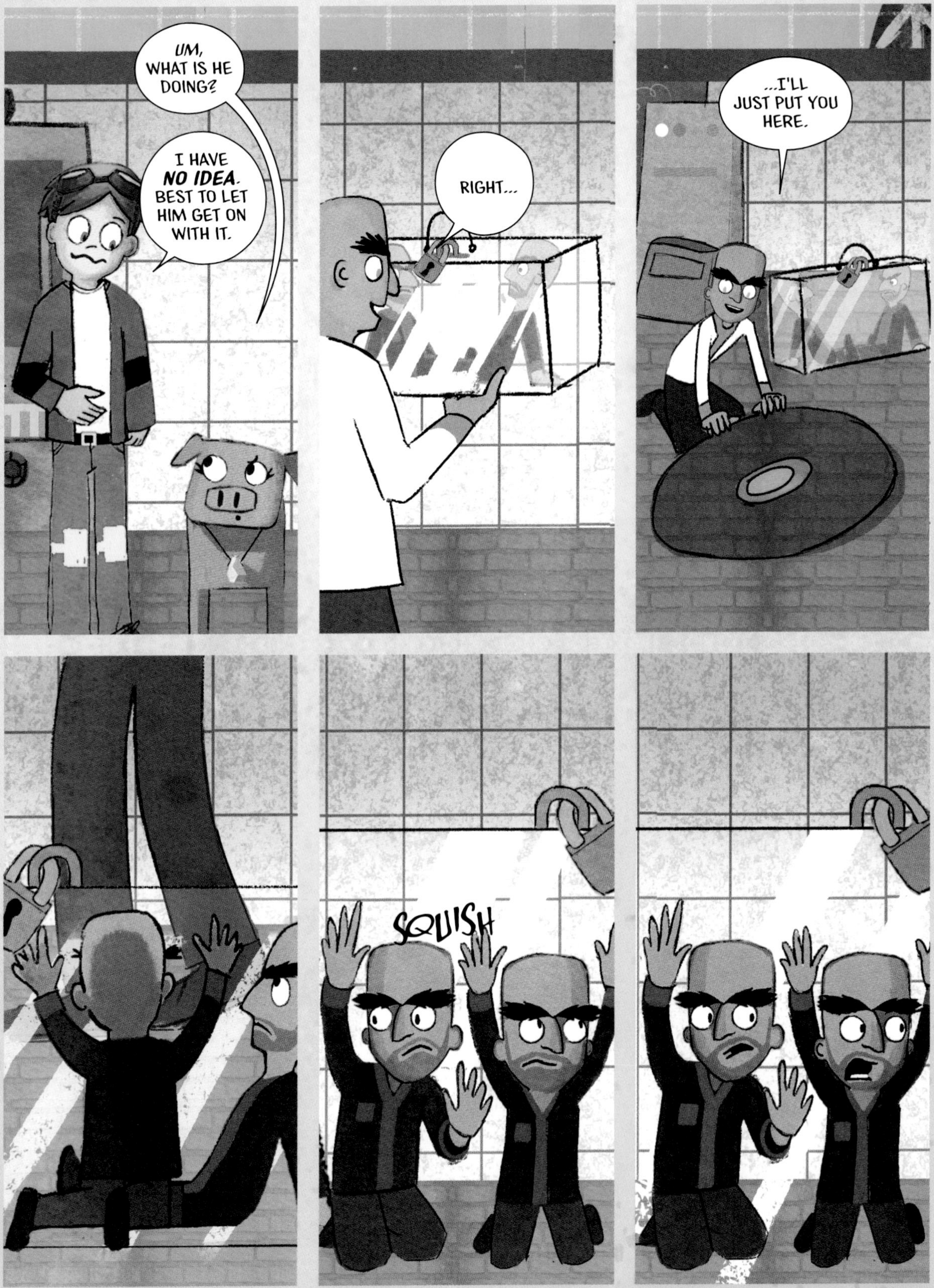
UM, WHAT IS HE DOING?
I HAVE NO IDEA. BEST TO LET HIM GET ON WITH IT.
RIGHT...
...I'LL JUST PUT YOU HERE.
SQUISH

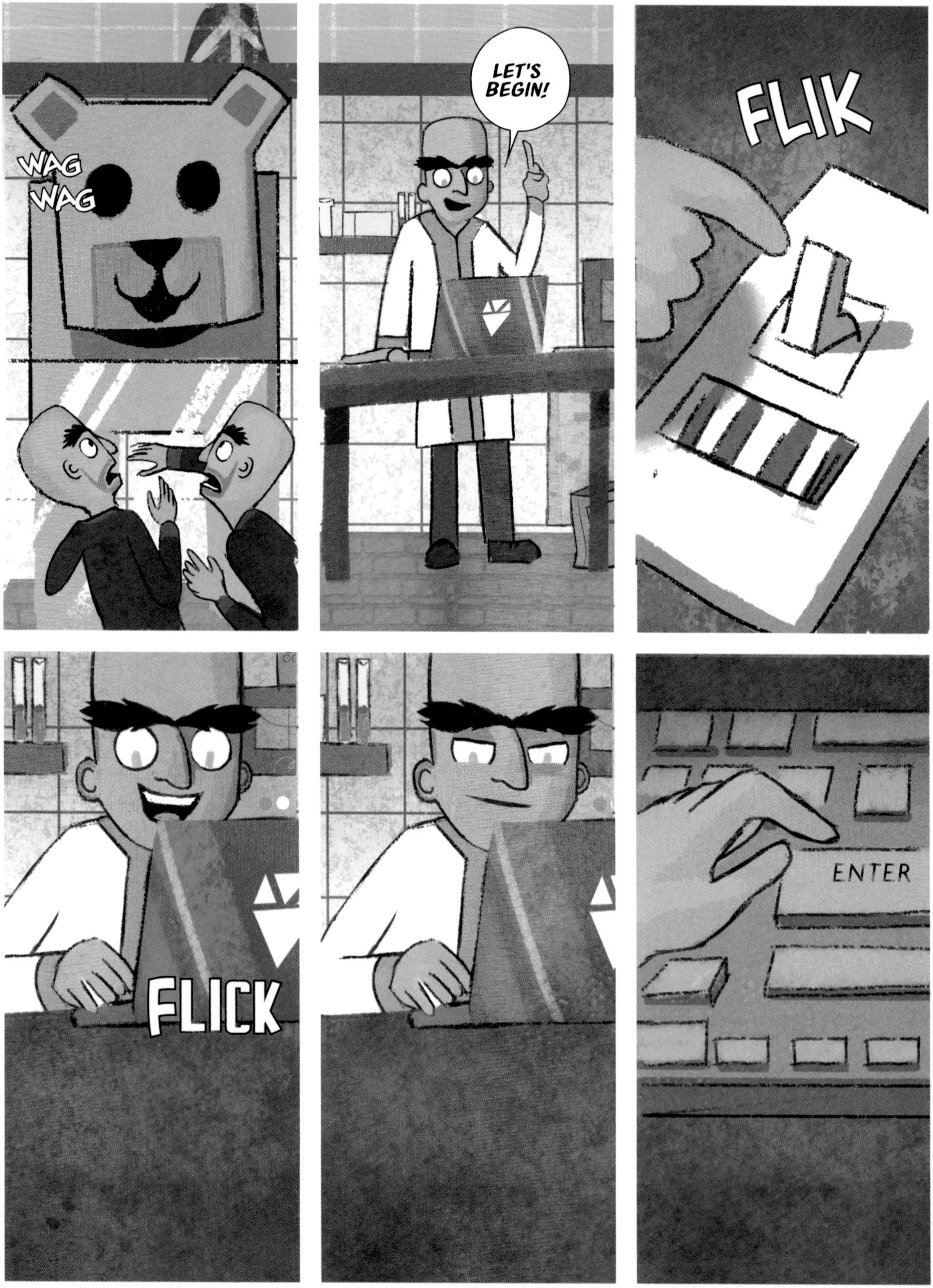
WAG
WAG
LET'S BEGIN!
FLIK
FLICK
ENTER

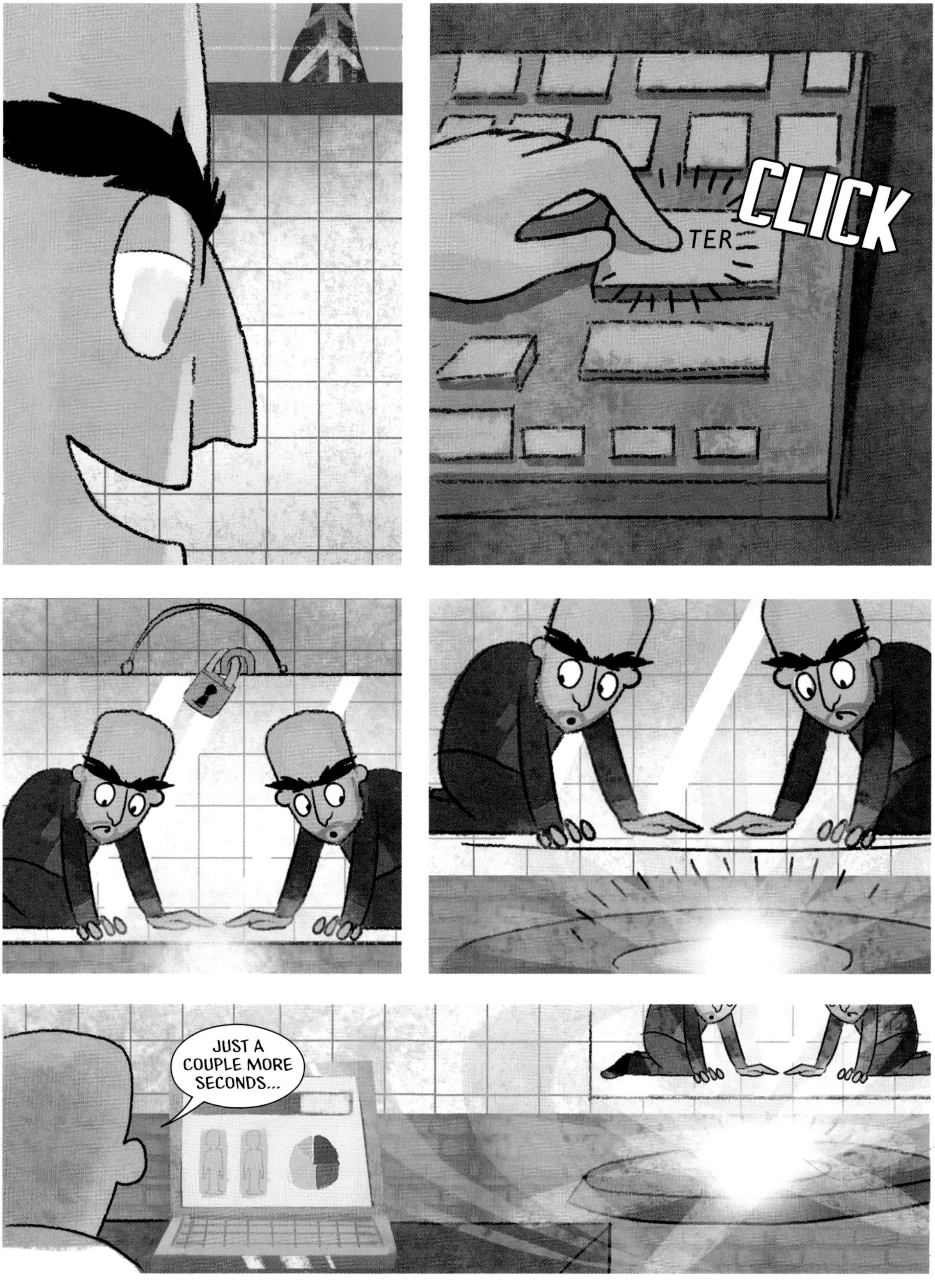

CLICK
TER
JUST A COUPLE MORE SECONDS...

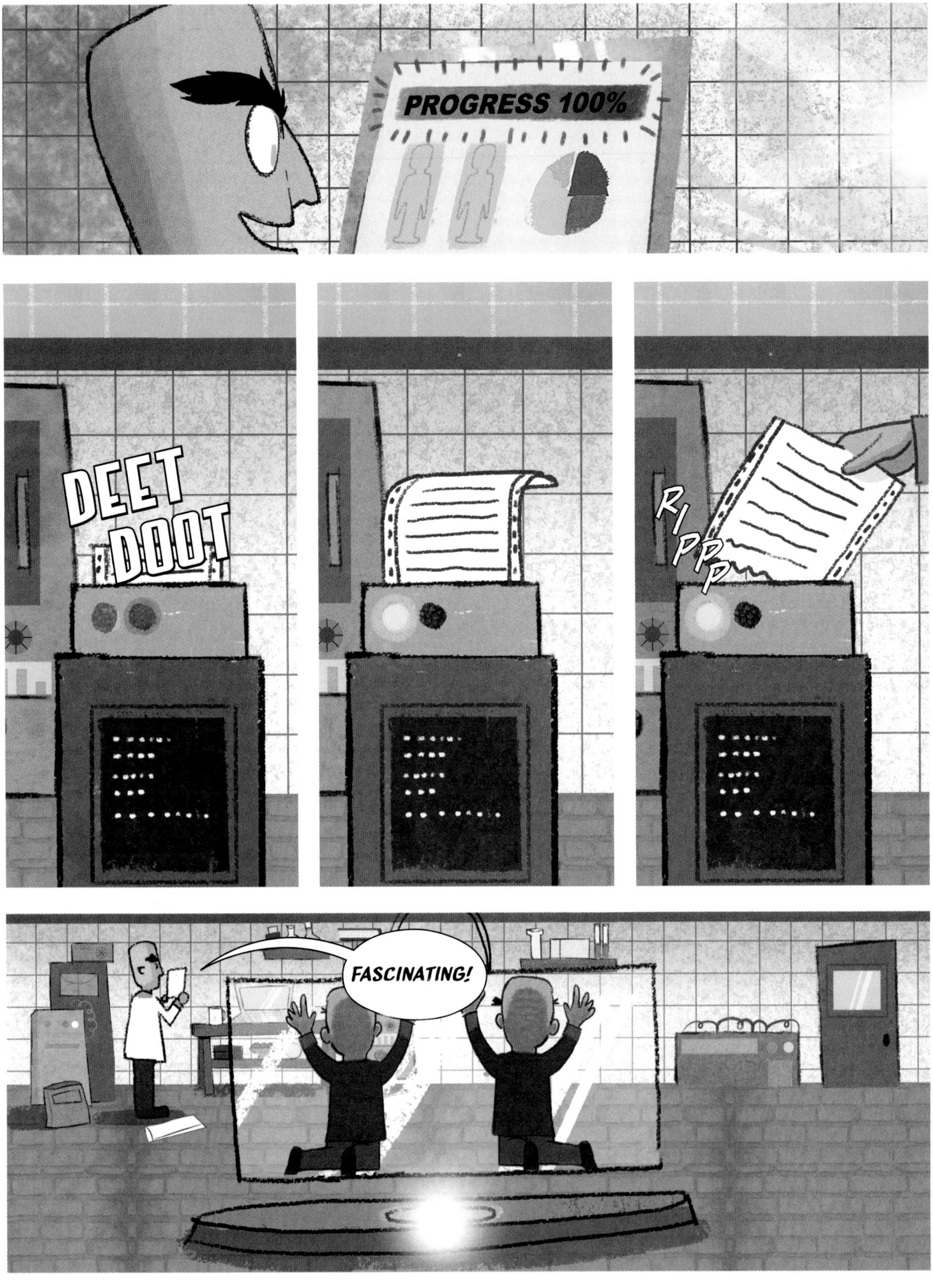
PROGRESS 100%
DEET DOOT
RIPPP
FASCINATING!

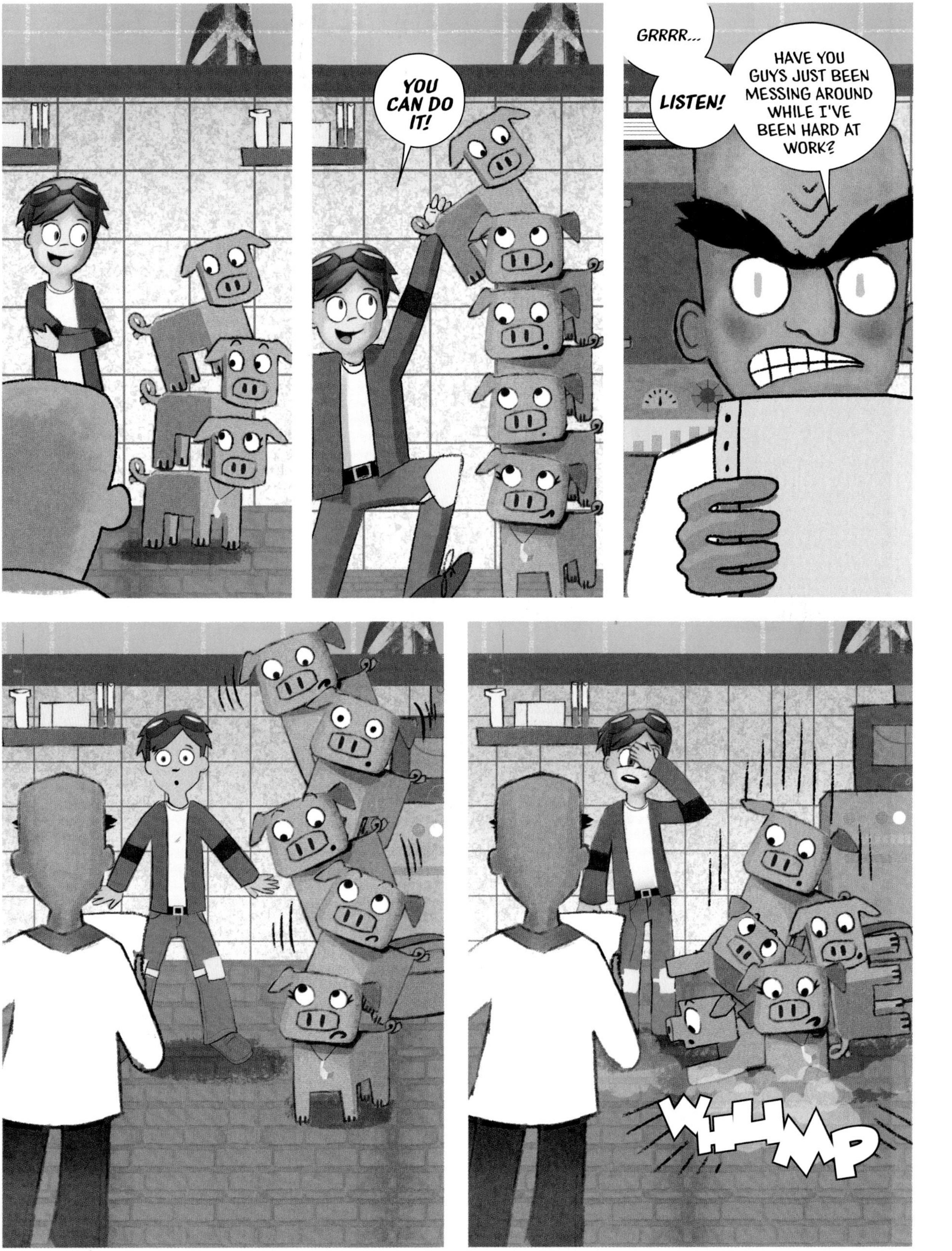
YOU CAN DO IT!
GRRRR...
LISTEN!
HAVE YOU GUYS JUST BEEN MESSING AROUND WHILE I'VE BEEN HARD AT WORK?
WHUMP

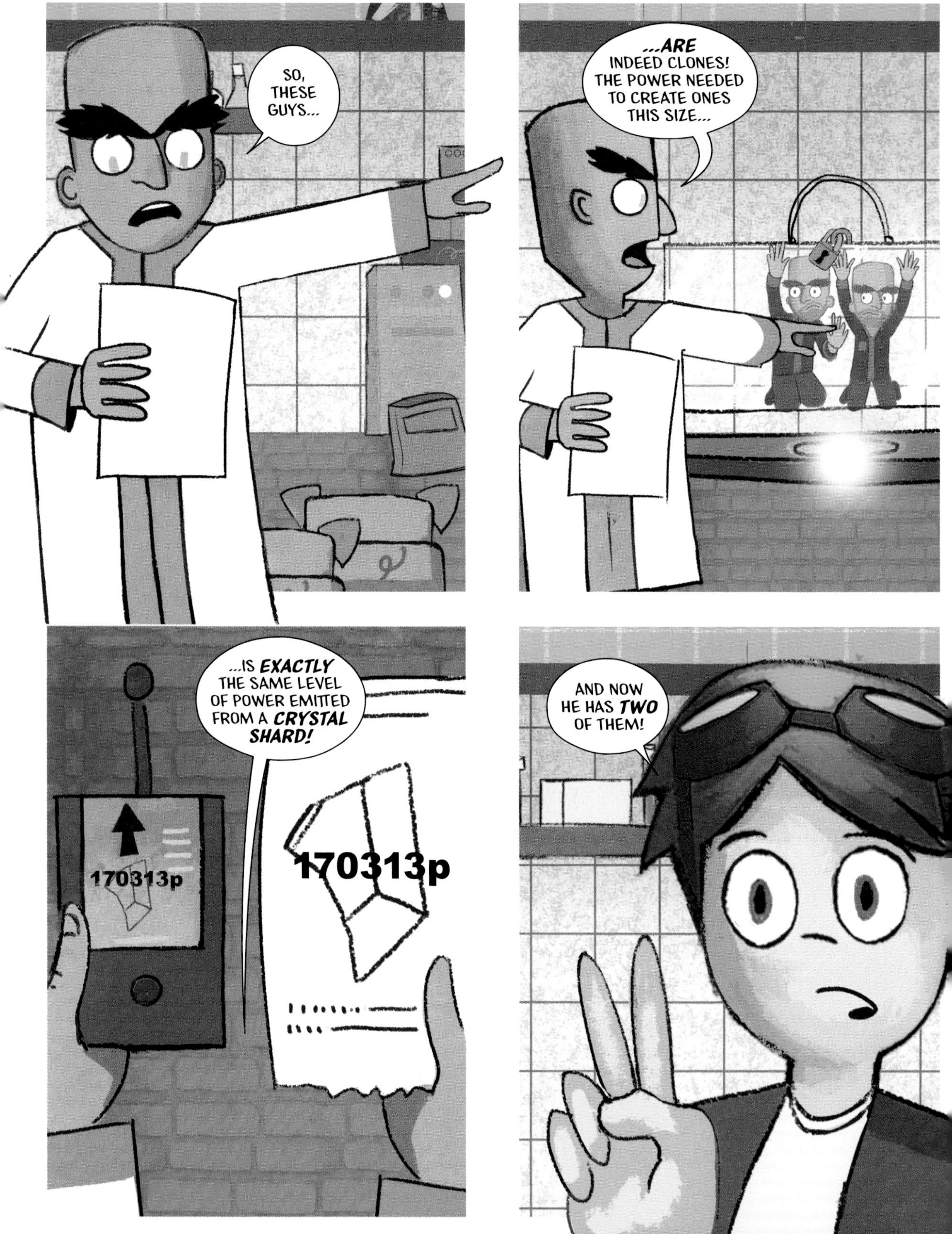
SO, THESE GUYS...
...ARE INDEED CLONES! THE POWER NEEDED TO CREATE ONES THIS SIZE...
...IS EXACTLY THE SAME LEVEL OF POWER EMITTED FROM A CRYSTAL SHARD!
170313p
170313p
AND NOW HE HAS TWO OF THEM!

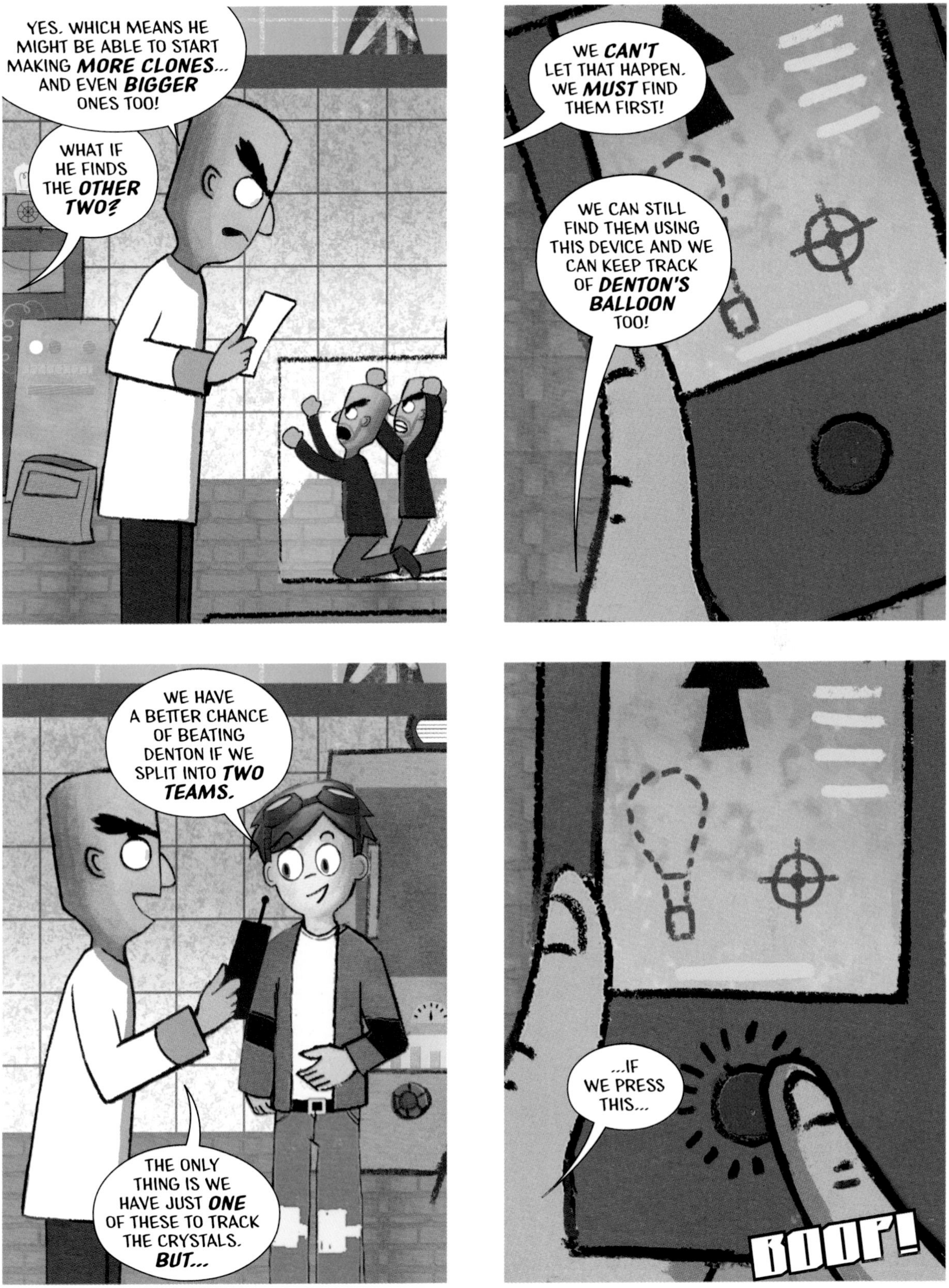
YES. WHICH MEANS HE MIGHT BE ABLE TO START MAKING **MORE CLONES...** AND EVEN **BIGGER** ONES TOO!
WHAT IF HE FINDS THE **OTHER TWO?**
WE **CAN'T** LET THAT HAPPEN. WE **MUST** FIND THEM FIRST!
WE CAN STILL FIND THEM USING THIS DEVICE AND WE CAN KEEP TRACK OF **DENTON'S BALLOON** TOO!
WE HAVE A BETTER CHANCE OF BEATING DENTON IF WE SPLIT INTO **TWO TEAMS.**
THE ONLY THING IS WE HAVE JUST **ONE** OF THESE TO TRACK THE CRYSTALS. **BUT...**
...IF WE PRESS THIS...
BOOP!

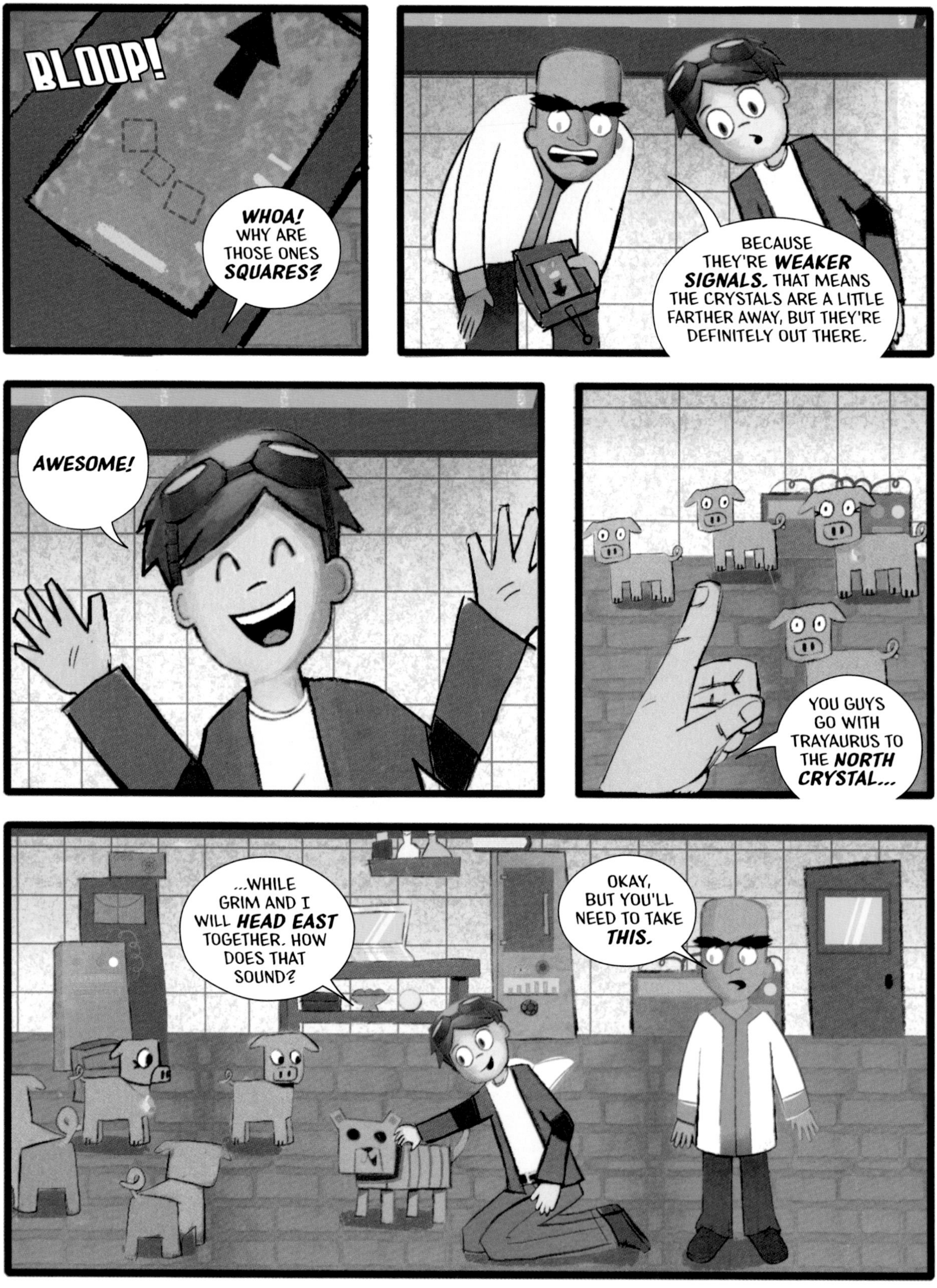
BLOOP!
WHOA! WHY ARE THOSE ONES SQUARES?
BECAUSE THEY'RE WEAKER SIGNALS. THAT MEANS THE CRYSTALS ARE A LITTLE FARTHER AWAY, BUT THEY'RE DEFINITELY OUT THERE.
AWESOME!
YOU GUYS GO WITH TRAYAURUS TO THE NORTH CRYSTAL...
...WHILE GRIM AND I WILL HEAD EAST TOGETHER. HOW DOES THAT SOUND?
OKAY, BUT YOU'LL NEED TO TAKE THIS.

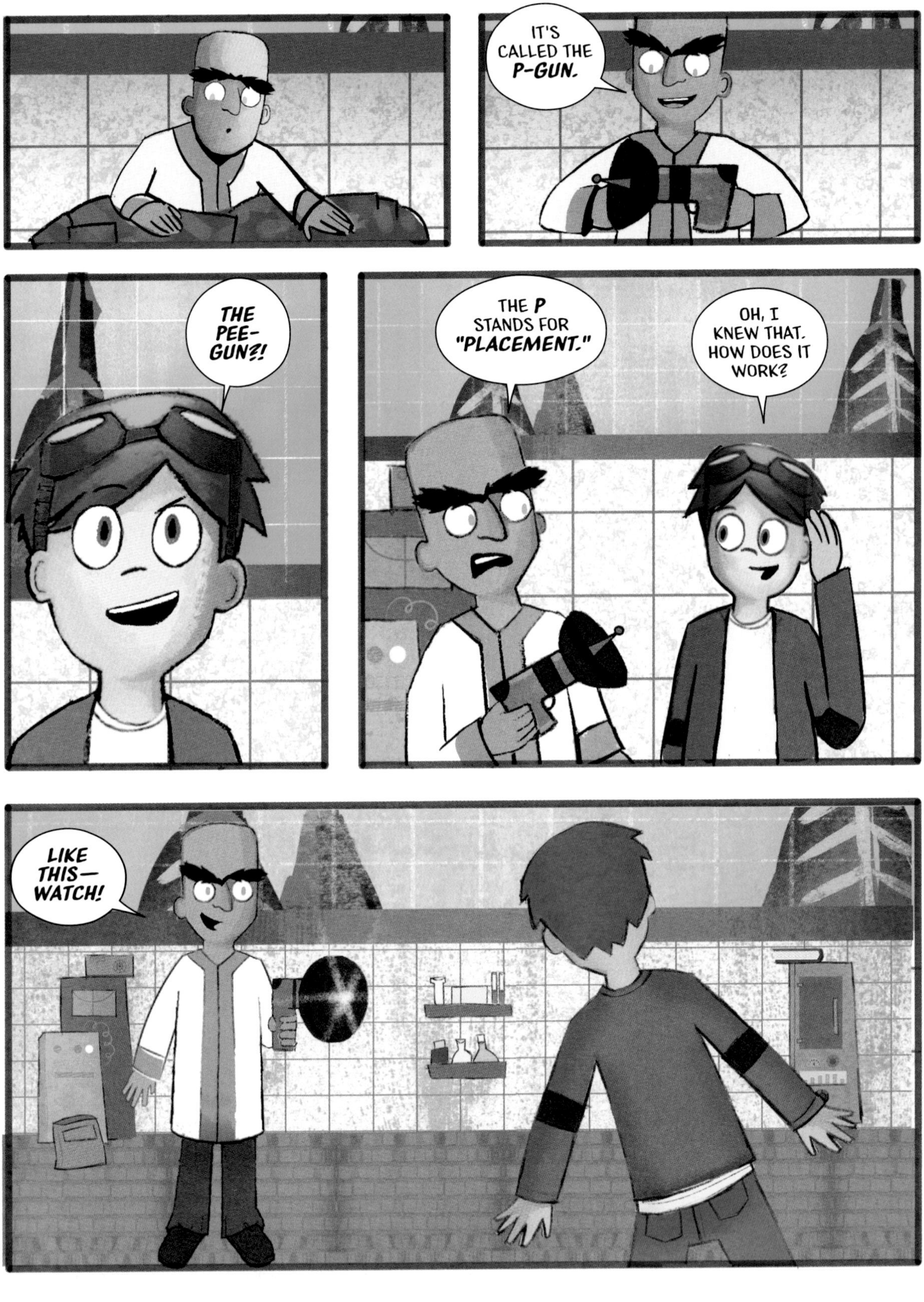
IT'S CALLED THE P-GUN.
THE PEE-GUN?!
THE P STANDS FOR "PLACEMENT."
OH, I KNEW THAT. HOW DOES IT WORK?
LIKE THIS—WATCH!

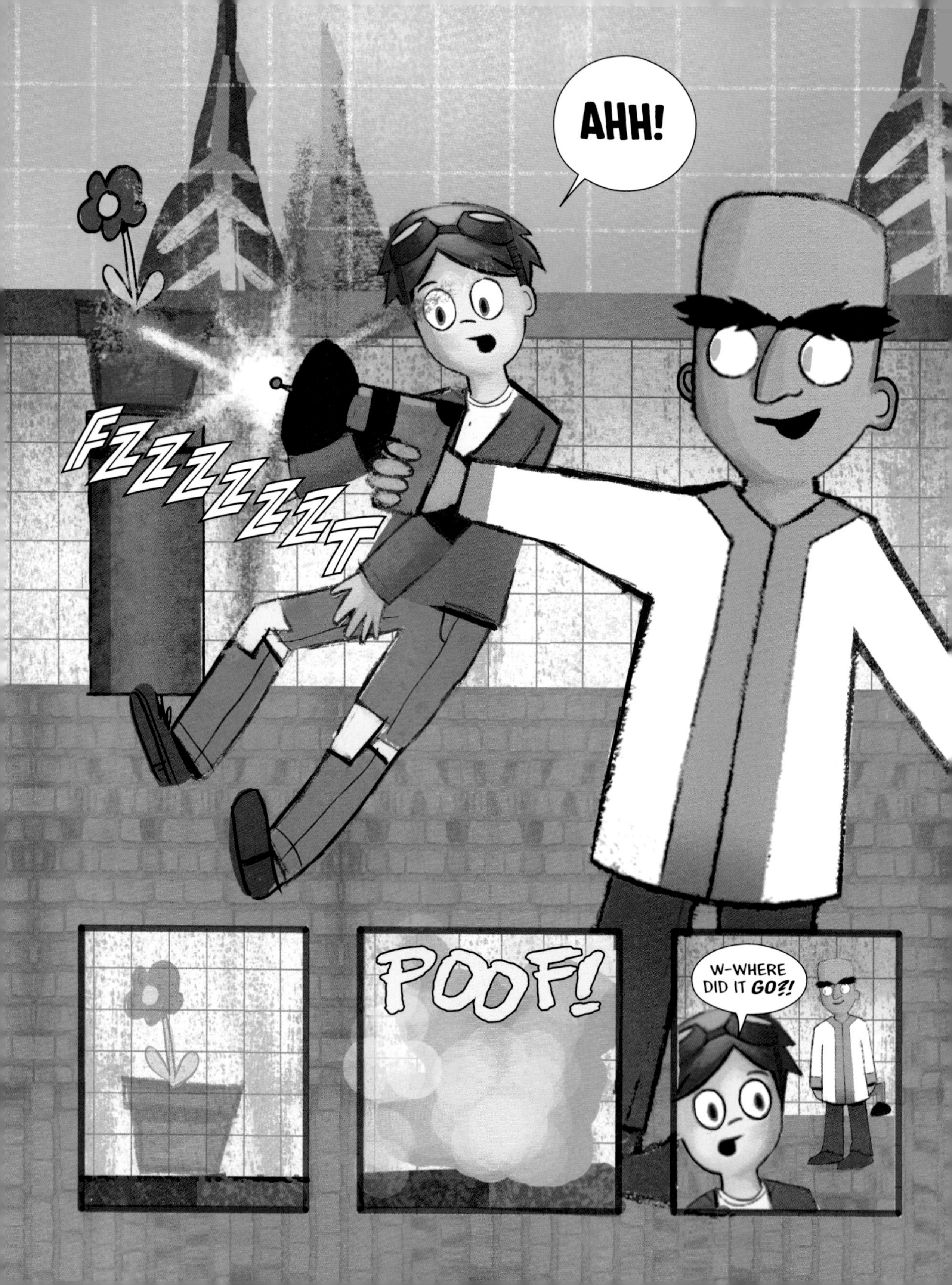
AHH!
FZZZZZZZT
POOF!
W-WHERE DID IT GO?!

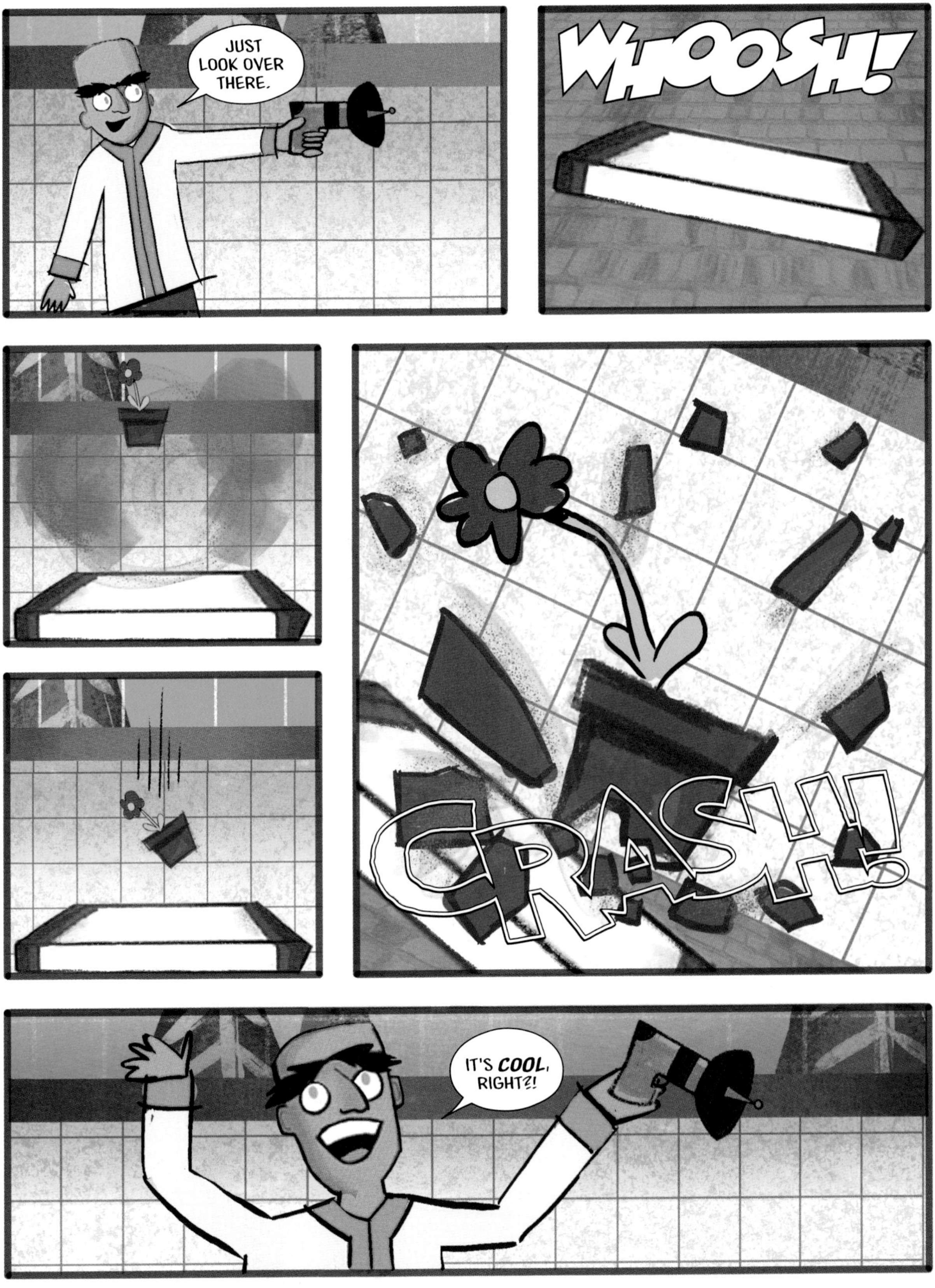
JUST LOOK OVER THERE.
WHOOSH!
CRASH!
IT'S COOL, RIGHT?!

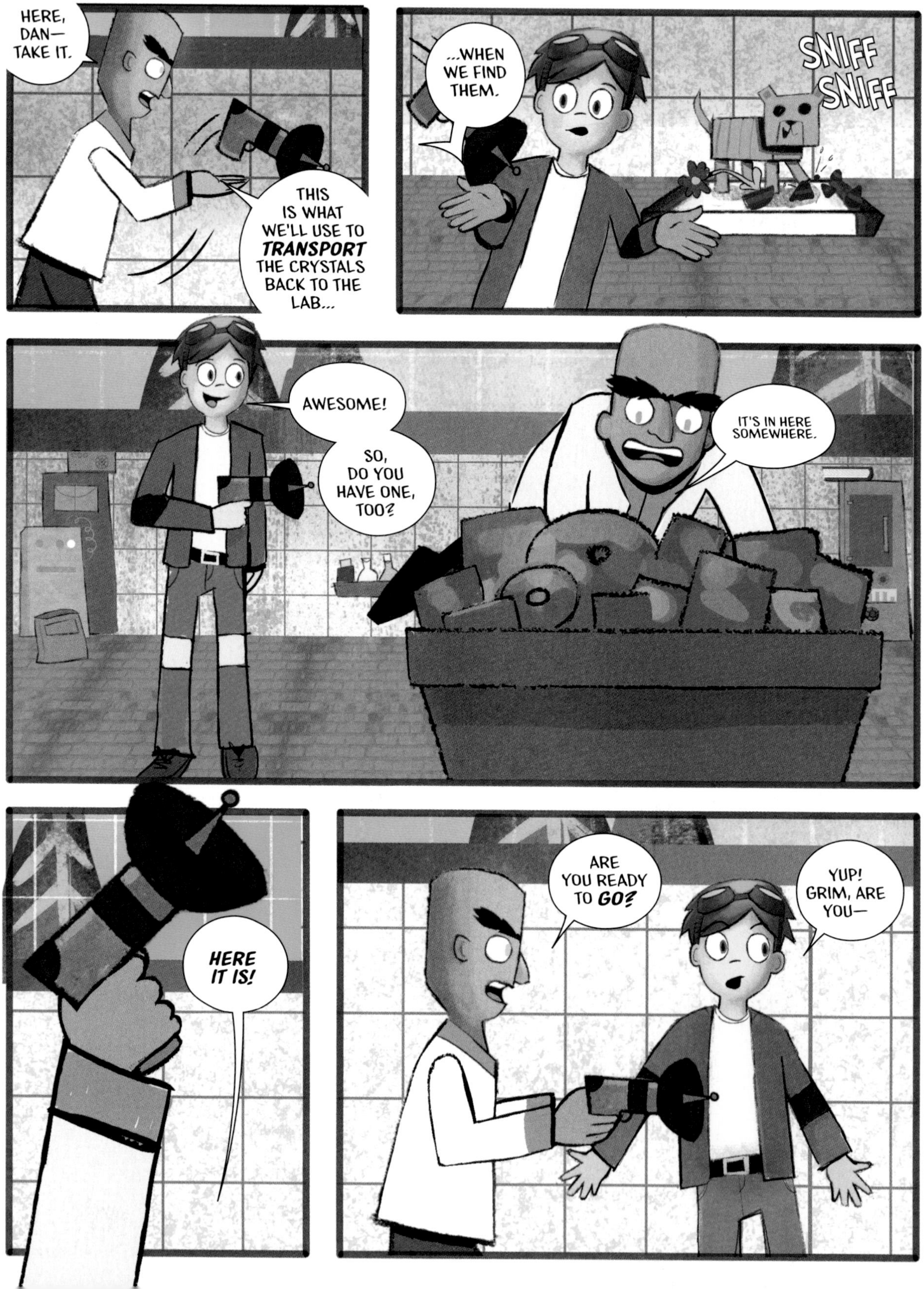
HERE, DAN— TAKE IT.
THIS IS WHAT WE'LL USE TO *TRANSPORT* THE CRYSTALS BACK TO THE LAB...
...WHEN WE FIND THEM.
SNIFF SNIFF
AWESOME!
SO, DO YOU HAVE ONE, TOO?
IT'S IN HERE SOMEWHERE.
HERE IT IS!
ARE YOU READY TO *GO?*
YUP! GRIM, ARE YOU—

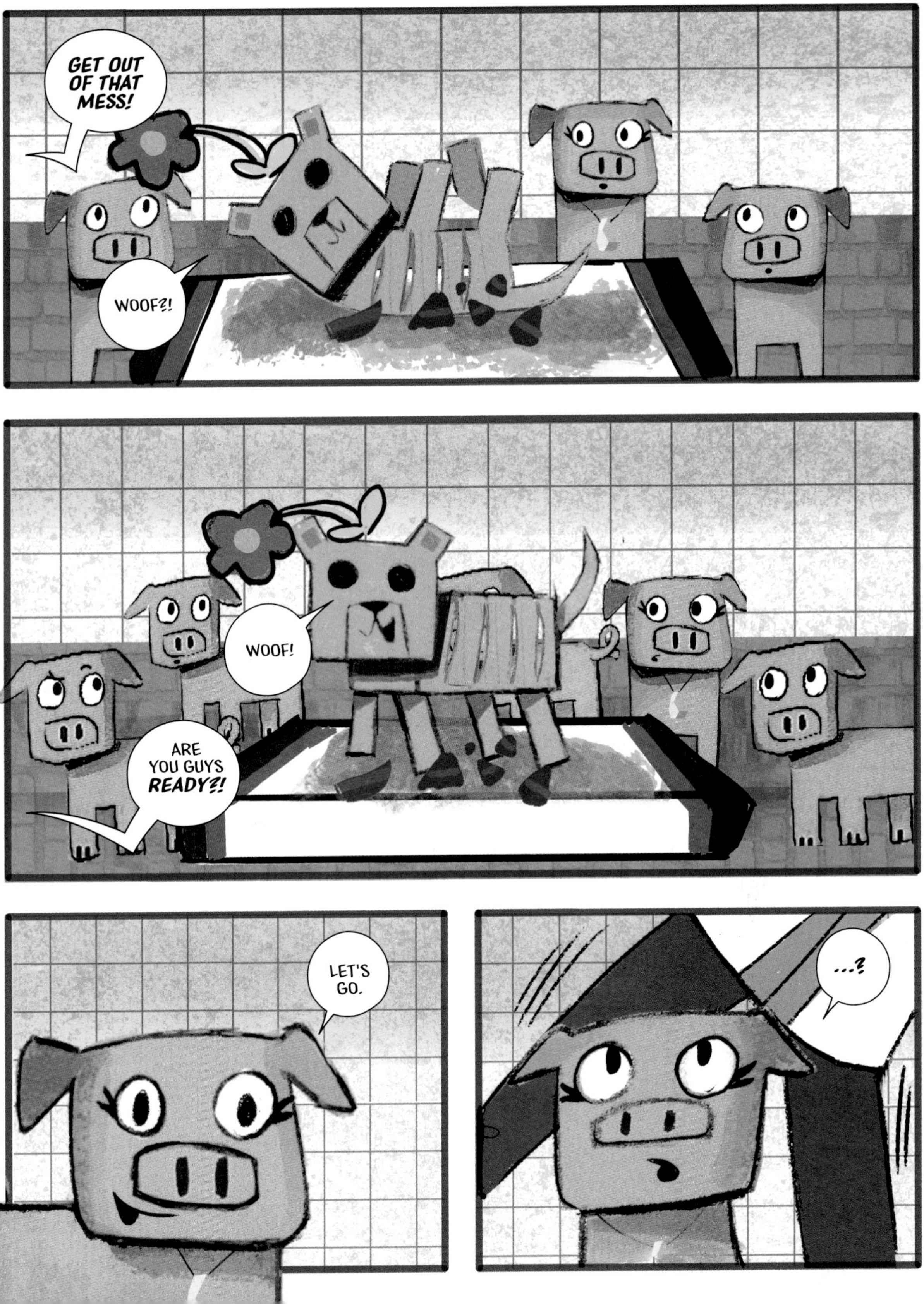
GET OUT OF THAT MESS!
WOOF?!
WOOF!
ARE YOU GUYS READY?!
LET'S GO.
...?

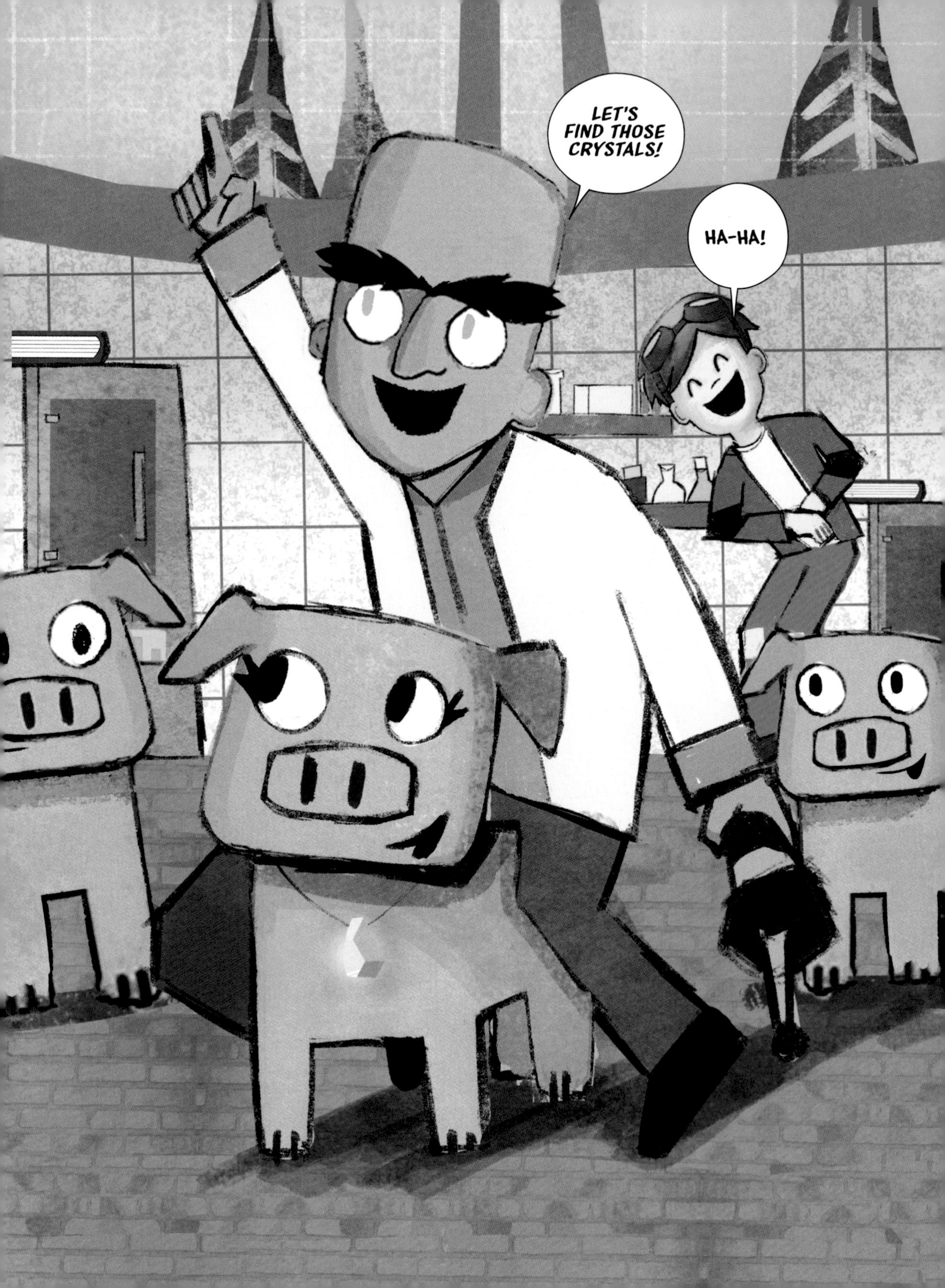
LET'S FIND THOSE CRYSTALS!
HA-HA!

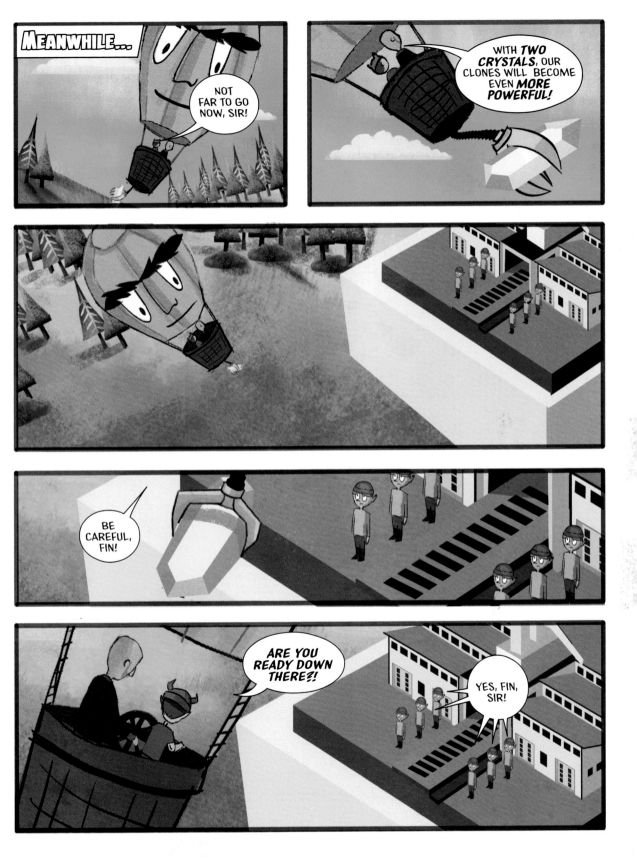

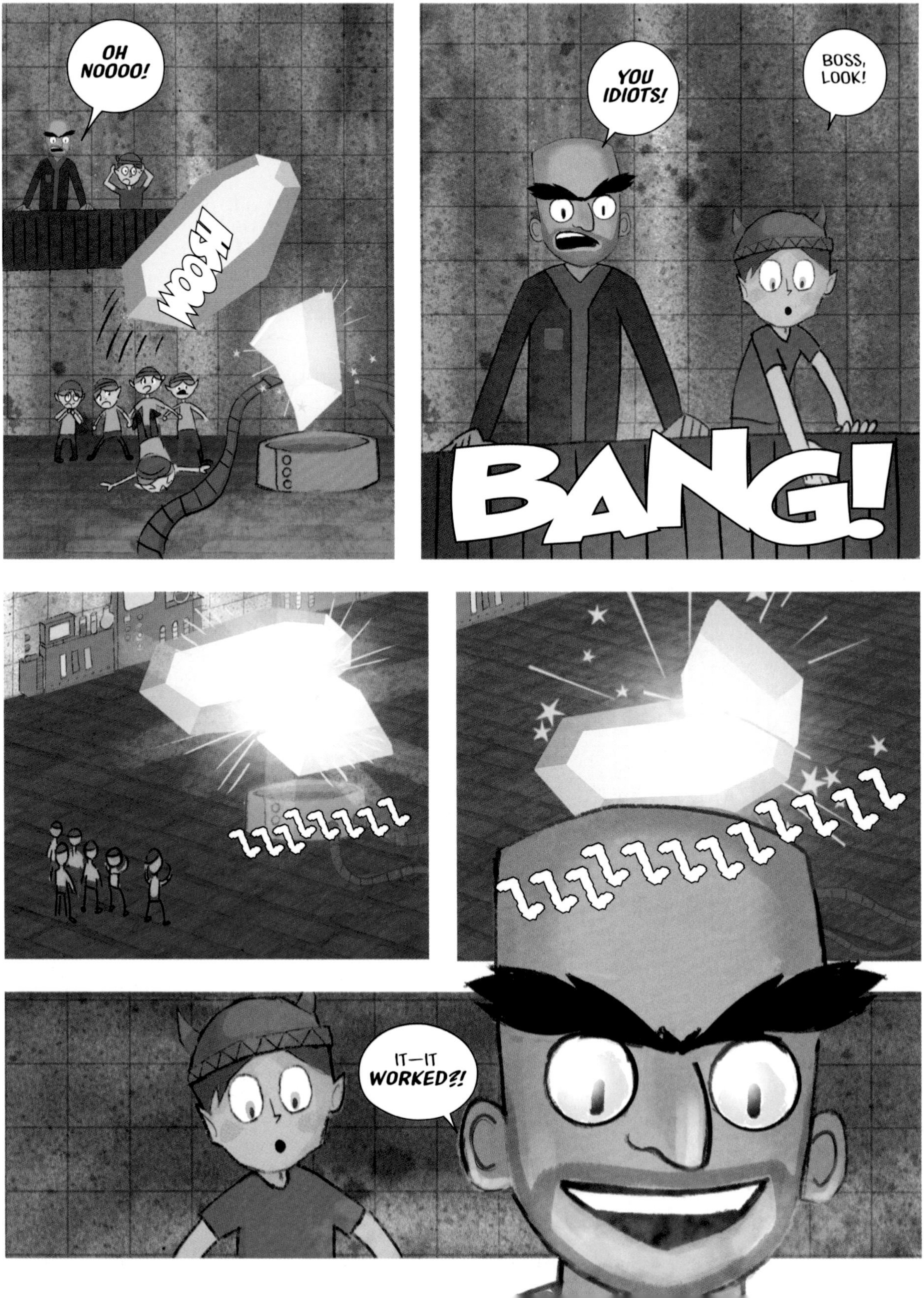
OH NOOOO!
FHSOOM
YOU IDIOTS!
BOSS, LOOK!
BANG!
ZZZZZZZZ
ZZZZZZZZZZZZZZ
IT—IT WORKED?!

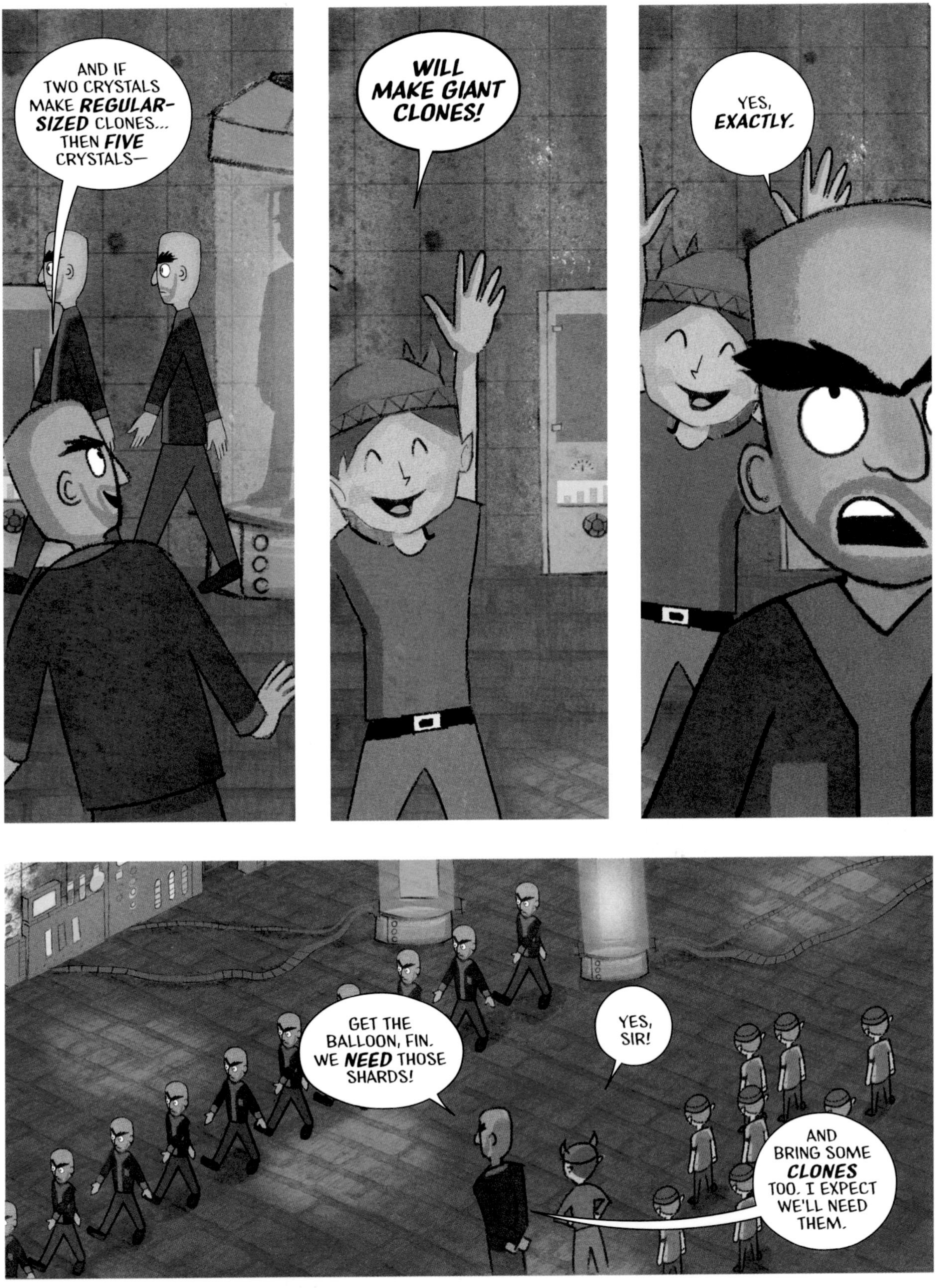
AND IF TWO CRYSTALS MAKE REGULAR-SIZED CLONES... THEN FIVE CRYSTALS—
WILL MAKE GIANT CLONES!
YES, EXACTLY.
GET THE BALLOON, FIN. WE NEED THOSE SHARDS!
YES, SIR!
AND BRING SOME CLONES TOO. I EXPECT WE'LL NEED THEM.

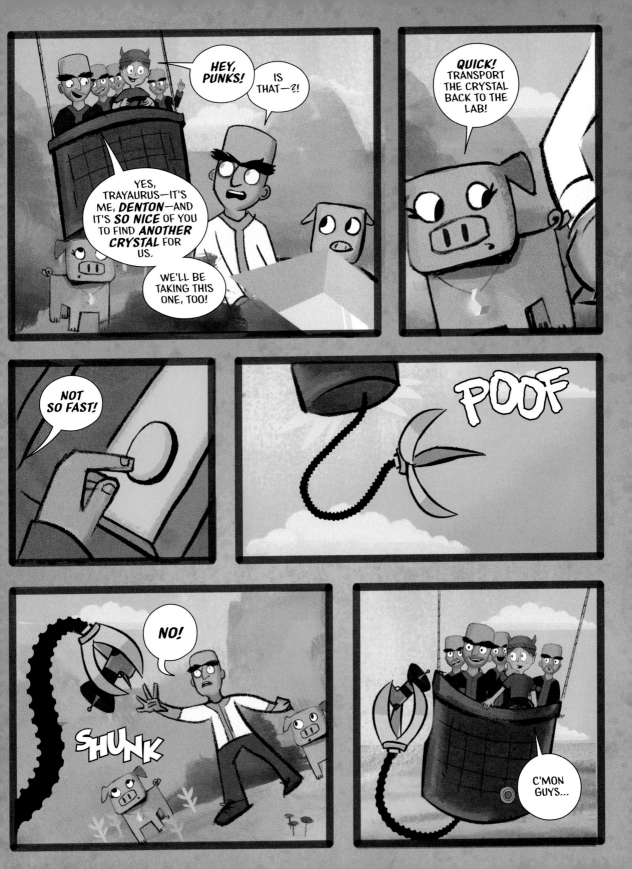

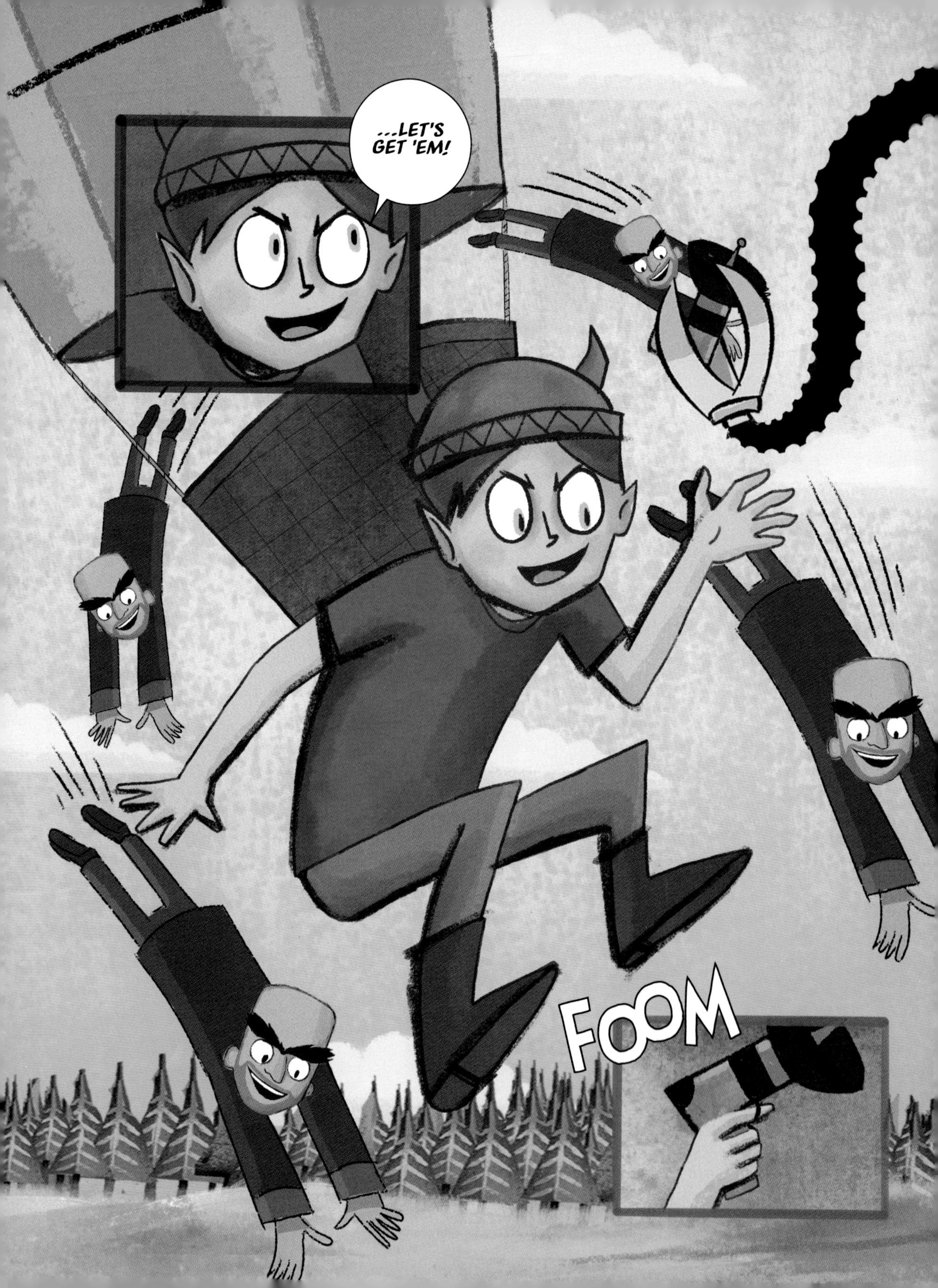
...LET'S GET 'EM!
FOOM

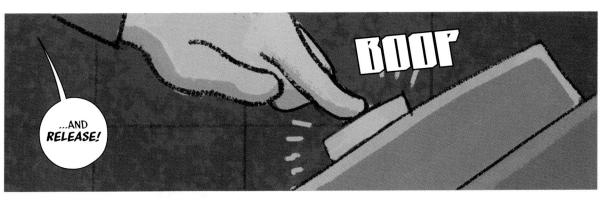

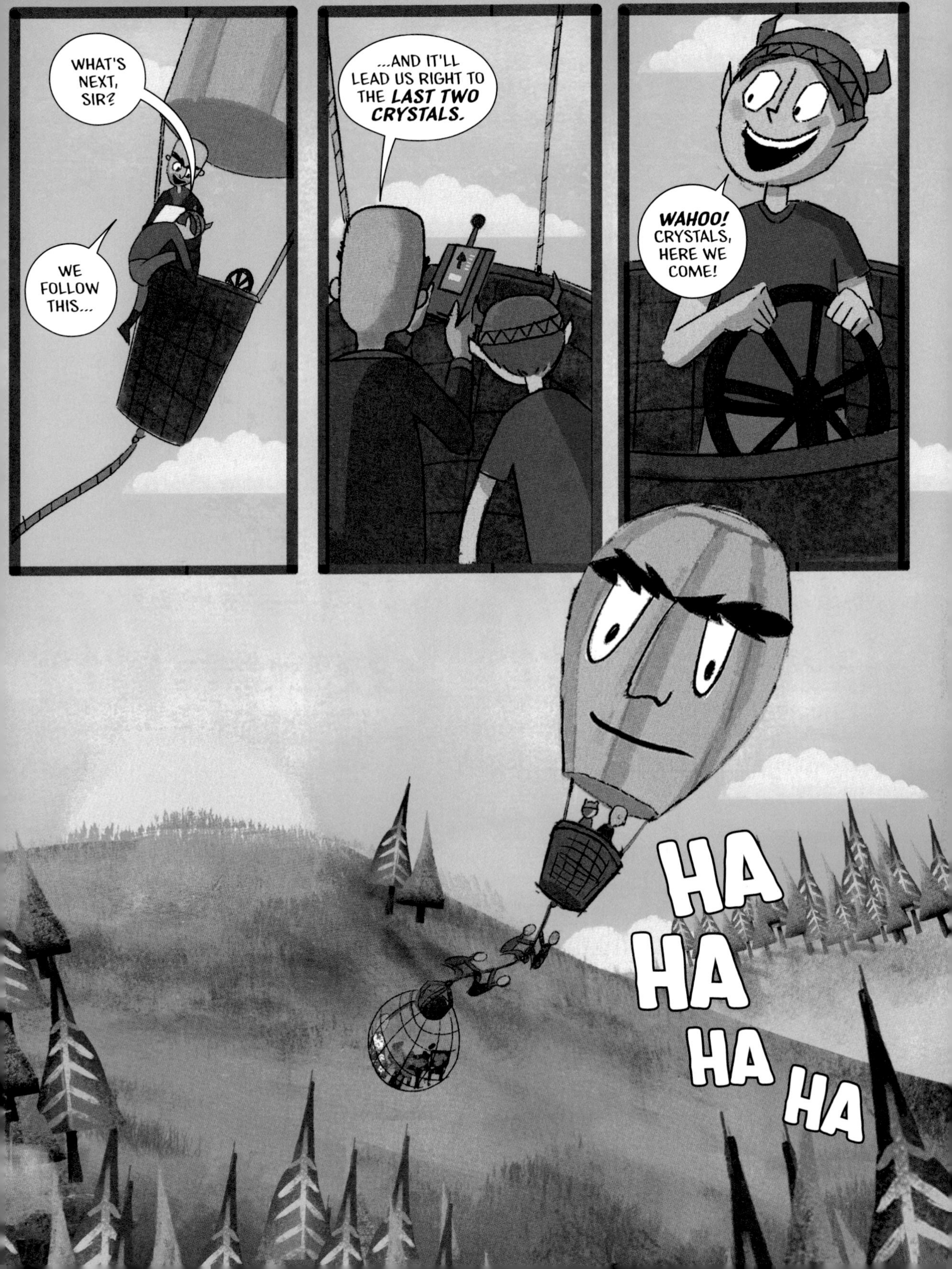
WHAT'S NEXT, SIR?
WE FOLLOW THIS...
...AND IT'LL LEAD US RIGHT TO THE LAST TWO CRYSTALS.
WAHOO! CRYSTALS, HERE WE COME!
HA HA HA HA

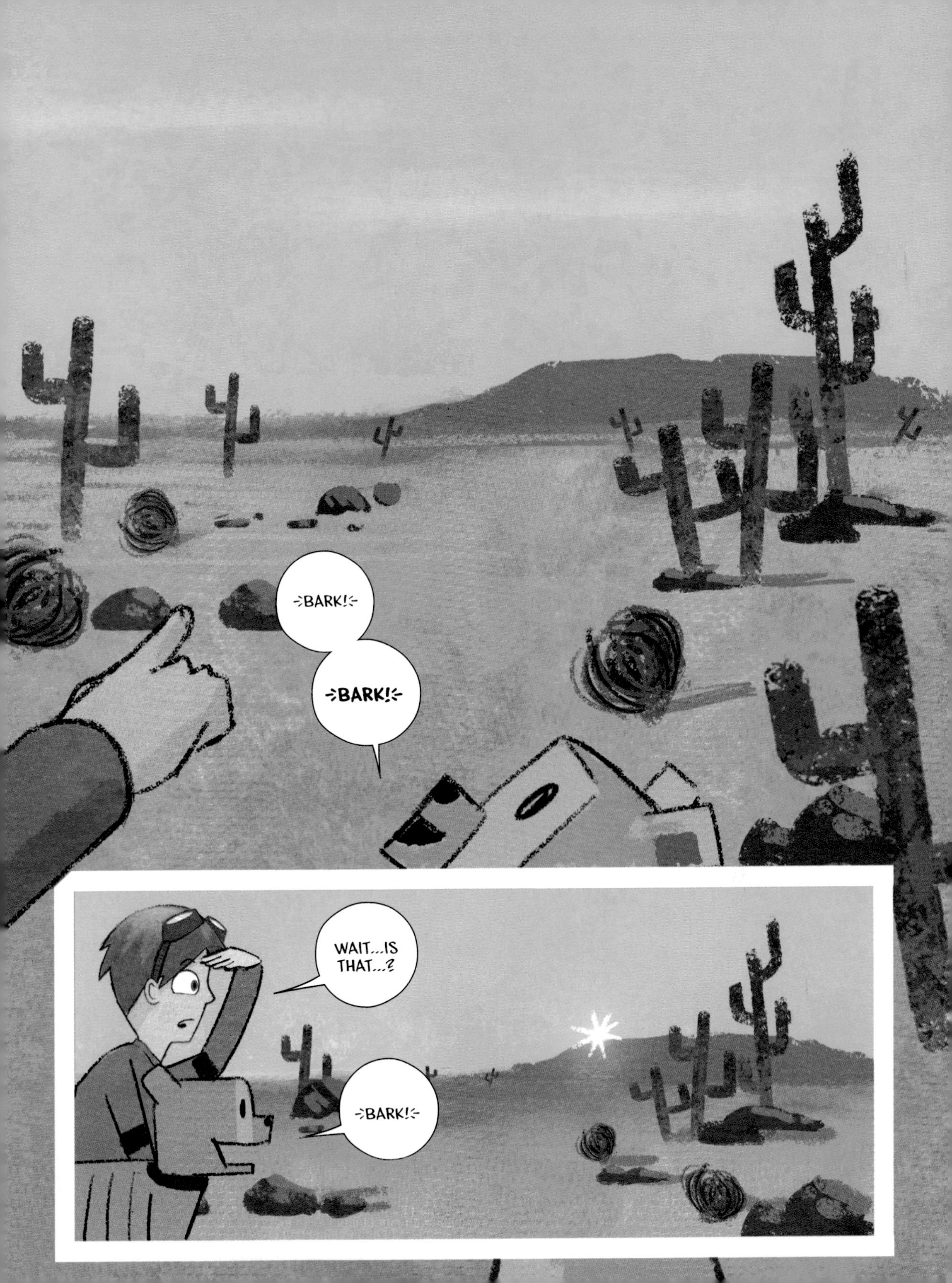
BARK!
BARK!
WAIT...IS THAT...?
BARK!

FINALLY!

YES!

IT'S THE CRYSTAL! THAT'S LUCKY.

÷BARK!÷

GRIM, SEE IF YOU CAN DIG IT OUT.

GOOD JOB, GRIM. NOW MOVE ASIDE WHILE I SEND THIS HOME!

READY... AIM...

DIG DIG DIG

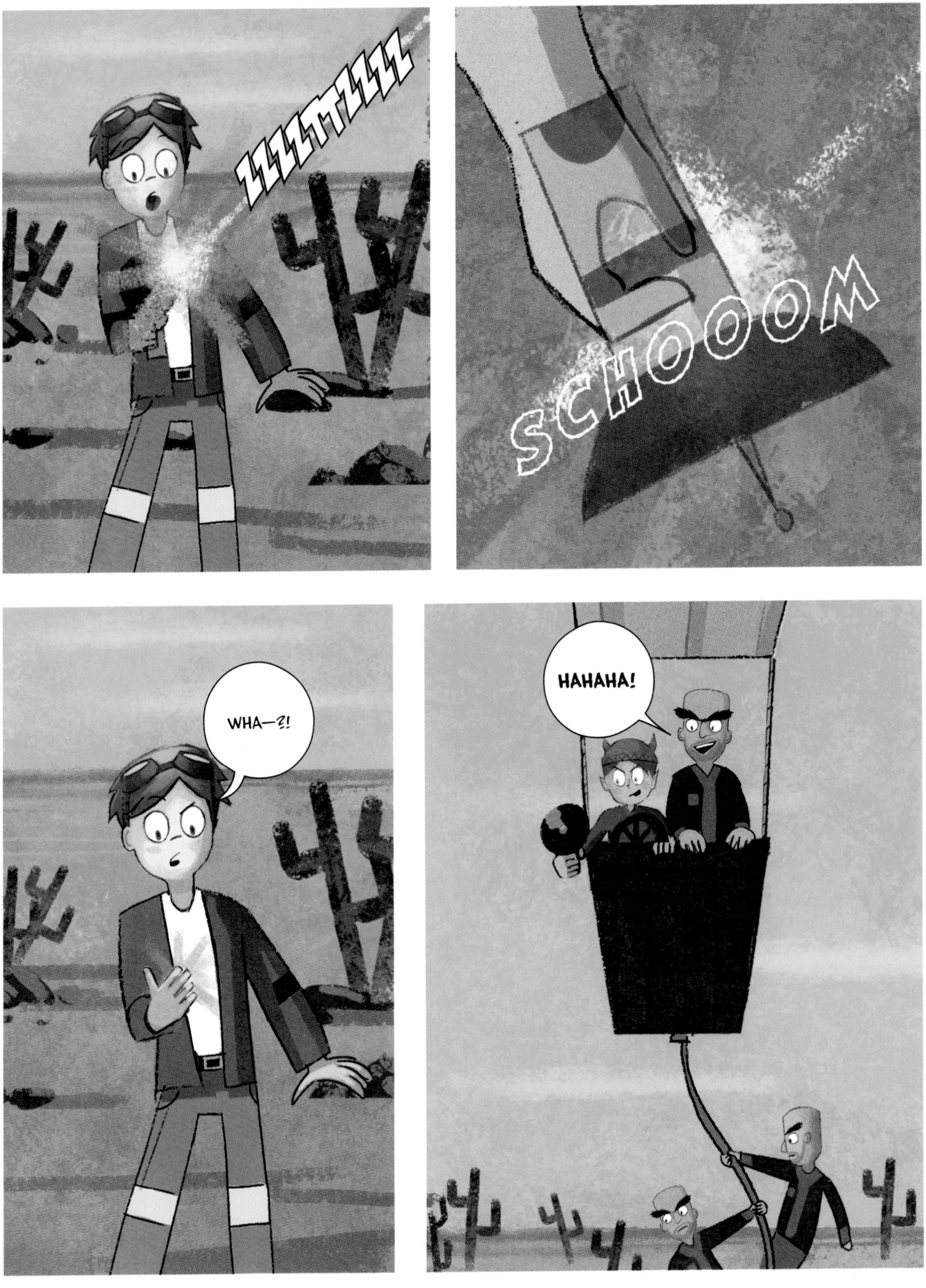
ZZZZZTTZZZZZ
SCHOOOM
WHA—?!
HAHAHA!

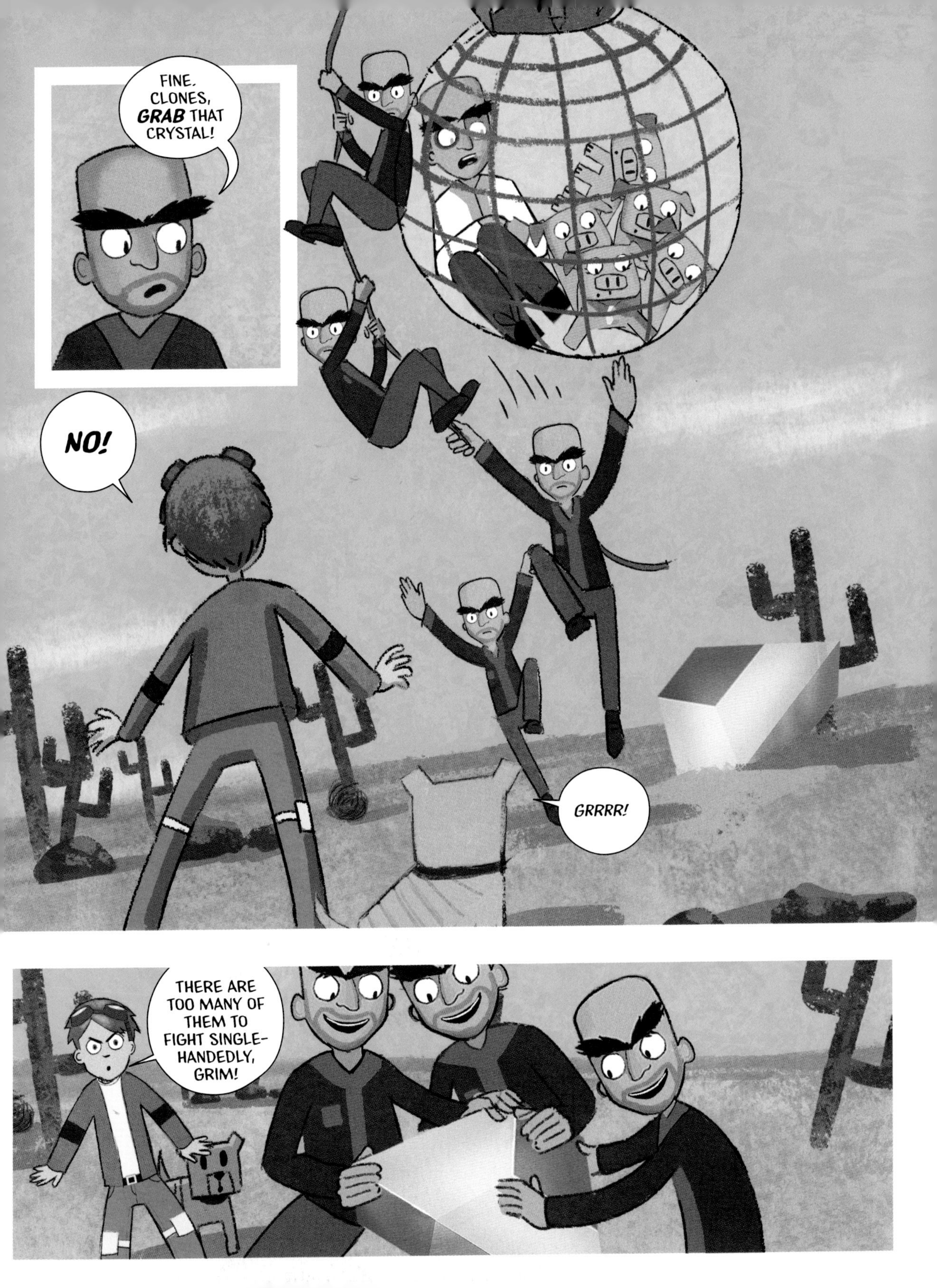
FINE. CLONES, **GRAB** THAT CRYSTAL!
NO!
GRRRR!
THERE ARE TOO MANY OF THEM TO FIGHT SINGLE-HANDEDLY, GRIM!

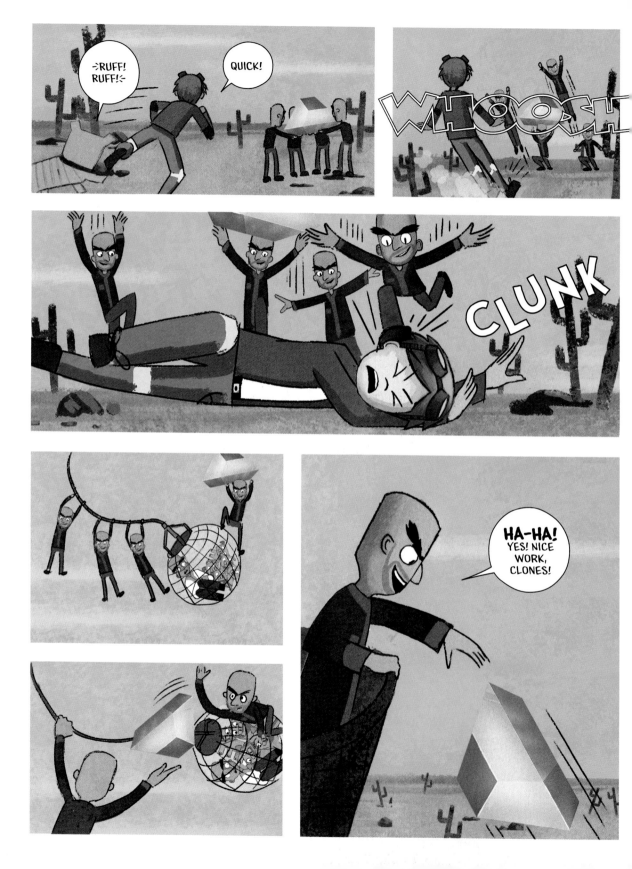

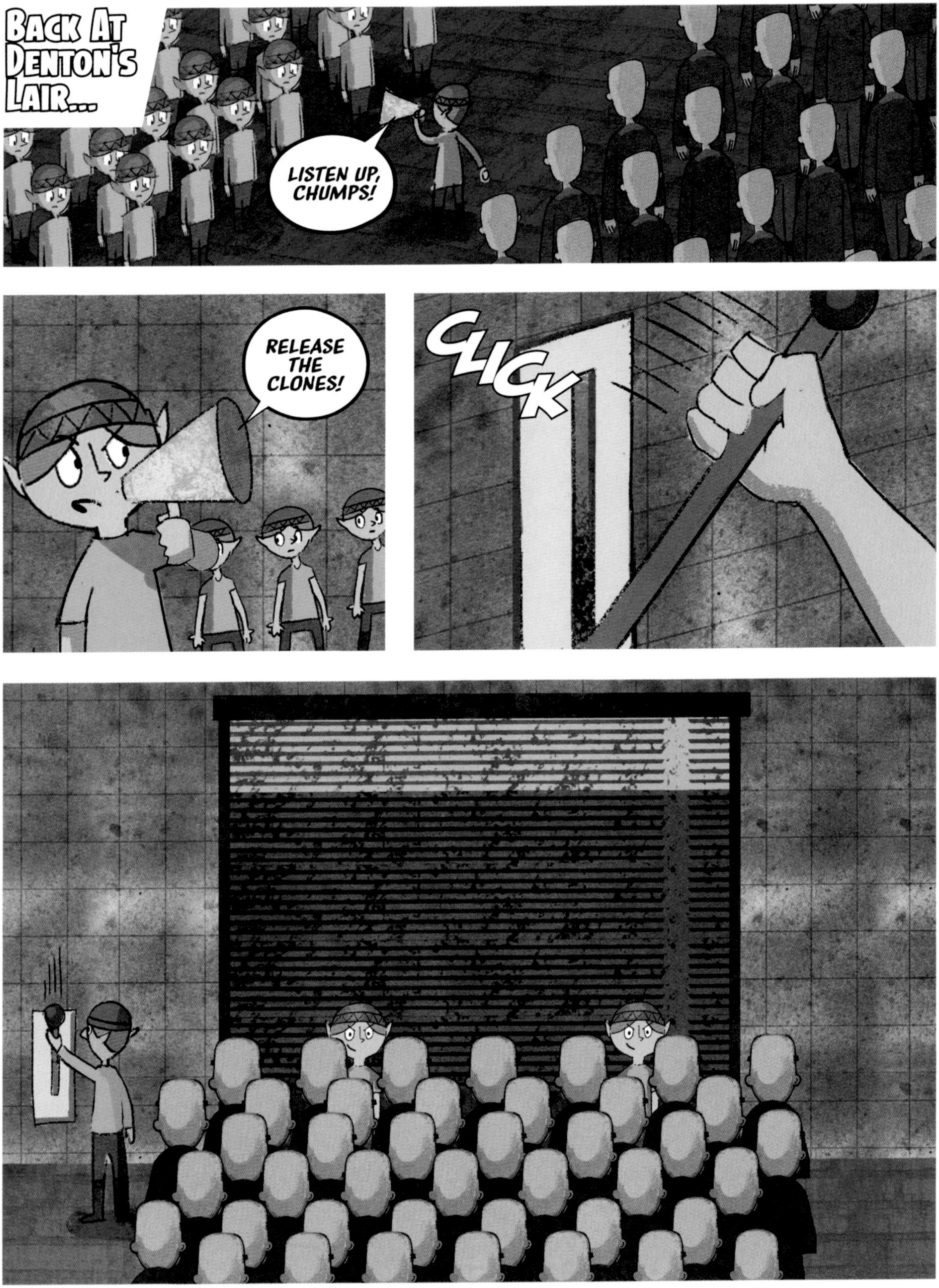
BACK AT DENTON'S LAIR...
LISTEN UP, CHUMPS!
RELEASE THE CLONES!
CLICK

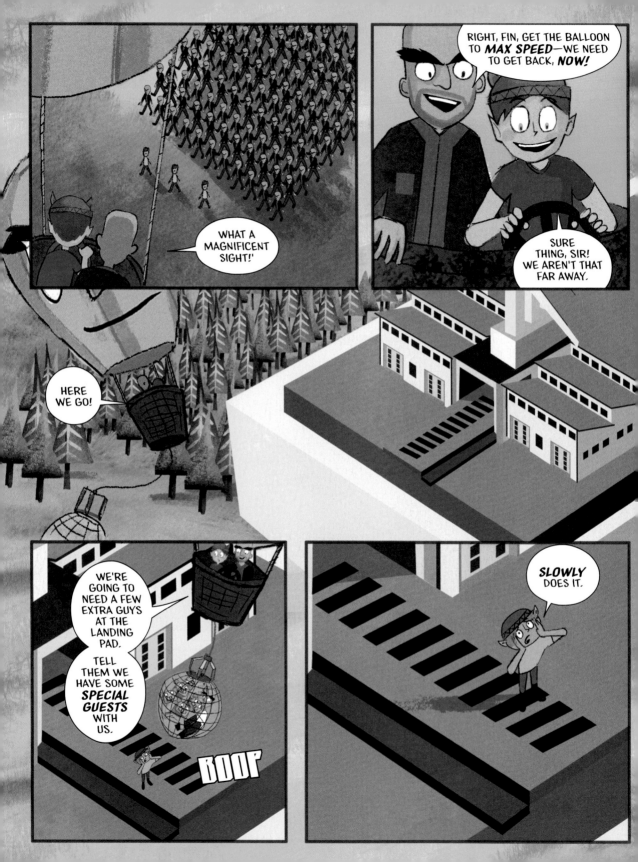

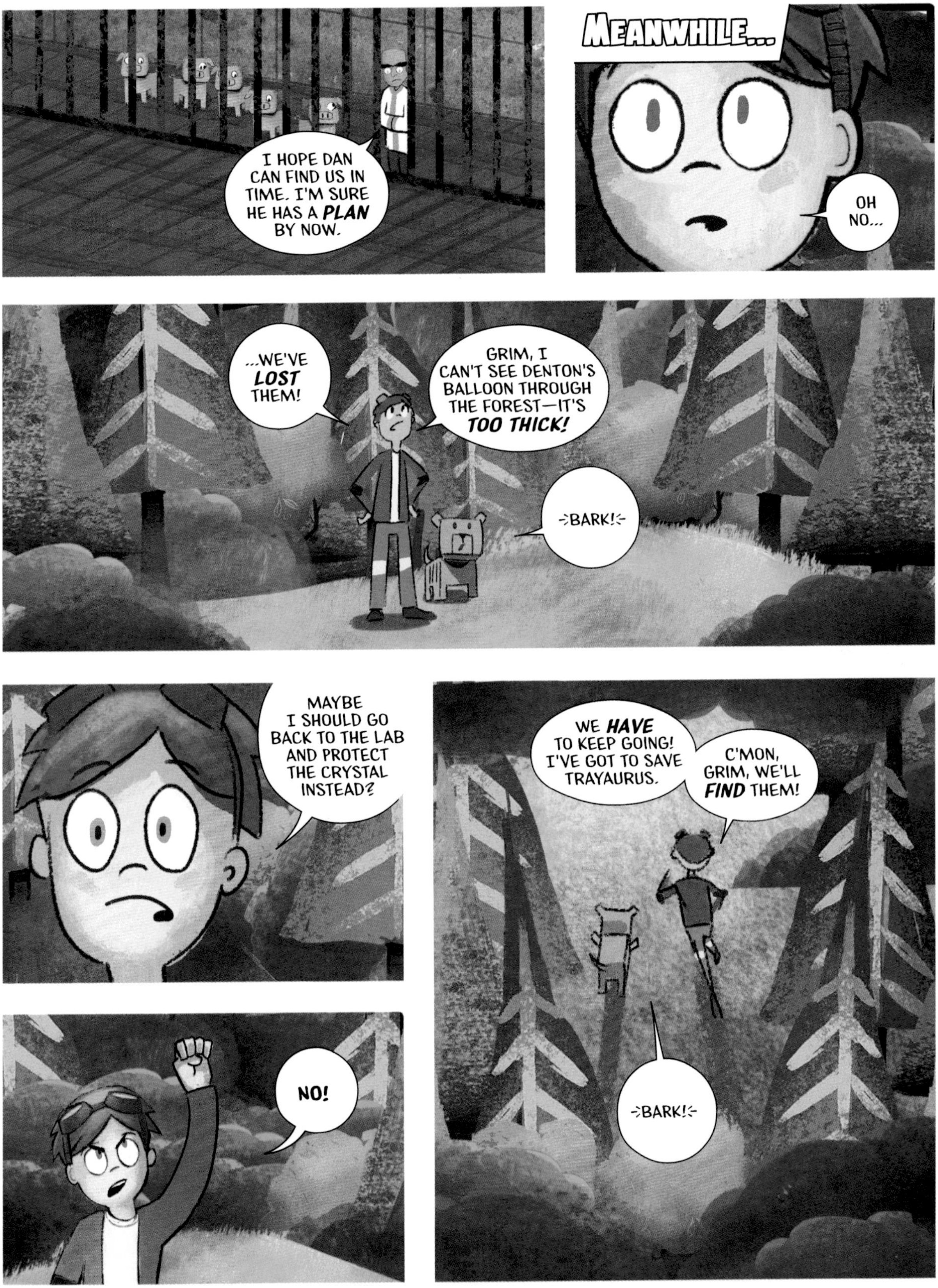
I HOPE DAN CAN FIND US IN TIME. I'M SURE HE HAS A *PLAN* BY NOW.
MEANWHILE...
OH NO...
...WE'VE *LOST* THEM!
GRIM, I CAN'T SEE DENTON'S BALLOON THROUGH THE FOREST—IT'S *TOO THICK!*
BARK!
MAYBE I SHOULD GO BACK TO THE LAB AND PROTECT THE CRYSTAL INSTEAD?
NO!
WE *HAVE* TO KEEP GOING! I'VE GOT TO SAVE TRAYAURUS.
C'MON, GRIM, WE'LL *FIND* THEM!
BARK!

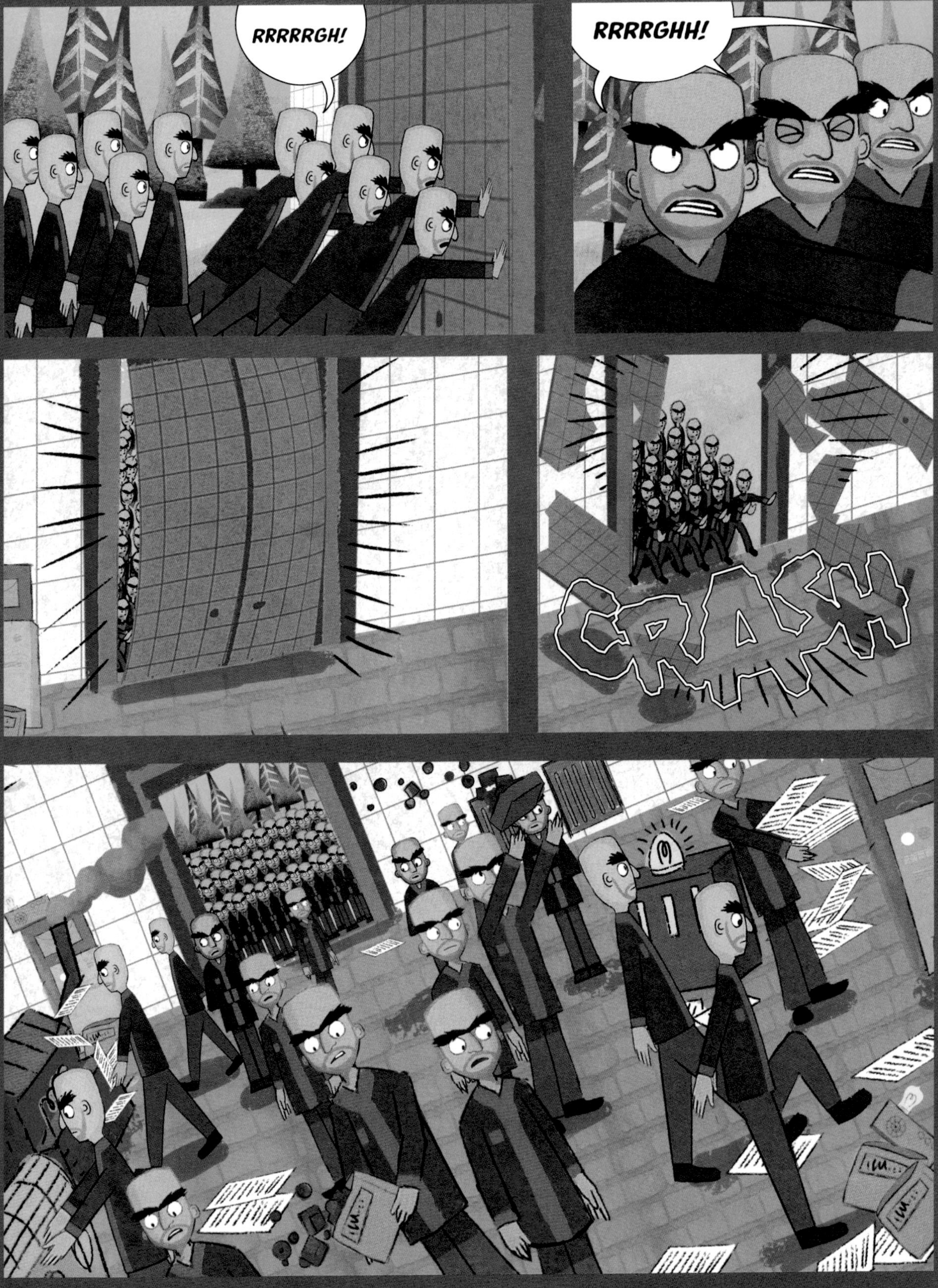
RRRRRGH!
RRRRGHH!
CRASH

OOOOHHH.... AAGGGHHH!

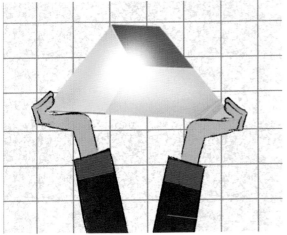

EXCELLENT! YOU FOUND IT! GOOD WORK!

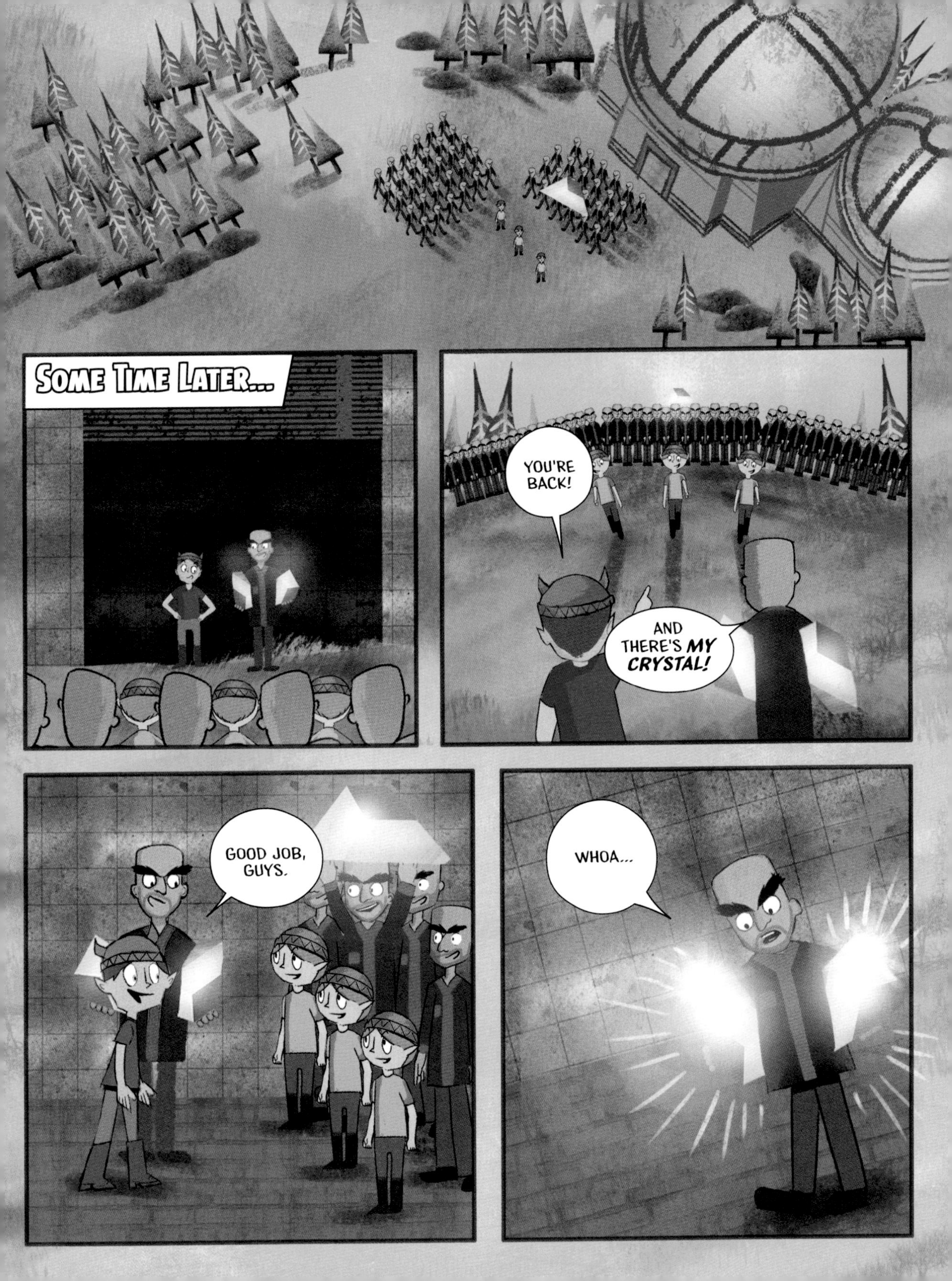
SOME TIME LATER...
YOU'RE BACK!
AND THERE'S MY CRYSTAL!
GOOD JOB, GUYS.
WHOA...

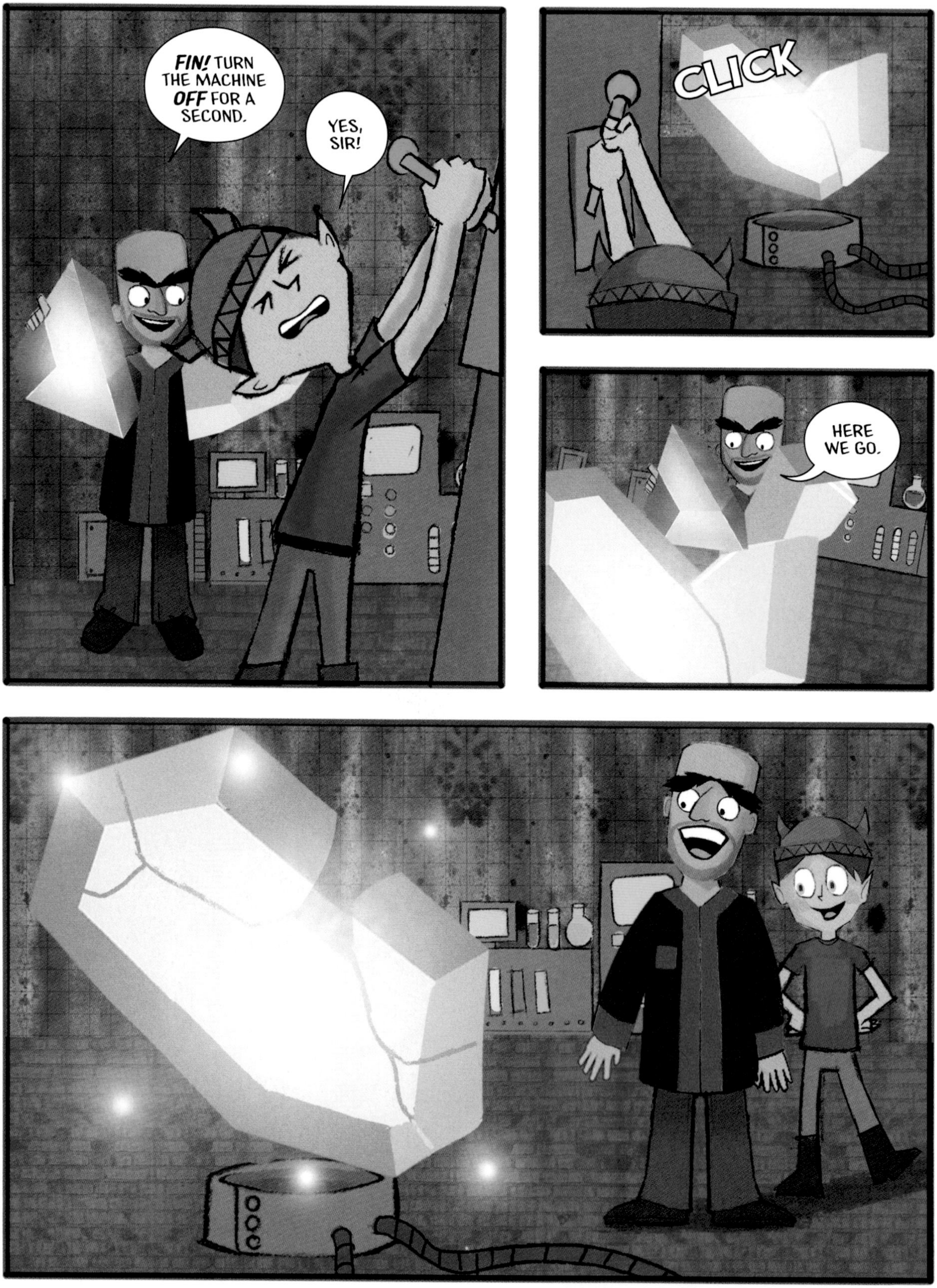
FIN! TURN THE MACHINE **OFF** FOR A SECOND.
YES, SIR!
CLICK
HERE WE GO.

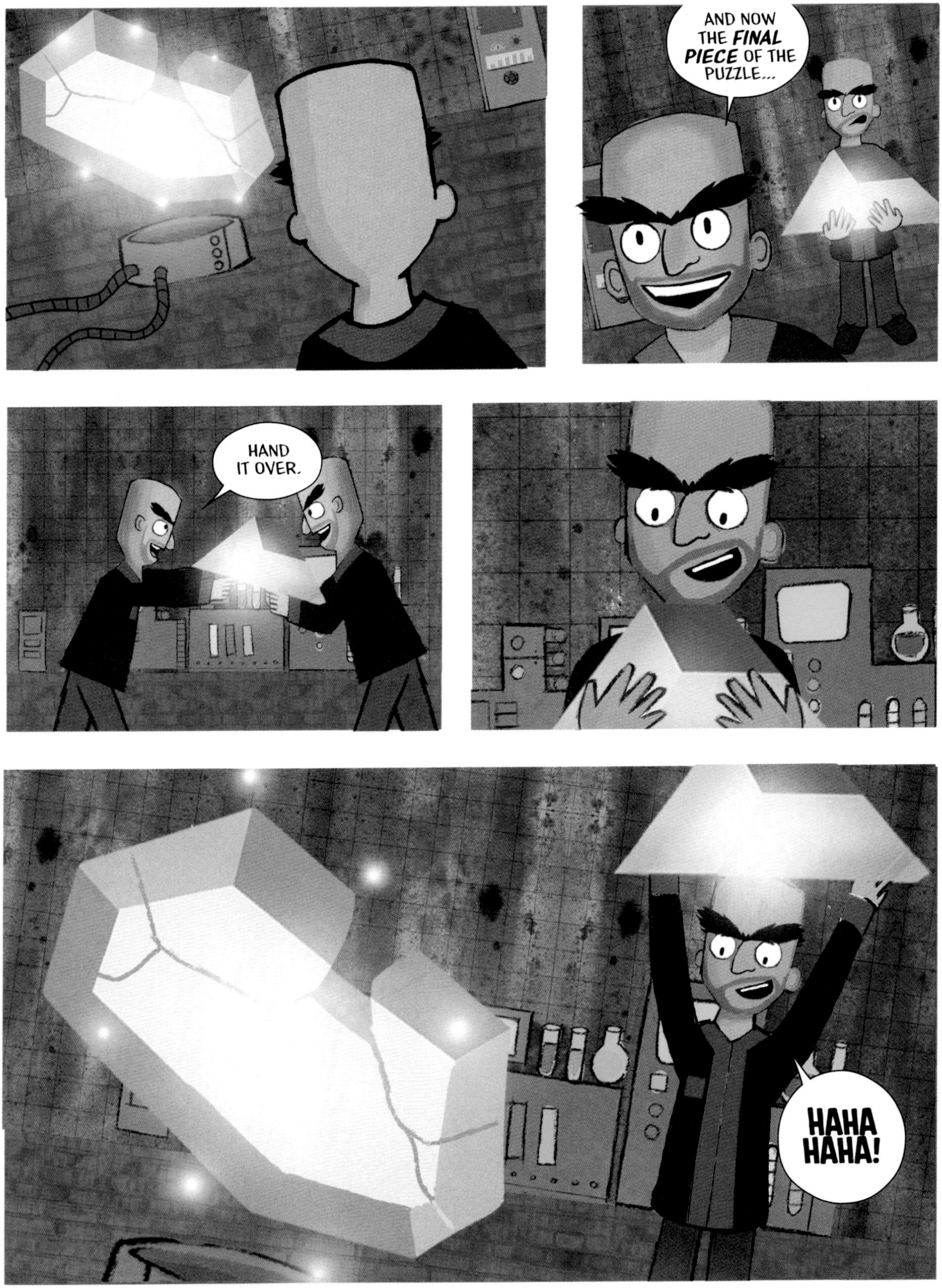
AND NOW THE *FINAL PIECE* OF THE PUZZLE...
HAND IT OVER.
HAHA HAHA!

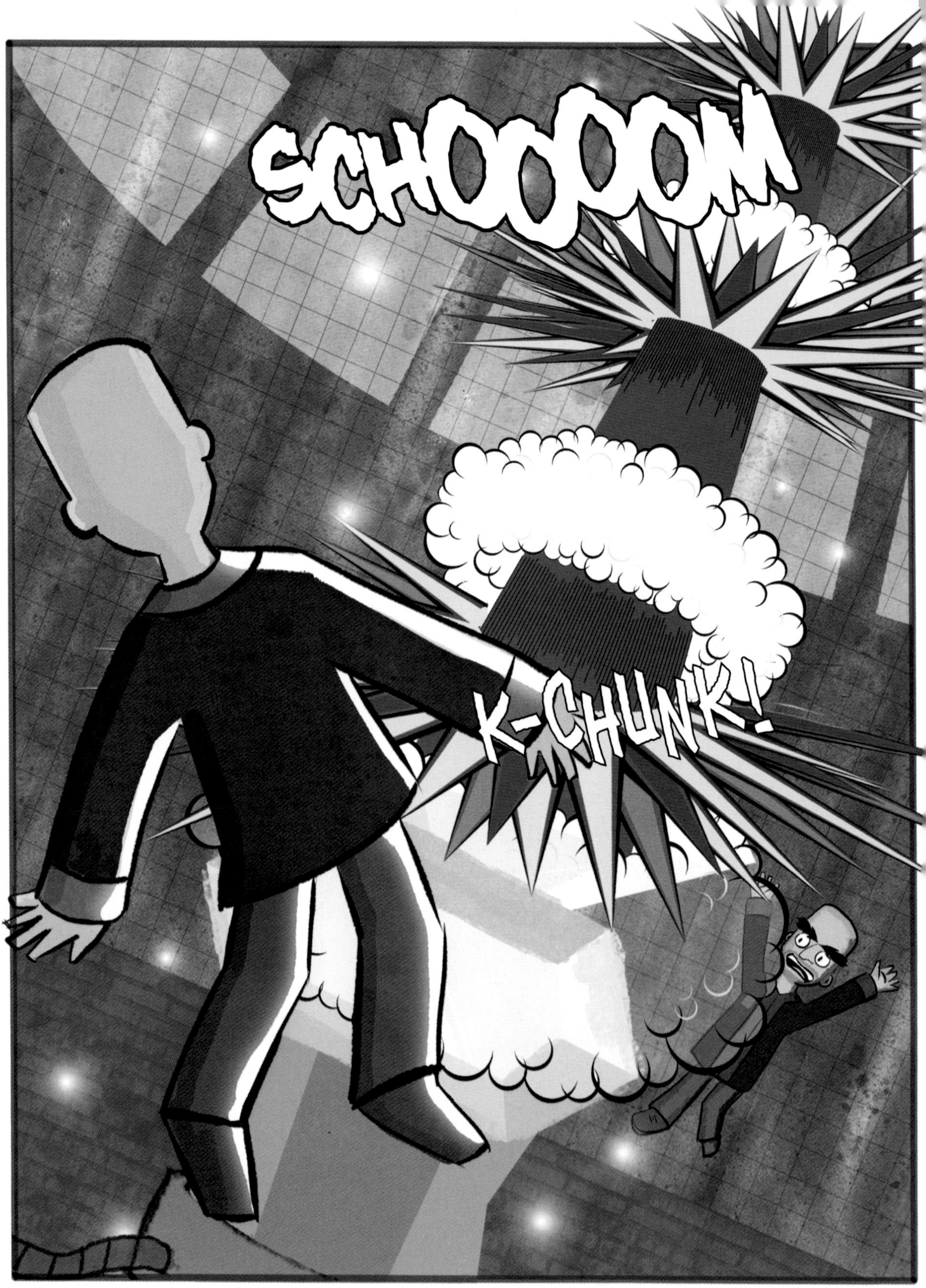
SCHOOOOOM
K-CHUNK!

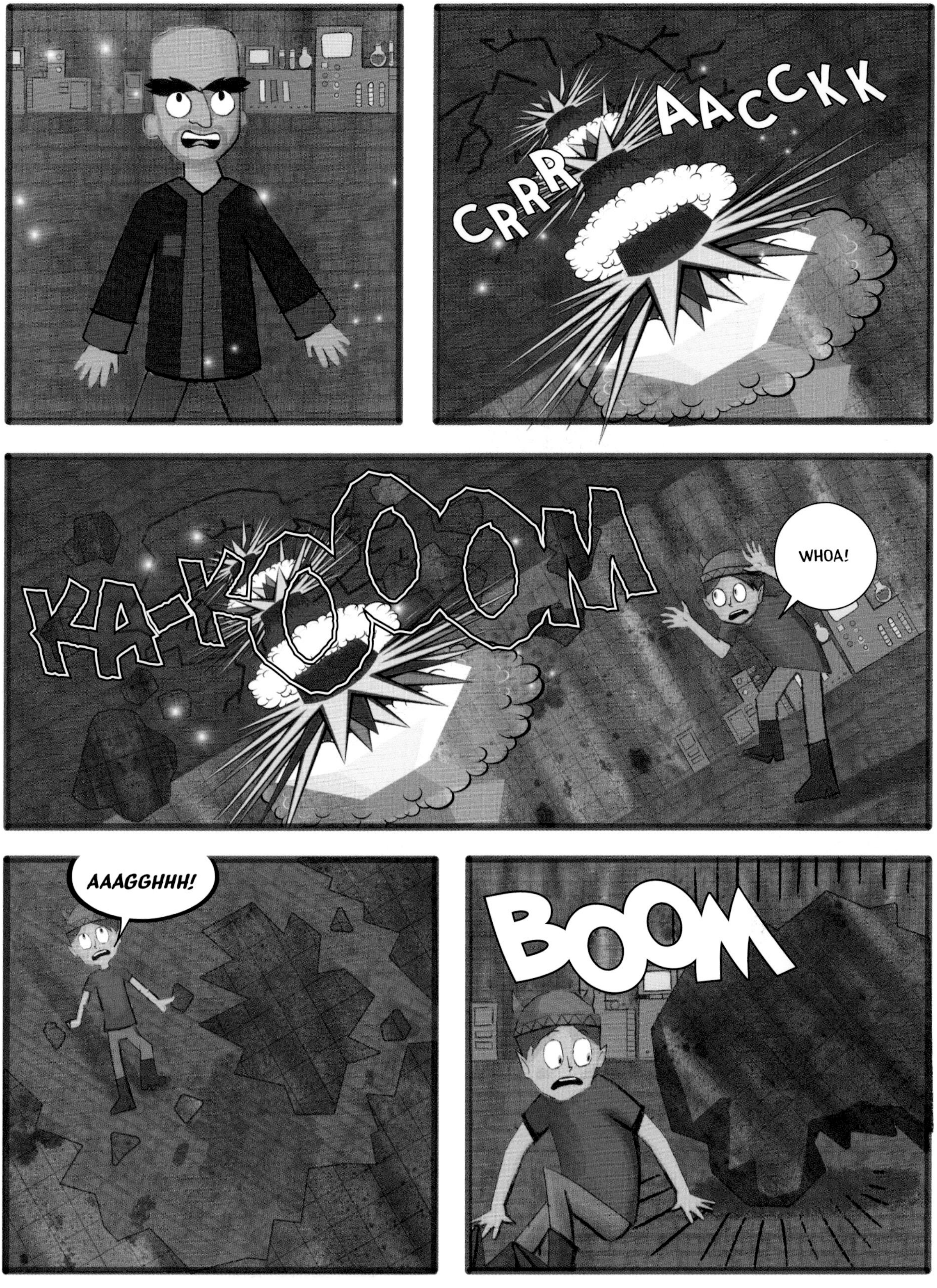
CRRR AACCKK
KA-KOOOOM
WHOA!
AAAGGHHH!
BOOM

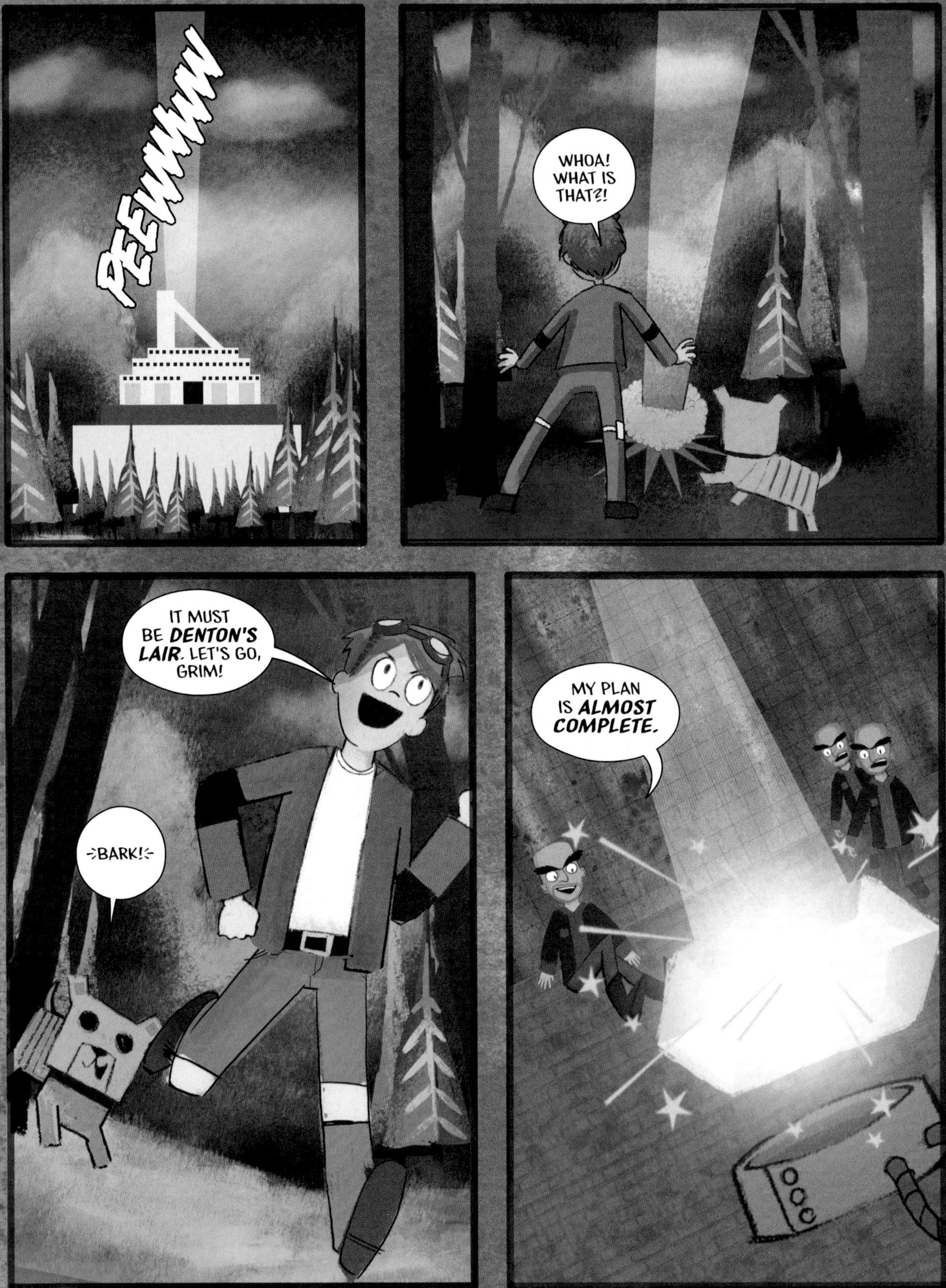
PEEWWWW
WHOA! WHAT IS THAT?!
IT MUST BE DENTON'S LAIR. LET'S GO, GRIM!
BARK!
MY PLAN IS ALMOST COMPLETE.

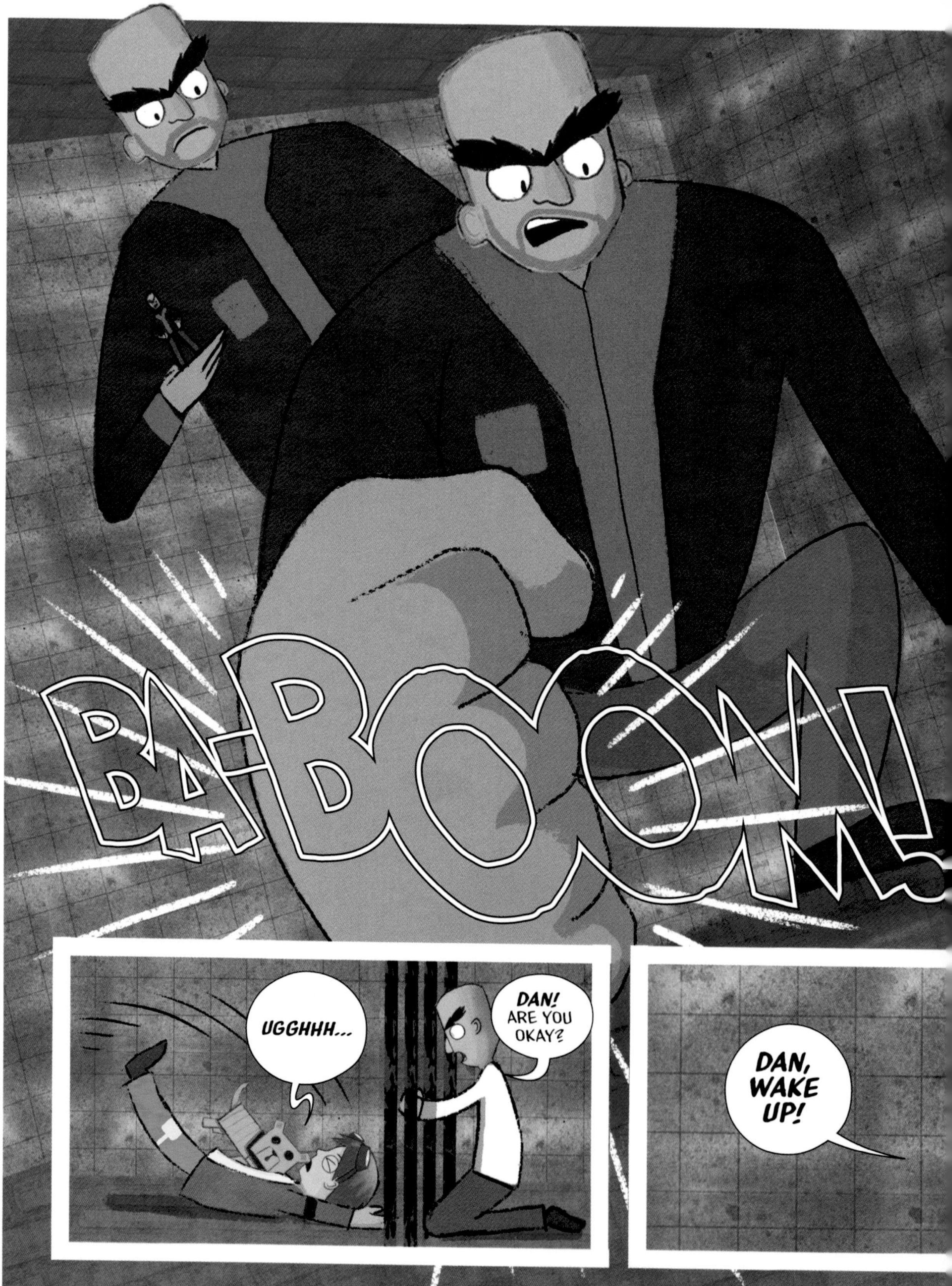
BA-BOOM!
UGGHHH...
DAN! ARE YOU OKAY?
DAN, WAKE UP!

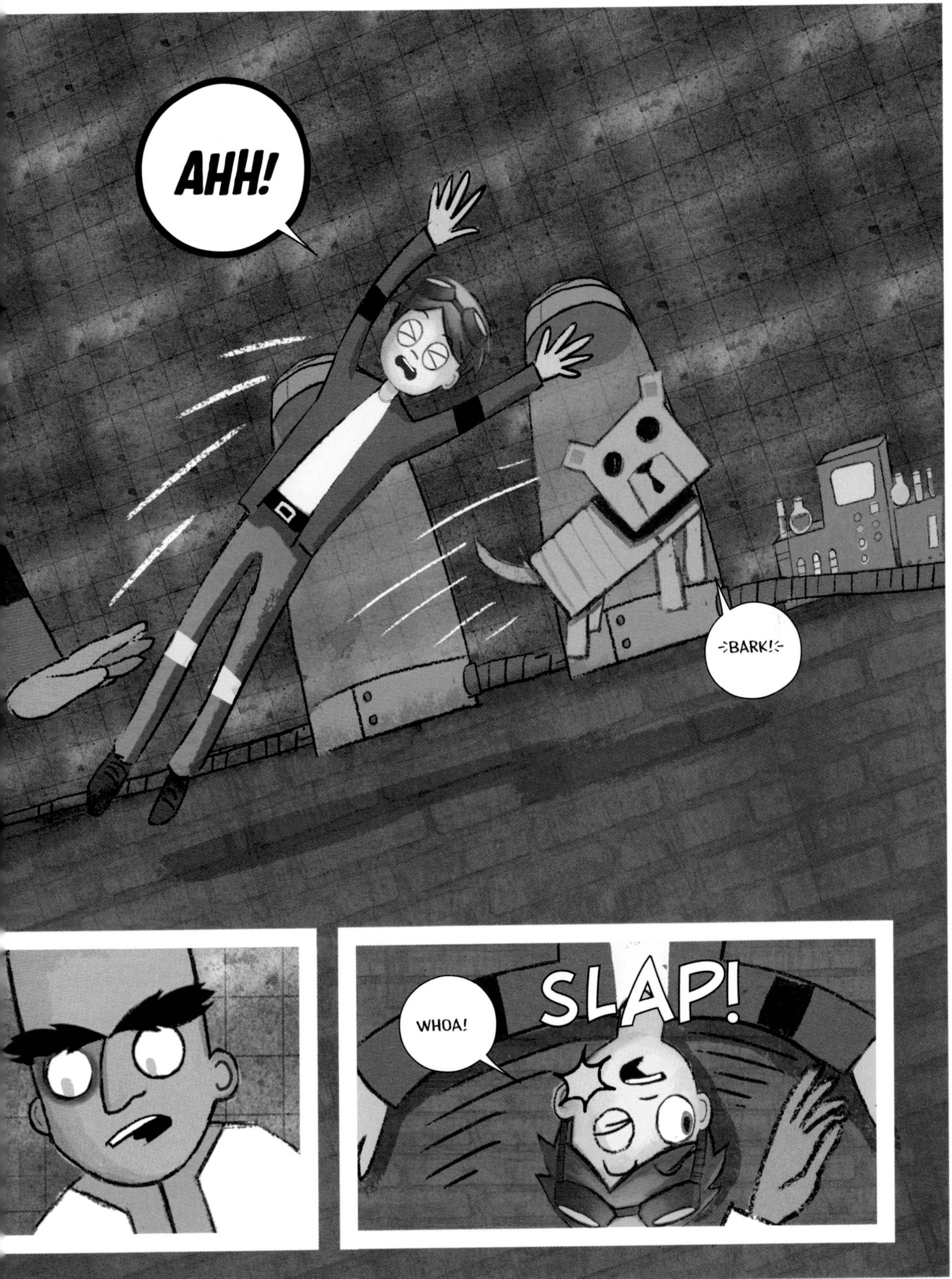
AHH!
BARK!
WHOA!
SLAP!

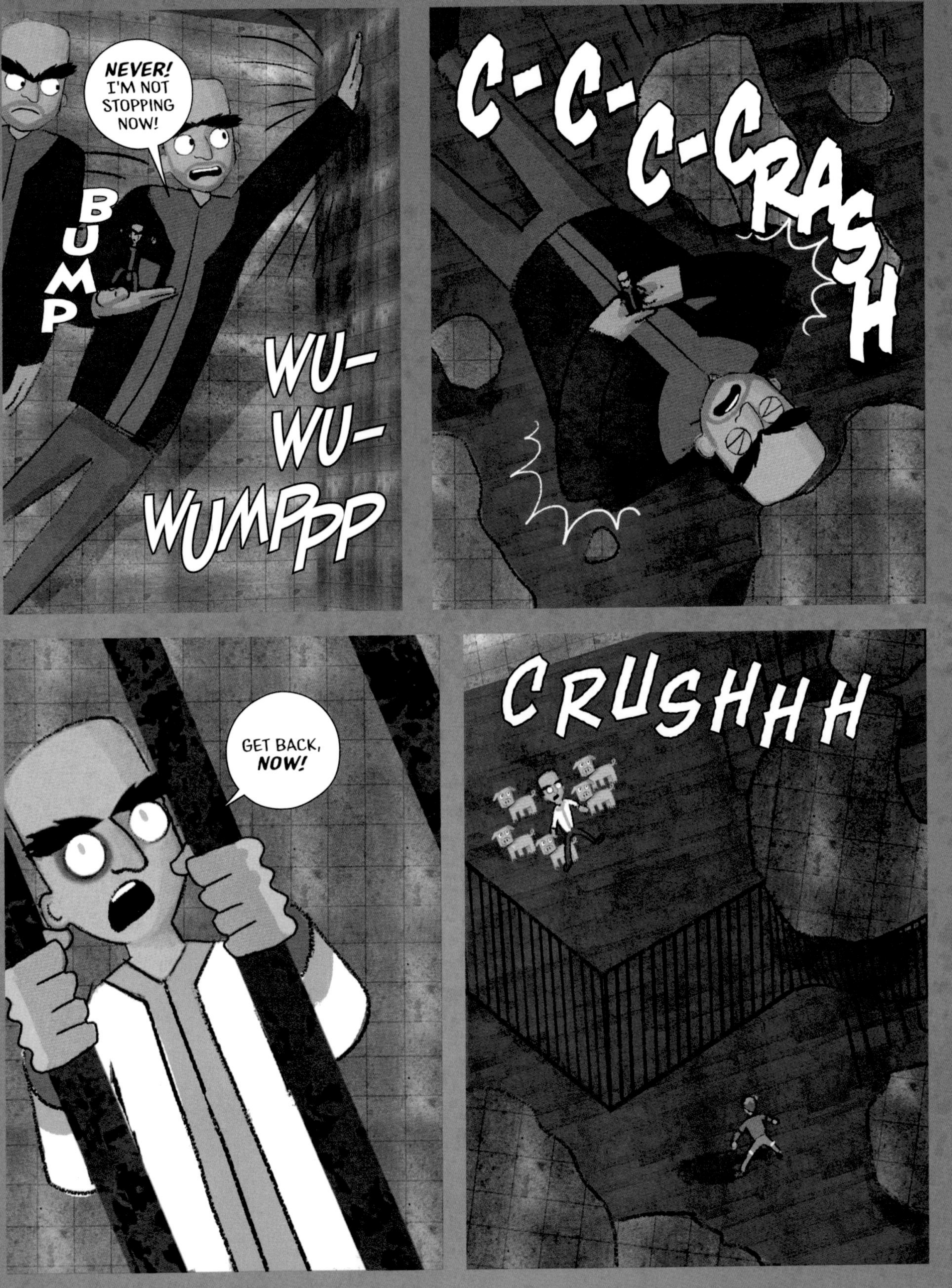
NEVER! I'M NOT STOPPING NOW!
BUMP
WU-WU-WUMPPP
C-C-C-CRASH
GET BACK, NOW!
CRUSHHH

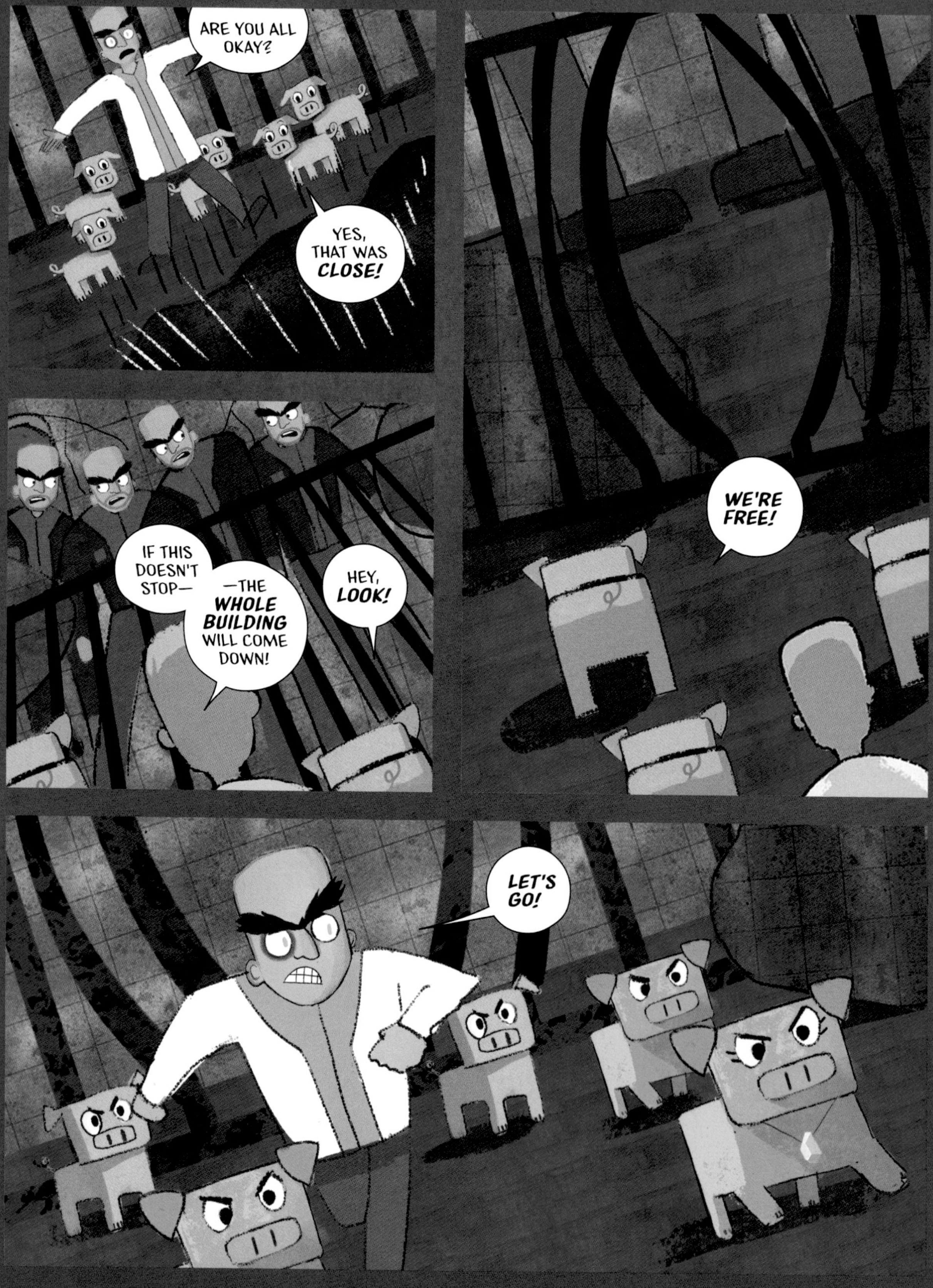
ARE YOU ALL OKAY?
YES, THAT WAS CLOSE!
WE'RE FREE!
IF THIS DOESN'T STOP—
—THE WHOLE BUILDING WILL COME DOWN!
HEY, LOOK!
LET'S GO!

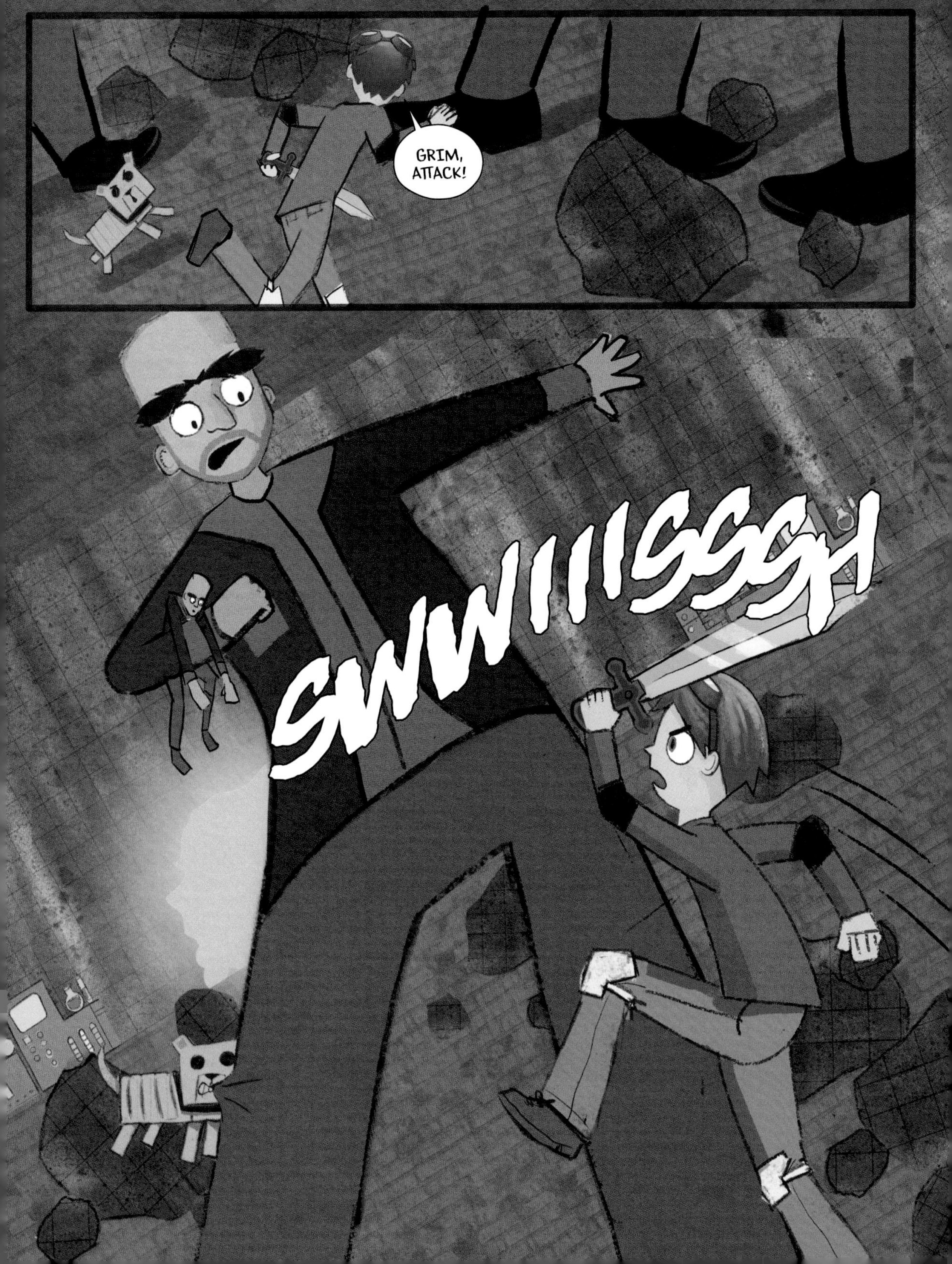
GRIM, ATTACK!
SWWIIISSSH

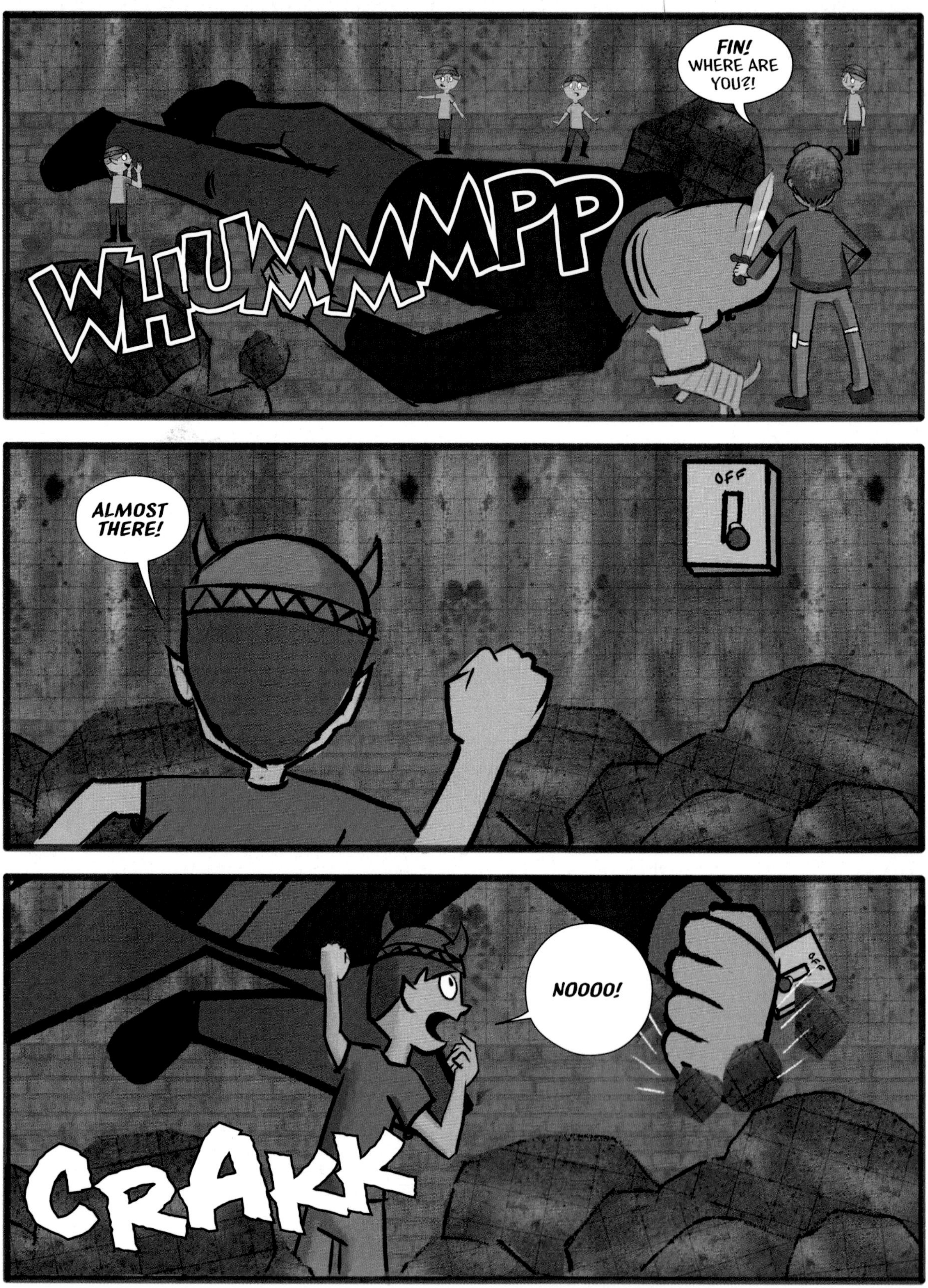
FIN! WHERE ARE YOU?!
WHUMMMPP
ALMOST THERE!
OFF
NOOOO!
OFF
CRAKK

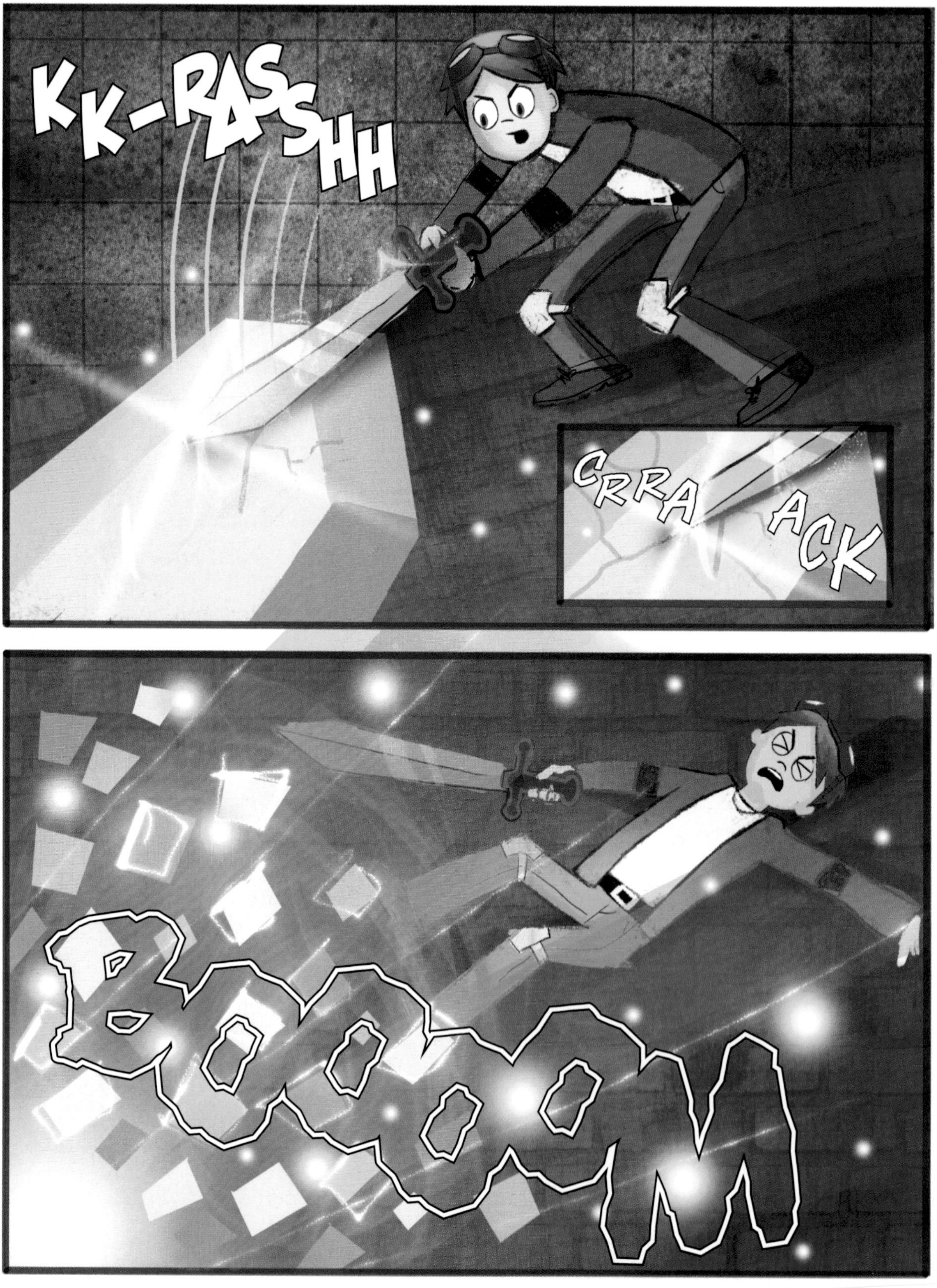
KK-RASSHH
CRRA ACK
BOOOOM

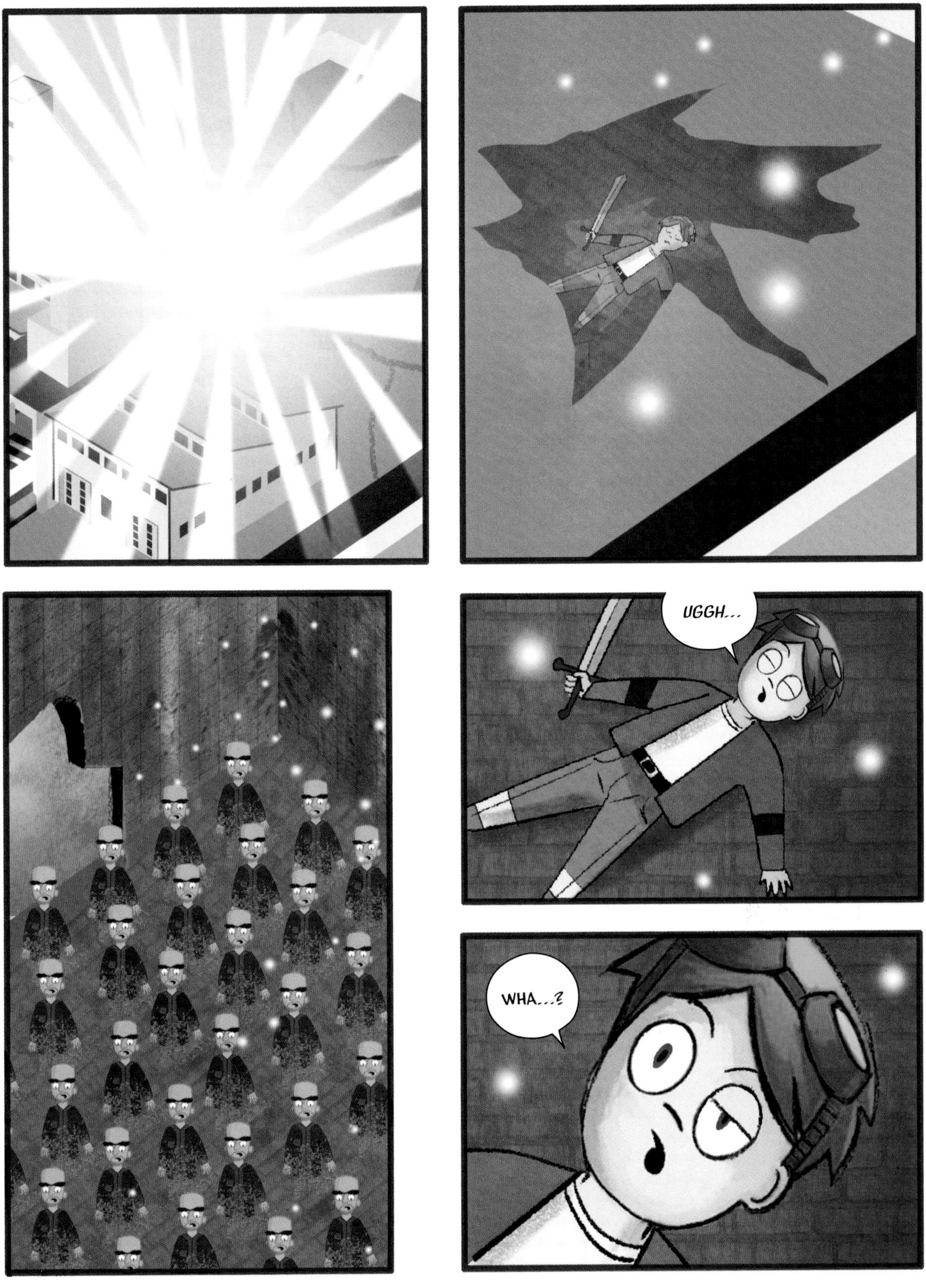
UGGH...
WHA...?

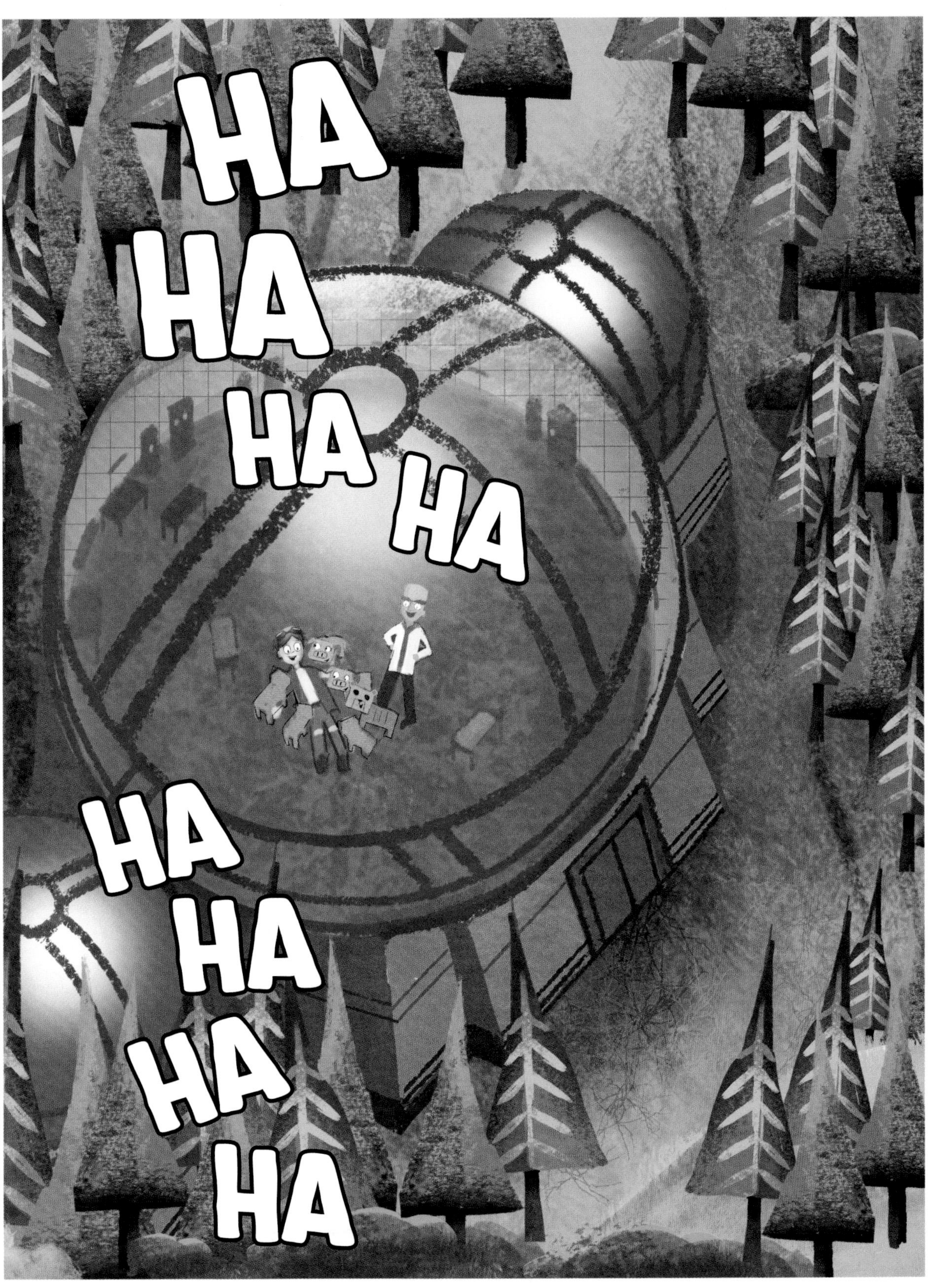
HA
HA
HA
HA
HA
HA
HA
HA

MEET TEAM DANTDM...

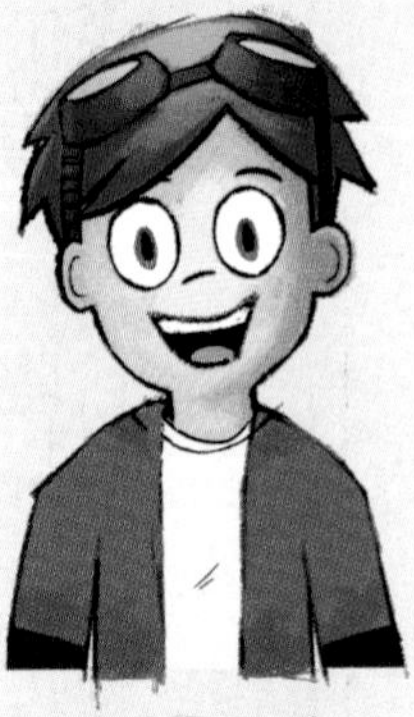

DANTDM

WROTE THE STORY LINE, CREATED THE CHARACTERS, AND OVERSAW THE WHOLE BOOK THAT YOU'RE READING TODAY!

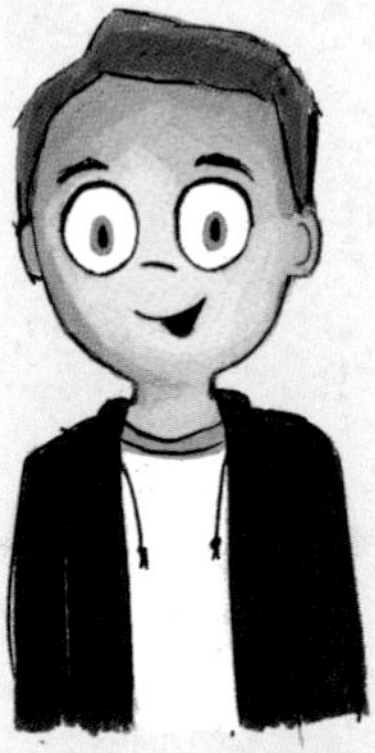

MIKE MARTS

IS THE PERSON WHO BROKE DOWN DAN'S SCRIPT AND CREATED THE COOL, FAST-PACED NARRATIVE TO ACCOMPANY THE PICTURES.

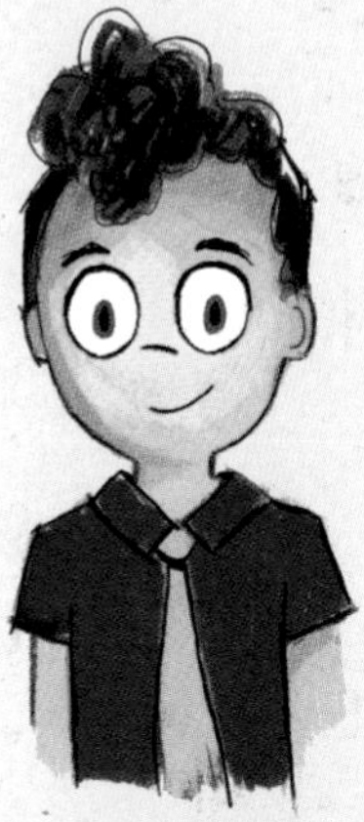

CORY PETIT

IS THE MASTERMIND BEHIND THE AWESOME VISUAL SOUND EFFECTS, LETTERING, AND SPEECH BUBBLES.

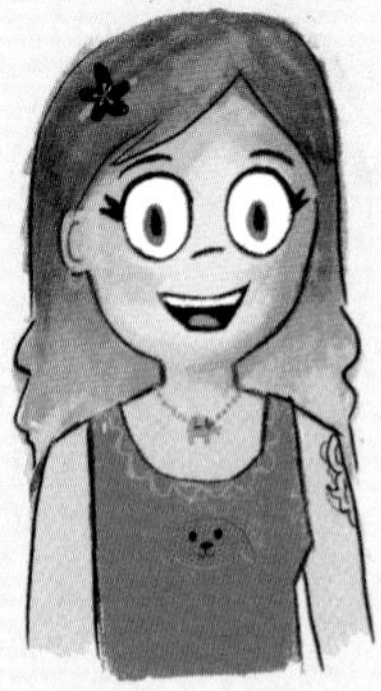

DOREEN MULRYAN

IS THE WONDERFULLY CREATIVE ARTIST WHO SET THE STYLE FOR THE STORY AND TRANSFORMED DAN'S WORDS INTO PICTURES.

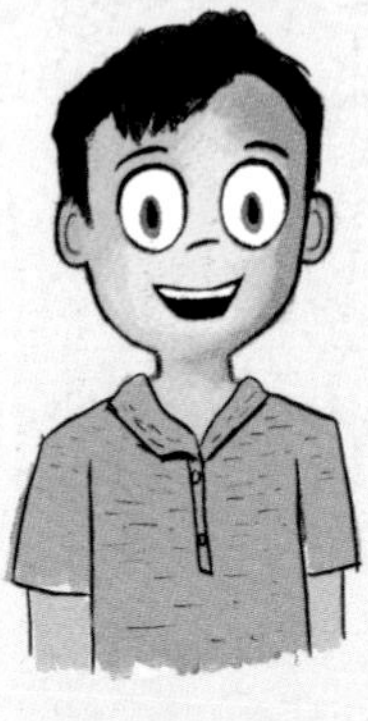

MIKE LOVE

IS THE EXTREMELY TALENTED SUPPORT ARTIST WHO HELPED BRING THE WORLD OF DANTDM TO LIFE.

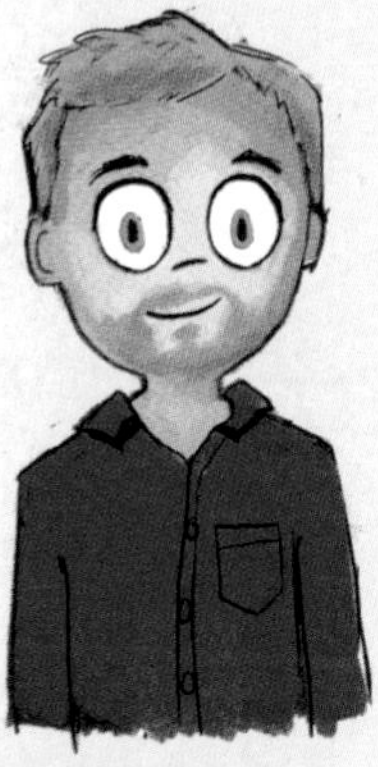

JULYAN BAYES

IS THE DESIGNER WHO HELPED TO ADD THAT ALL-IMPORTANT SPARKLE TO THE REST OF THE BOOK.

A SPECIAL THANK-YOU TO
EMMA KUBERT, LISA FOWLER LUBERA, MARKI WOLFSON, JARED OSBORN, AND DAVID FORREST AND HIS TEAM AT KINETIC UNDERGROUND.